The Librarian Stereotype:

Deconstructing Perceptions and Presentations of Information Work

Edited by

Nicole Pagowsky and Miriam Rigby

Association of College and Research Libraries
A division of the American Library Association
Chicago 2014

The paper used in this publication meets the minimum requirements of American National Standard for Information Sciences–Permanence of Paper for Printed Library Materials, ANSI Z39.48-1992. ∞

Library of Congress Cataloging-in-Publication Data

The librarian stereotype : deconstructing perceptions and presentations of information work / edited by Nicole Pagowsky and Miriam E. Rigby.
    page cm
  ISBN 978-0-8389-8704-9 (pbk. : alk. paper) 1. Librarians--Public opinion. 2. Librarians--Professional ethics. 3. Librarians--Psychology. 4. Library science--Public opinion. 5. Libraries and society--Public opinion. I. Pagowsky, Nicole. II. Rigby, Miriam E.
  Z682.L537 2014
  020.92--dc23
                        2014013675

Cover design by Dorothy Gambrell

Table of Contents

Acknowledgements

This project has been a truly collaborative effort, and without the contributions of many this book would not exist. We first extend thanks to our authors for writing compelling chapters and their dedication to taking revisions with grace. The topic of this book is expansive and at times ventures into risky territory, where authors needed to be bold in order to support their more critical points of view. We thank them for being outspoken and working to enact positive change in our profession.

We also extend a heartfelt thanks to Kathryn Deiss for her guidance and enthusiasm during this project. Kathryn has provided us with the perfect mix of mentoring, trust, and encouragement, and her support, along with the backing of ACRL Press, has helped us make this book exceptional.

Both Emily Drabinski and Marie Radford have contributed wonderful advice for us novice editors, and we appreciate the time and thought they put into answering our questions or making suggestions about process and approach.

Dorothy Gambrell has been extremely generous in designing the book's cover and illustrating a chapter. Out of the kindness of her heart, and her fondness for libraries and librarians, she requested only a price that librarians could afford. We hope you will visit her artist sites for the Cat & Girl comic (http://catandgirl.com) and her infographic-based project, Very Small Array (www.verysmallarray.com), and consider supporting an independent artist.

We also greatly thank our peer-reviewers: Meghan Bean, Jenny Benevento, Damon Campbell, Erica DeFrain, Laura DeLancey, Emily Drabinski, Allie Flanary, Jenna Freedman, Lia Friedman, Aliqae Geraci, Leo Lo, Kelly McElroy, Erin Pappas, Sheila Rabun, John Russell, Cassie Schmitt, Maura Seale, Yen Tran, and David Woken. Often in the conversation of research, these more invisible discussions go unnoted, but we think it is important to offer acknowledgement and thanks for the invaluable insight shared along the way to the final product.

Last but not least, we thank our friends and family for supporting us in this process, as well as our institutions, the University of Arizona Libraries and the University of Oregon Libraries. And of course we want to say a big thank you to all of the real-life librarians and other information professionals whose interest and participation in our presentations, webinars, and online conversations motivated us to produce this book.

Embracing the Melancholy

How the Author Renounced Moloch and the
Conga Line for Sweet Conversations on Paper,
to the Air of "Second Hand Rose"

James V. Carmichael Jr.

> This is the exalted melancholy of our fate that every Thou
> in our world must become an It.
>
> —Dag Hammarskjöld[1]

What Stereotype?

I grew up in a provincial and historic southern town without a public
library but with an old social library established in 1893 that had been
turned over to the city to run.[2] On my one visit as a small boy (my parents
were readers, and I had my hands full working through their library), I
discovered a novel with a three-noun title, one of which was *Mandolin*. The
only feature of the novel that sticks with me is the opening scene in which
a señorita peers through a keyhole at a matador who is undressing. The
librarian, who was the only other person besides my guardian and myself
in this rather largish one-story brick building with a domed skylight—inspired by the British Museum—checked the book out to me, but a week
later at home, I received a private note from her on which she had carefully
placed a bluebird sticker in the upper left-hand corner and had written in
her impeccably neat script, "Dear Jimmy, I did not see the book you were

checking out until after you left the building. Why don't you bring that one back and let me find one you would really like to read?" I did not give it up until it was due.

Although this story predates the Broadway musical *The Music Man*, I can state unequivocally that the play in no way exaggerates the puritanism of small-town American mores. At a jumble sale at the supposedly free-wheeling Episcopal church (we were Presbyterians), a docent wanted to refuse to sell me a paperback entitled *French Short Stories* by de Maupassant and the other usual French *fin de siècle* literary suspects. The woman kept pointing out the word *French* in the title to her coworker while raising her eyebrows provocatively as if the bodice-ripper cover art could not adequately convey its depravity. My guardian intervened, however, and I received satisfaction for my dime.

It is the librarian of the first anecdote I want to describe, however. She came from a locally renowned family, and her father was simply "the judge." She was a spinster in her 60s who stayed with her parents in the old home place supposedly to care for them although they could have just as easily been caring for her. They occupied a second-row pew in front of my family in church, and the librarian always plugged in her hearing aid before the sermon. At the library, she wore a gingham dress, rolled stockings, and—yes—tennis shoes. Her hair was braided around her head, and I picture her in a nimbus of flyaway strands and dust motes with her back to a window. She wore no makeup whatsoever, and her face was freckled with age spots. It wasn't until I was in library school 20-odd years later, voting for Jimmy Carter at that same library, that it occurred to me that I had grown up with the very paragon of librarians, an embodiment of the despised stereotype, and that I had loved her almost as much as I loved my Aunt Willie Mae, a woman of the same generation and ilk. During Halloween of 1963, while I was abroad at a French boarding school, the librarian had a breakdown brought on by the discovery that the assistant city manager had been cashing the paychecks that she faithfully turned back over to the city because she did not need the public funds as much as the city did. She died several years after the scandal. I never understood how anyone could deride a soul so selfless because I—an "old maid in britches"

as Scarlett O'Hara might have called me—marveled at the librarian's belief, indeed, faith, in her work. What need did she have for television or
commerce?

I married one week out of college with a French degree. My wife and
I were both weekend hippies, which made passing high-security clearance
in the defense industry problematic, and I was soon laid off. I finally settled
in trust administration in a now-defunct Atlanta bank for six years. Half-
way through, my father died and my marriage, a re-creation of the relations
of the Montagues and the Capulets, finally sputtered out. It was harder
and harder to hide disenchantment, and I was eventually terminated at my
bank job, where I felt like the embodiment of inappropriate aptitude. My
vocational test showed me to be perfectly suited for the Catholic ministry,
which must have derailed my father, who had arranged the test, at least
temporarily. I unsuccessfully applied to the Navy: I aced their electron-
ics exam—which worried me considerably because I can't plug in a cof-
feepot without second-guessing myself—but did not pass the masculinity test (unwritten). I sat in the backyard one Sunday afternoon while my
mother gazed worriedly out the window and wondered what I could do
for a living, besides converting to Catholicism and joining a monastery,
that would not mortify her. I remembered visiting my sister and her hus-
band at Duke University, where I was shown the Flowers Collection of
Rare Books, and envying the assistant who was dusting and polishing the
covers of the leather-bound books. Maybe I could dust books. Thus, albeit
unknowingly, I filled one of the worst stereotypes in the male librarian inventory: he who is a librarian because he's failed at other work.[3]

Little did I realize when I entered the master's program at the Division
of Librarianship at Emory University that St. Jerome was patron saint of librarians—the monastic ideal! Nor did I anticipate feeling for the first time
as if I had come home to a world I had left behind with my French degree:
literature, philosophy, religion, art, dance, theater, film, music. Lunches
became interesting again. I no longer had to feign interest in football and
basketball scores or the latest stock-market wiz. I especially enjoyed the
arduous hours trying to shake answers out of reference books for the multiple hard-knocks reference courses I took. I even enjoyed advanced cata-

loging, during which our instructor devised a laboratory game where one drew cards with various elements of MARC2 format (example: title = 1 card; space = 1 card; semicolon = 1 card; space = 1 card) until one had a complete catalog card.

I accepted a job as a rare books cataloger in Milledgeville, Georgia—a perfectly preserved antebellum town that had served as the state capital until 1868. It had escaped Sherman's torch during the Civil War although perhaps all but one home was thoroughly emptied by the marauders.[4] I actually never had a chance to catalog rare books because the regular cataloger moved back to Florida, and I learned OCLC copy cataloging in about a week on the beehive dedicated terminal. Meanwhile, I allied myself with a gay group in Atlanta, and, in an attempt to quit smoking, I picked up needlepoint. Soon I was inundated in pillows I had started as Christmas projects, and as the library was always looking for an exhibit with which to stuff its cases, I soon mounted my projects, and the local paper ran a large color photograph of me in a three-piece suit lying amid my pillows like Burt Reynolds in *Playgirl*, only fully clothed. I received one phone call at home from a vaguely threatening male voice that asked, "Don't you think people are going to think you are kind of weird?" Not to be flummoxed, I cited Henry Fonda and Rosey Grier as paragons among male needle-pointers. He hung up. Shortly thereafter, my new director suggested that I needed a doctorate to teach the reference course that I was then in my fifth year of offering to school media specialists seeking certification. I wasn't quite sure how to take that suggestion, but I applied to doctoral programs and kept hoping that someday I might meet the Nureyev-looking guy who posed for the librarian photo in the 1982 *Occupational Outlook Handbook*. I did not, but who's counting?

Making an It of a Thou

Skip a few years. I am a doctoral student, reading Garrison's study of late Victorian public librarians in America and focusing on Melvil Dewey's first library school classes at Columbia and Albany, and stumble across the fact that those female "acolytes" who later left the profession for marriage felt that they had betrayed "a sacred trust."[5] I don't recognize these characters because even at my most sentimental, I have always recognized the steel grip behind the velvet gloves of the women I have known, including a great-grandmother who was five years old when General Sherman came marauding, a grandmother who taught Latin until she married in 1903, another grandmother who was a school principal, my mother who was a self-taught school librarian and a second-grade teacher until she married in 1938, and an ex-wife who read a science fiction novel while her wedding train was being arranged to march down the aisle: worthy opponents all.

Garrison's work confirmed that librarians' cultural capital was passé: too many Protestant, white, sexually repressed librarians and far too many male ministers (mainly) among their early leaders. I learned through a sociology of occupations course that I took with the eminent editor of *Social Forces*, Richard L. Simpson, that librarianship was a feminized semi-profession, one that had been occupied by men who then hired women to do the busy work cheaply. In class, Simpson recanted the essay written with his wife in 1969 just as militant feminism was forcing sociologists to revise their theories of power and professionalism.[6]

Do librarians only come in vocational flavors? I certainly used to think so, much like Mrs. Delia Foreacre Sneed, later Lee (1868–1947), who opined that reference librarians were "born" not "made" and described reference skills as an "art."[7] Needless to say, the same artistic crown may be granted to catalogers and not only those who share the OCD gene; in fact, the present author could easily spend $1,500 at an office supply store to get his life in alphabetical order in color-coded folders. Then he would be sidelined for 15 years by the bon mots of various Bloomsbury writers of the 20th-century teens and twenties he would dream of incorporating into a revised taxonomy of literary dysfunction: *Non Sequiturs R Us.*

Managers must certainly be born, not made, although I imagine it is still pedagogical heresy to say so since for the last 50 years or so, library education programs have been touting the value of managerial skills for all. People who succeed in rising to the top of big hierarchically organized academic libraries seem to practice the same low-affect tactics of control and manipulation that Walmart managers do, whatever sex they happen to be. The only touchy-feely managers I've ever known worked in smaller private institutions. In public institutions, directors seem uniformly pained and self-involved, with the saving qualifier of a sense of humor in a minority of cases. Then again, my experience with the upper echelons is extremely limited and is tainted by my years working as a grunt in an aircraft factory and a mainline southern bank to which I would drive from home at 5:30 a.m. every morning to avoid the kind of rush-hour conga line I joined every afternoon in the desperate attempt to escape the city.

I know that libraries are "just" businesses; however, after teaching academic librarians and others for 25 years, I understand that they are (I am?) fundamentally different personality types from the young people I used to lunch with at the bank or sit next to in accounting and marketing classes at Georgia State University (term paper: starting an astrology store in Underground Atlanta: C–). I no longer fear being considered quaint and unmanly in not bowing to the dictates of Moloch. In 2000, when the Supreme Court decided the presidential election and I could see the approaching nonstop round-the-clock coverage of another network saga along the lines of Joey Buttafuoco, O. J. Simpson, Tanya Harding, Michael Kennedy Smith, and Princess Diana, I snipped the cable and dumped my television in the yard of an artist friend who makes sea creatures out of scrap. I banned the computer to my workplace. My three cats were very happy, and I have never looked back.

Back to my hometown librarian and the archetype fail-male librarian: the only sociological problem here is in my own head. There was a golden moment in my doctoral program that brought this fully to bear on my life. During those years, I stayed sane thanks to a recovery program, and as in all self-help organizations, there were some very intimidating and socially controlling people who did not like nonconformists. One woman had forbidden her followers to have anything to do with me because I wasn't doing things or behaving the way she thought I ought to. Asked to speak to a large assembly one night at which the woman and her acolytes were perched on the edge of their seats, ready to pounce—the regular speaker had failed to show up—I appeared in a 19th-century Alexander Hamilton costume in distressed green velvet: knee breeches, white stockings, long vest and coat with gold lace braid and brass buttons, tea-stained white lace jabot at my neck, and long lace cuffs draping out of my coat sleeves. I had found the outfit in an antique shop in Cameron, North Carolina, on my 40th birthday after my mother had died. "All of what you see tonight," I explained, "used to be on the inside of my head. Now it's out here. I've come a long way, baby." I spoke on for 45 minutes, completely at ease. My nemesis could not intimidate me because the only nemesis I had to fear was inside my own head.

A similar experience happened a decade later at the 1998 IFLA conference in Amsterdam, where I had been asked to appear on a censorship program to talk about homosexuality and libraries in the United States. I was on a double bill with the national librarian of Belgium, who was talking about the historical problems that had attended the language split between Flemish and French speakers in the country, similar to that of French and English speakers in Quebec and Quebec separatism within Anglophone Canada. I had travelled with my friend Deb White from Pittsboro, who happened to also be my *coiffeuse*. We schmoozed well together and were both similarly disposed to bursts of southern irony amid the well-traveled corridors of European tourism. "My God," she had said when we arrived in Reykjavik, "what is wrong with these people? They are beautiful people, but they are all dressed like they are going to a funeral. They need some color!" Both of us tried our best to supply that ingredient in abundance wherever we went. We could be heard from the top of glaciers—those kinds of voices that carry because of regional inflection and emphasis and way too many cigarettes growing up.

At any rate, when we arrived at the conference laden with bags from the Amsterdam street market filled with fabric, quilts, old furs, tassels, and bits of trim I was bringing home for a living room overhaul, we came to the room where the speakers were to read their papers, all pre-printed in conference proceedings; Wayne Wiegand, then teaching at the University of Wisconsin, caught me outside the door. It was his encouragement that had led me to pursue the male librarian survey that led to my 15 minutes of fame in the *Library Journal* for noticing that there were male librarians who had stereotype problems too, the main one of which was the perception that male librarians might be gay.[8]

Moreover, I had published the comments of the male librarians who recounted being hit on by women or complained of having to clean up the vomit in the lobby of their public library or do the heavy lifting *because* they were male, so a panel of distinguished female respondents including Kathleen Heim de la Peña McCook, Suzanne Hildenbrand, and Dallas Shaffer commented on reverse sexism, etc., all in a very supportive and enthralling way.

Wayne said, "Jim, you may not read your paper. I forbid you to do that. They can read it in the proceedings. Just *speak*." So when my turn came, after the Belgian librarian had delivered his paper word for word in the finest old-world style, I bundled up with my bags; came to the podium; introduced "My hairdresser, Debra;" and started unpacking the bags, describing our activity in the market that morning, and asking the audience whether they thought that a fascination with fabric—fondling and owning it, not producing it, or wearing a slightly ratty rabbit jacket with just enough shoulder padding to look tailored but not like it was cut for Joan Crawford—was an indicator of male homosexuality because there was nothing in my personal life (other than being attracted to men and women in an affectionate but not necessarily sexual way) except my passion for color and line, china, and a tendency to roll my eyes to give me away: no lover, anyway. Maybe I would be like my friend Martha who had talked me into readiness for the doctoral program. She used to say that she was going to have all female pallbearers because no man had ever taken her out while she was alive, and she was damned if one was ever going to do it after she was dead. The room cracked up. We had a lively exchange aided by James Anderson of Rutgers, there in lieu of fellow faculty member Pamela Spence Richards (1941–1999), also of Rutgers, who had solicited the paper and invited Anderson, along with his partner, my friend Debra, and me to stay with her at her summer home in Holland, only to be diagnosed with a brain tumor from which she never recovered.

I'm not through with that story either. Pamela Spence Richards and I discovered, after I had known and revered her for years in the meetings of the Library History Round Table where she was the authority on Soviet-era Russian libraries and information problems, that her mother and my father had had an affairette in 1937. Her mother was a taxi dancer in Atlanta and he was in the state legislature fighting for railway rate reform. She presented herself as an actress rather than a dancer, and my father, ever the soul of Protestant rectitude, disparaged her lack of complete and total honesty. A good thing too, my mother might say, because she and my father married in 1938.

Librarianship is the vehicle through which all of these scenes and wardrobe changes occurred: coincidences that were not really coincidences—serendipity of the highest order. These miracles and the people who were the medium for them came to me through the rich heritage of librarianship, which, like Christian Evangelism, does its best work while being on the sidelines of social reform rather than the center of policy making, for example, in Congress. I understand that librarianship is a business, but that is not *all* or even *mainly* what it is, and the same can be said for any school or university you care to name. For many people, the fact that all institutions are businesses first and services second is an indication of how far astray capitalism has led us. After all, Carnegie, Rosenwald, Rockefeller, and others did not contribute to libraries and educational centers to make them profit centers or bureaucratic structures whose primary purpose was to remain indestructible and perpetuate themselves; rather, they gave money to libraries, schools, universities, and museums because those entities were good for society.

The post-9/11 American computer-generated dysphoria, so well described in Thomas Pynchon's mordantly funny novel *The Bleeding Edge* (2013), is evident in the divisive spirit, social and economic inequality, and preposterous televised rhetoric by which a large portion of the citizenry of both political parties of the United States live. The United States seems to be caught in an exit-less maze of conundrums—medical, intellectual, ideological, and spiritual. These are not the kinds of problems that can always be solved by theory, formula, data, or assessment. We all know too well the nature of the problems, if we know that there is a problem at all. Those who don't know there is a crisis or at least a radical re-posturing of positions are living in what that crazy old drug-addled radical plutocrat

William S. Burroughs called *The Soft Machine*, lulled into complacency by the blinking lights, the alienation, the comforting company of electronic media.[9] In such a world, deep thought and deliberate statements and actions are called for and hopefully will be forthcoming, along with generous portions of humor. Libraries and the literature confirm one comforting truth that no politico or zealot wants to hear: humans are foolish; they err, but if they persevere, they can forgive themselves and each other and move forward.

Maybe there really are two kinds of human beings as one of my favorite students once proposed in a social sciences literature class: those who are always looking forward for the main advantage and those melancholic souls who look backwards and try to learn from their mistakes. As one observer of modern folly recently observed, breaking the cycle of relentless and dehumanizing "progress"

> is about slowness, and about finding alternatives to alienation that accompanies a sweater knitted by a machine in a sweatshop in a country you know nothing about, or jam made by a giant corporation that has terrible environmental and labor practices and might be tied to the death of honeybees or the poisoning of farmworkers. It's an attempt to put the world back together again, in its materials but also its time and labor. It's both laughably small and heroically ambitious.[10]

There is a balance, of course, just as there are far more types of human being than any one person or author can account for. Librarians can speak for all of those people whatever allegiance they claim and whatever wardrobe they wear—entrepreneurs, maiden aunts, accountants, lovers of bodice rippers, fanzine fashionistas, deconstruction divas, gay anorexics in designer hair shirts, exotic musky-voiced singers of the last known unknown language in the world—or is this just *nostalgie de la boue*? Do we have to go back to caves and try it that way for a while until the bombs stop falling, as Sabrina suggested in Thornton Wilder's *The Skin of Our Teeth*? I choose to think not. I think it is the very latest thing, and it is fit for very long-term wear.

Revising My Thou

For a start, maybe I better quit buying and collecting and start sharing.

Perhaps the profession needs to petition the new Pope Francis, who seems to be a stellar person, to change the patron saint of librarians from St. Jerome, who was always rather cranky—a result of eating all those locusts with honey, no doubt—to Hypatia, the last great Greek philosopher, who was martyred by a Christian mob in Alexandria in 415 CE. She sounds much more like the kind of saint we need in these troubled times.

I will lengthen my list of correspondents to practice what is left of my penmanship and sharpen my ability to express myself. In addition to dear Virginia in Lincoln, Nebraska, and dear Sandy in Milwaukee, Wisconsin, I will also occasionally write reflective letters to my two sisters so that everything we express won't be trapped in the dynamics of dysfunction.

I will learn how to breathe mindfully.

I will claim ownership of my librarian wardrobe, not only what I wear, but what I own as part of me, what I value as a professional, and I will accept no professional truths as personal gospel unless I believe it is so. My inside, vintage or not, should be as carefully nurtured as the external image I project. That should keep me busy for a while.

Notes

1. Hammarskjöld's translation of Martin Buber's *I and Thou* from German, on which Hammarskjöld was working at the time his plane crashed in Nbola, Zambia, on September 18, 1961; quotation from Michael Ignatieff, "The Faith of a Hero," review of *Hammarskjöld: A Life*, by Roger Lipsey, *New York Review of Books* 60, no. 17 (November 7, 2013), www.nybooks.com/articles/archives/2013/nov/07/dag-hammarskjold-faith-hero.
2. Sadie T. Gober, *The First Hundred Years, Georgia* (Atlanta, GA: Walter W. Brown, 1935), 433–37.
3. Arnold P. Sable, "The Sexuality of the Library Profession: The Male and the Female Librarian," *Wilson Library Bulletin* 43 (1969): 748–51.
4. James C. Bonner, *Milledgeville* (Athens: University of Georgia Press, 1978), 190.
5. Dee Garrison, *Apostles of Culture* (New York: Free Press, 1979), 176.
6. Richard L. Simpson and Ida M. Simpson, "Women and Bureaucracy in the Semi-Professions," in *The Semi-Professions and Their Organization,* ed. Amitai Etzioni (New York: Free Press, 1969), 196–265.
7. James V. Carmichael Jr., "Atlanta's Female Librarians, 1883–1915," *Journal of Library History* 21 (Spring 1986): 376–99.
8. James V. Carmichael Jr., "Gender Issues in the Workplace: Male Librarians Tell Their Side," *American Libraries* 25, no. 3 (March 1994): 227–30.

9.   William S. Burroughs, *The Soft Machine* (New York: Olympia Press, 1961).
10. Rebecca Solnit, "In the Day of the Postman," Diary, *London Review of Books* 35, no. 16 (August 29, 2013), www.lrb.co.uk/v35/n16/rebecca-solnit/diary.

Bibliography

Bonner, James C. *Milledgeville: Georgia's Antebellum Capital*. Athens: University of Georgia Press, 1978.

Burroughs, William S. *The Soft Machine*. New York: Olympia Press, 1961.

Carmichael, James V., Jr. "Atlanta's Female Librarians, 1883–1915." *Journal of Library History* 21, no. 2 (Spring 1986): 376–99.

———. "Gender Issues in the Workplace: Male Librarians Tell Their Side." *American Libraries* 25, no. 3 (March 1994): 227–30.

Garrison, Dee. *Apostles of Culture: The Public Librarian in American Society, 1876–1920*. New York: Free Press, 1979.

Gober, Sadie T. *The First Hundred Years: A Short History of Cobb County, Georgia*. Atlanta, GA: Walter W. Brown, 1935.

Ignatieff, Michael. Review of *Hammarskjöld: A Life*, by Roger Lipsey. *New York Review of Books* 60, no. 17 (November 7, 2013), www.nybooks.com/articles/archives/2013/nov/07/dag-hammarskjold-faith-hero.

Sable, Arnold P. "The Sexuality of the Library Profession: The Male and the Female Librarian." *Wilson Library Bulletin* 43 (1969): 748–51.

Simpson, Richard L., and Ida M. Simpson. "Women and Bureaucracy in the Semi-Professions." In *The Semi-Professions and Their Organization,* edited by Amitai Etzioni, 196–265. New York: Free Press, 1969.

Solnit, Rebecca. "In the Day of the Postman." Diary, *London Review of Books* 35, no. 16 (August 29, 2013): 32–33, www.lrb.co.uk/v35/n16/rebecca-solnit/diary.

CHAPTER 1

Contextualizing Ourselves
The Identity Politics of the Librarian Stereotype

Nicole Pagowsky and Miriam Rigby

Librarians are in the business of presentation.* Whether we are presenting information or presenting ourselves to the public, it is a constant of
the profession. And all of our constituents—especially our served communities—judge our presentation, consciously and subconsciously, as to
whether they can see us as reliable, authoritative, approachable sources of
information. Therefore, it is only natural for us to turn a reflexive eye on
ourselves, analyzing our presentation-of-self. Librarians have done this
in droves—from image-based blogs and reflective essays to a selection of
scholarly works addressing librarians in popular culture and other dimen-
sions of librarian-representation. What is rare, however, is the application
of ethnographic research and the incorporation of theory from the broader
social sciences into our examinations of how librarians present themselves
and how they are perceived.

We, the editors, come to librarianship through anthropological and
sociopsychological discourse communities that provide us with the lenses
through which we frame our understanding of our profession. Through
these lenses, we have engaged with librarianship to make sense of how we
can do our best work; to study how others perceive us, stereotype us, and
understand us; to better address the ongoing critiques and discussions of
the value of libraries. Articulating the value of libraries and librarians is
the zeitgeist of 21st-century librarianship; one does not need to look far to
find articles about the fading importance of libraries or about yet another

---

* Throughout this chapter, we will be using the terms *librarian* and *information professional* interchangeably as these issues apply to many in a broader sense of the field, although *librarians*
  specifically tend to be what are addressed in much of the literature related to our topics.

library being closed due to deprioritization in budgets. Value concern has been the subject of myriad conferences and publications. And with valuing comes examination of librarians, both serious and flippant, which often pulls from classic librarian stereotypes, whether appearance-, attitude-, or skill-based.

We have been fascinated by these discussions and the resulting engagement by our colleagues in person and online. On the one hand, there is a sense that the stereotype discussions are exhausted, and though there is excellent work being done in the realm of stating the value of libraries and librarians, there is a common sentiment that we should not have to state and restate our value so regularly. Yet, on the other hand, these discussions invariably become wonderfully passionate and multifaceted arguments on the demographics, presentation, and purpose of librarianship—topics that are important and, we argue, will continue to carry weight as long as there is any question as to the value of librarianship and libraries. In response to these discussions, and stemming from our predispositions to sociocultural inquiry, we have explored venues of presentation-of-self, first with Nicole Pagowsky's venture into counteracting stereotypes, vis-à-vis sartorialism, with the *Librarian Wardrobe* blog since 2010 and subsequent invited lectures on the topic.[*] Miriam Rigby wrote on presentation-of-self in an essay for *College and Research Libraries News* on outreach and networking with faculty as well as in a chapter on how to approach outreach as a new subject librarian in the forthcoming book *Sudden Selector's Guide to Anthropology Resources*.[1] Additionally, these topics have been addressed in our joint projects of a series of conference and webinar panels on librarian stereotypes.[2]

To provide more background, *Librarian Wardrobe* catalogs how information professionals dress for work via a primarily photograph-based blog, with the majority of content being self-submitted. On its face, the blog demonstrates clothing choice; however, its underlying purpose is to

---

[*] Nicole Pagowsky, *Librarian Wardrobe* (blog), 2014, http://librarianwardrobe.com; presentations and lectures include LIM College's Fashion Symposium in NYC, Museum of Contemporary Art Tucson, and Maricopa County Library District Staff Day.

visually clarify that there is no longer a unifying stereotype for librarians: librarians dress differently and have varying interests and job descriptions. Many Internet searches for librarian style, images of librarians in general, or pictures of specific items of clothing (stereotypical or not) lead a variety of individuals to the blog, librarians and non-librarians alike, which implies stereotypes are still fixed in the public mind if there are searches for "librarian glasses," "shushing librarian," "librarian shoes," "hipster librarian style," and "sexy librarian."[†] If our stereotypes have focus on clothing, then to some degree we must dissect our clothing. In *The Language of Fashion*, Roland Barthes posits,

> Clothing allows man to "assume his freedom," to constitute himself as he chooses, even if what he has chosen to be represents what others have chosen for him…. Clothing is very close to this phenomenon; it seems that it has interested writers and philosophers because of its links with personality, of its capacity to change one's being for another; personality makes fashion, it makes clothing; but inversely, clothing makes personality. There is certainly a dialectic between these two elements.[3]

Clothing, and the rest of one's appearance, communicates. Art and design theorist Malcolm Barnard examines semiotics, noting, "Fashion and clothing are ways in which inequalities of social and economic status are made to appear right and legitimate, and therefore acceptable, not only to those in positions of dominance, but also to those in positions of subservience. The term used to describe this situation is hegemony."[4]

The structures of power need to be examined, challenged, and reconfigured if we are going to take hold of our image and have more control over our identity. Positioning current, everyday images of librarians in the public eye is one way in which to dispel notions of shushing spinsters, which—perhaps surprisingly to some—still exist. Typically, the focus of librarian image in the discourse has been directed toward popular media,

---

† All are actual search terms that have directed people to *Librarian Wardrobe*, though it is not certain how some of these terms led readers to the blog.

but it is useful for librarians to examine how we present ourselves in an ongoing basis and how this presentation impacts public perceptions. Moreover, library use is not the only thing affected by stereotype impressions; other relevant issues to consider include professional status, pay, and integration in campuses and communities.

A number of articles provide scholarly insight on the topic, as we will discuss in brief and which the chapter authors of this volume weave into their analyses to great effect. Noteworthy books are rarer. A few recent examples of books touching on issues of the presentation of librarianship include Ray Tevis and Brenda Tevis's 2005 book, *The Image of Librarians in Cinema,* which looks at how librarians have been represented in film.[5] Ruth Kneale's *You Don't Look Like a Librarian* from 2009 explores librarians' perspectives on stereotypes and presentation, comparing representation in pop culture with anecdotes.[6] Moving away from popular culture and media studies, William C. Welburn, Janice Welburn, and Beth McNeil explore the collaborative nature of advocacy in academic libraries through their edited volume, *Advocacy, Outreach and the Nation's Academic Libraries.*[7] And Lauren Comito, Aliqae Geraci, and Christian Zabriskie provide an actionable resource for library advocacy and valuing with *Grassroots Library Advocacy,* demonstrating ways in which to improve visibility, relationships, and messaging to the public for all types of libraries.[8]

Looking back over the decades, we find that books of in-depth scholarly engagement with similar issues of image emerge about every 10 years, sometimes in flurries. In the early 2000s, a solid engagement of librarian image and activist librarianship was provided by K. R. Roberto and Jessamyn West with *Revolting Librarians Redux: Radical Librarians Speak Out.*[9] The early-to-mid-1990s offered a number of titles, including the International Federation of Library Associations and Institutions–sponsored contribution of *The Image of the Library and Information Profession: How We See Ourselves* and Mary Jane Scherdin's *Discovering Librarians: Profiles of a Profession.*[10] One more decade back, we encounter another flurry with Pauline Wilson's 1982 volume, *Stereotype and Status: Librarians in the Unit-*

ed States and Kathleen de la Peña McCook's 1983 *The Status of Women in Librarianship: Historical, Sociological, and Economic Issues.*[11] These related topics continue to be relevant.

Our vision for *The Librarian Stereotype: Deconstructing Presentations and Perceptions of Information Work* is to revitalize this conversation with a strong focus on empirical research and a mix of historical, anthropological, sociological, and literary analysis of the presentation of information professions. This work fills a gap in the literature, going beyond a documentation of popular culture stereotypes of librarians and how to craft a personal brand to a scholarly examination of how these stereotypes exist in this decade, what they mean, and how to use and shape them advantageously for the profession. As *deconstructing* is used in the title of this book, we can look to Gayatri Chakravorty Spivak in her study of Jacques Derrida's notion of the term, where Spivak states, "[Deconstruction] is constantly and persistently looking into how truths are produced."[12] Examining truth production is what we are hoping to do from the discussions within and beyond this book.

The discussion surrounding librarian stereotypes has questioned whether studying perceptions has any impact on decreasing barriers to library use and improving the status of librarianship. In the article "Images and Perceptions as Barriers to Use of Library Staff and Services," Tracey Green stresses that it is not so much the stereotype, but rather users not fully understanding what librarians *do* that creates barriers to public use and detriment to librarians' status; further, she argues that the value of information needs to be in the spotlight for the subsequent valuing of libraries and librarians.[13] Although the value of our work should take the spotlight, when librarian stereotypes have a strong presence, they activate heuristics, or mental shortcuts, for defining what librarians do. Abigail Luthmann, in "Librarians, Professionalism and Image: Stereotype and Reality," agrees that the focus should be turned toward what librarians do and that most stereotype-related angst is misfocused and based on self-victimization, which serves to further promulgate circulating stereotypes.[14] Luthmann interprets this anxiety as unnecessary because stereotype obsession comes from within the profession rather than externally, and it would be more useful to respond with positive behavior. Freeing ourselves as a profession from this anxiety would be immensely beneficial to both our image and self-esteem, but we argue that anxiety and self-examination are two separate issues, the latter of which we should be engaged in. Both Project Information Literacy and the ERIAL Project have demonstrated how these points resonate for academic libraries through ethnographic and large-scale studies of students' research habits, showing that students do not typically understand what librarians do or how they can get help.[15] Lack of knowledge or misunderstanding in this capacity further impedes students in actually using the library and asking for help from librarians, feeding into a cycle of stress and confusion. This feeling of being lost and overwhelmed is referred to as "library anxiety," and it plays a role in how users interact with the library and librarians.[16] Considering user anxiety and role of the library, Gary Radford, in "Flaubert, Foucault, and the Bibliotheque Fantastique: Toward a Postmodern Epistemology for Library Science," draws the user into the issue of power relations, demonstrating how negative stereotypes of librarians can translate into negative (self-)expectations for users: "This stereotype may, at first glance, seem trivial and unimportant, but … such images serve to reinforce, in their very triviality and harmlessness, a particular network of power relations that connect the librarian, the user, and the text."[17] Henceforth, the relationship between the stereotype, the librarian and library, and the user "does not, and cannot, lead to a satisfying and productive library experience."[18] Users' exposure to these stereotypes can wind up reinforcing library anxiety, resulting in a snowball effect.

Clearly, informing users about the library and creating greater awareness about what librarians do can help allay this fear, but it also must be understood that users having anxiety—or simply negative impressions of librarians—may be intentionally avoiding the library and its positive messages based on their standing perceptions. Taking a proactive and multifaceted approach would be more effective. Responding with positive behavior will reach users who are already engaging with us. However, if we limit ourselves to this tactic alone, we risk missing many nonusers for whom the library is foreboding, anxiety inducing, or seemingly irrelevant and who may continue to know of libraries and librarians only through our stereotypes. Although from within the profession these stereotypes seem clearly outdated and irrelevant, this is not necessarily true for the public. Changing the conversation about the roles of librarians and the function of libraries should coincide with improving librarian image and status to dissolve lingering public assumptions of who librarians are and what librarians do. When considering how image influences perceptions, we can see that there is a lot more at play regarding stereotypes when we look to gender studies, sociopsychology, and anthropological perspectives.

Decades of social science research has tackled issues of how people present themselves and how people interact, and some of this has been applied within library and information science. Noted sociologist Erving Goffman stands out as a particularly prominent theorist, and though his work has been expanded upon by others since the 1960s and 70s, his groundwork on how people present themselves and interact with others remains fundamental and highly applicable to the day-to-day life of librarians. Marie Radford incorporates Goffman's analysis of "footing" and rituals of interaction into her 2006 article "Encountering Virtual Users: A Qualitative Investigation of Interpersonal Communication in Chat Reference."[19] Terrence Epperson and Alan Zemel similarly draw on Radford's work and directly upon Goffman in their analysis of language use in chat reference interactions.[20] Likewise, in chapter 9 of this volume, in her analysis of tattoos and library workers, Erin Pappas incorporates Goffman's work on how context affects an individual's self and presentation thereof. Goffman describes how an individual does not have one single "self" that they present in all situations.[21] For instance, the self presented to close friends may differ from what is presented to family; presentation of self shifts even more significantly as the distance from a core group increases.

The self presented can also shift for each individual interacted with depending on the context in which the interaction takes place.

This translates into our work as librarians, whether in public services or otherwise, as people enter into interactions with us already burdened with expectations. How we present ourselves shapes those expectations and our ongoing relationships—both positively and negatively. And whether one is actively concerned or not with occupational stereotypes or personal image and presentation, these influence how others see us and interact with us. Written while the author was a student of library science in 1988, Mary Land's article "Librarians' Image and Users' Attitudes to Reference Interviews" explored the detrimental nature of librarian stereotypes and how users' perceptions affected their use of libraries and librarians.[22] A major barrier is even identifying who is a librarian as they are not necessarily distinguishable from any other library worker or even from any other adult in the library. After identifying a librarian, other factors influencing user-success and confidence include "approachability, identity, warmth, openness, and body language of the librarian."[23]

This suggests that even active users, who are already in a library with research questions, carry preconceived notions that might hinder or help their access to information, depending on what they encounter and how librarians presents themselves. We risk losing the engagement of potential lifelong users of libraries if we fail to present ourselves as welcoming, accessible, engaged, and savvy. Imagine, then, how this carries over to people who are less aware of the usefulness of librarians. If we cannot communicate our value through librarian imagery seen beyond the walls of our libraries, then we lose that many more users who know of us only through stereotype and hearsay.

Consider further those questioning whether to fund a library or a competing service. If library-related stereotypes mislead potential donors, our trustees, or government agencies, we risk losing necessary funding and related support. Library workers are outspoken when it comes to intellectual freedom and other issues that affect library users, but we have not been nearly as vocal on our own behalf. Some good work is being done by a number of bodies within librarianship already, and we must be ready to join and support their efforts as well as push other causes forward. OCLC's report, *From Awareness to Funding: A Study of Library Support in America*, addresses the need for library advocacy and evaluates how advocacy and marketing campaigns can best influence those who fund libraries—especially voting taxpayers.[24] The intertwining of our image and value thus extends to the "value" of librarianship on a monetary level; our image must communicate our value to those who fund us. Some donors may be happy to will their estates to their vision of a large book warehouse, but they, over the course of time, are dying off. The first library super political action committee (super PAC), EveryLibrary, is leading the charge in library advocacy in the United States, and its fundamental message is that the public's perception of "librarians" (meaning anyone working in a library) drives behavior at the polls.[25] EveryLibrary is taking this understanding and its fundraising power as a super PAC to help spread positive librarian image campaigns and help small library groups around the United States in their local ballot initiatives.

Concerns over value and advocacy can feed right back in to our anxiety; even more so in women-dominated professions, in which perception anxiety is commonplace.* In James V. Carmichael Jr.'s trailblazing article "The Gay Librarian: A Comparative Analysis of Attitudes towards Professional Gender Issues," he explains that "stereotype and status concerns are obsessive in all low-status, marginal professions."[26] Discussion surrounding status and stereotypes of librarians enters into gendered space and touches on problems with inequality in women-dominated professions as a whole. Marie L. Radford and Gary P. Radford astutely state in "Librarians and Party Girls: Cultural Studies and the Meaning of the Librarian" that "[stereotyping] creates a regime of representation that ultimately constricts the power and economic status of a gendered profession—librarianship."[27]

---

* *Female-dominated* might be more grammatically correct, but here as well as in the rest of this chapter, we are focusing on gender-referencing terms, rather than sex, as one does not have to be biologically female to identify as a woman.

Looking at the American Library Association–Allied Professional Association's (ALA-APA) median salary comparison chart, adapted from the Bureau of Labor Statistics, it is clear that women-dominated fields, even when requiring more advanced education, have lower pay and status than those dominated by men.[28] This should not be surprising, but it is something that needs to be within our awareness to understand the effect stereotypes have. Melissa Lamont echoes this concern in "Gender, Technology, and Libraries" by highlighting that "the association of women's positions with lower wages and prestige serves to sustain the occupational segregation and justify the subtle discrimination that hinders women."[29] Lamont also notes the problem with symbolic representations of gendered fields, where "sometimes perception creates reality."[30] This speaks to both being aware of our stereotypes and the importance of diversity.

Considering respect for women in a professional capacity, the Radfords further note in their research on stereotypes and power relations (through the lens of Foucault), "There is a clear relationship between the representation and treatment of women and the low status of the library profession."[31] The Radfords argue that gendered, constructed "systems of difference" maintain hegemony.[32] Furthermore, it is essential to dig deeper into the stereotype to discover how it is perpetuated, who is hurt by it, and how can it be challenged and changed; we must "analyze the systems of power/knowledge that go to the very heart of what it means to be male and female, powerful and marginalized, valued and devalued."[33]

Naturally, women-dominated professions tend to face battles mirroring (first-world) feminism's overarching concerns. In the case of information work, we are dealing with asserting our value in a profession, which, on the face of it, is devalued due to stereotypes of subservience and caring. And this is how our worth is defined to the public. In an effort to provide solutions rather than just highlight the problem, ALA-APA points to a suggested course of action: first, "We must overcome the stereotype of the library worker as the selfless, dedicated and devoted worker, who is in the profession to do good and who will accept any pittance of pay;" second, we need to better inform the public of what librarians do and the special skills, education, and experience that are needed to be a successful librarian; and third, pay equity is a battle we should continue fighting, particularly because it is one way (among many) in which women are discriminated against.[34] As we similarly stress, the APA-ALA suggestions illustrate a multifaceted approach because stereotypes, perceived value, and public understanding of what librarians do are all intertwined.

Although these positive efforts exist and have been expanding in recent years, there are also efforts that are detrimental. In trying to create distance from stereotypes, librarians at times wind up hypocritically policing each other (e.g., why is he or she dressing too sexy, he or she looks too frumpy, he or she looks like a hipster, he or she looks so smug, I or we could do it better, he or she does not deserve that award/press/recognition). This kind of in-fighting makes it more difficult to bring librarianship and our value as professionals into a positive light in the public's eye and even our own. Is it any wonder that the information professions carry self-esteem issues and anxiety if we are constantly flagellating ourselves? It is also not surprising that when librarians have the opportunity to present themselves, the focus shifts off of their message and on to how they look. Even in positive feature stories where the true intent of the piece is to promote librarians for what they do, the focus instead turns so heavily on how the featured librarians (especially when they are women) look or do not look or should have looked that individuals get reduced to physical attributes only.

Discounting abilities and accomplishments to instead focus on appearance, whether intentional or not, is not unique to librarianship; there is plenty of harassment directed toward women online as well as objectification in other occupations.* Considering image-based commentary about

---

* See "Internet Harassment of Women: When Haters Do More than Hate," www.npr.org/2014/01/08/260757625/internet-harassment-of-women-when-haters-do-more-than-just-hate; "Female Athletes Judged by Sex Appeal," http://abcnews.go.com/Technology/story?id=119952; "Focus on Hillary Clinton's Appearance Sparks Criticism," http://now.org/update/focus-on-hillary-clinton-s-appearance-sparks-criticism.

librarians has come from both the public at large and within the field, the latter especially proves we have some work to do. Audre Lorde makes the charge in "The Master's Tools Will Not Dismantle the Master's House" that women should take a united front and work together for feminism's success from a perspective of intersectionality:* "As women, we have been taught either to ignore our differences, or to view them as causes for separation and suspicion rather than as forces for change. Without community, there is no liberation, only the most vulnerable and temporary armistice between an individual and her oppression…. In our world, divide and conquer must become define and empower."[35] This powerful statement applies to our efforts in making librarianship better respected: we should be working together to demonstrate our value and garner greater respect from our relative communities, whether it be in neighborhoods, on university campuses, in corporations, or online.†

Lest we think the problems and divisiveness surrounding image in information professions are unique, it is useful to note that other professions, and even ones that are not traditionally women-dominated, ponder questions of image and presentation as well. Our conversations perhaps feel more prevalent due to our closeness to them, but it is mostly a case of a filter bubble (or information avoidance) that we may miss these conversations happening outside of librarianship.[36] Throughout academia we find many discussions on the topic, both casual and scholarly. Fashion blogs are kept by academics and professionals as diverse as historians, pharmacologists, and lawyers.[37] For the 2013 annual conference of the American Anthropological Association, the prominent anthropology blog *Savage Minds* posted in true anthropological style a somewhat tongue-in-cheek, yet thorough analysis, "Conference Chic, or, How to Dress Like an Anthropologist," featuring observant gems such as "The unisex pan-ethnic

---

* Briefly described, *intersectionality* signifies overlapping systems of oppression.

† Not just women librarians but all librarians should be working together to improve our collective status as these concerns affect us all; however, this does not mean ignoring important differences between us, including the need for improving diversity in LIS and giving a greater voice to those not in the dominant group(s).

scarf is a must" and "There is a way in which disheveled chic is the perfect style for anthropologists. It can match any situation."[38]

In recent years, the *Chronicle of Higher Education* has run articles exploring "The Academic Wardrobe," "Looking like a Professor," and even a humorous take on RateMyProfessor.com's chili pepper indicator of professor hotness.[39] Some of these articles might suggest a need to conform to particular styles to succeed in particular fields. Yet there is also visible pushback from early career academics trying to reconfigure traditional styles and stereotypes, such as the article "Wearing Me Out."[40] Among many astute observations, the author writes, "If we have too-strict rules about what our colleagues should look like, we may exclude people who don't look exactly like most of us." Publishing anonymously as "Female Science Professor," the author indexes the genuine pressure and possible ridicule she faces relating to these issues. *Inside Higher Ed* has also broached the subject regularly—"Those Really Smart Clothes," "The Well-Dressed Academic," and "Why I (Usually) Wear a Tie."[41] Regarding a *New York Times* feature on stylish professors, "Class Acts,"[42] Dr. Tanisha R. Ford contemplates the power of privilege, or the lack thereof, on dress and adornment in the Ivory Tower:

> The reality is that scholars of color, women, and other groups whose bodies are read as non-normative have never been able to check their race, gender, religion, or sexual orientation at the door…. Our professionalism and our intellectual competence are largely judged by how we style ourselves … [and so we use] our fashion sense to define ourselves, our professionalism, and our research and teaching agendas on our own terms.[43]

We will return to engaging with privilege, but for now it is key to note that much of the discussion of appearance in academia stems out of structures of power and the (de)construction of traditional "norms."

Academic studies from across the humanities, social sciences, and sciences have also taken a reflexive look at appearance in academia. Social psychologists Nalini Ambady and Robert Rosenthal found that it took approximately 30 seconds (or less) of silent video to judge how a high school teacher would be evaluated in end-of-term evaluations.[44] Another study out of the field of communications found correlations between graduate student teaching assistants' appearance and student engagement.[45] We might compare both to how image and presentation affect how library users encounter librarians as Jennifer Bonnet and Ben McAlexander study in "First Impressions and the Reference Encounter: The Influence of Affect and Clothing on Librarian Approachability."[46] Additionally, a recent study published in the *Proceedings of the National Academy of Sciences* on the evaluation of musicians' performances found that judgments of a performance's quality based solely on audio were significantly different from judgments based on audio and visual input, with image strongly impacting judgments of otherwise identical performances.[47] A 2002 article, "Posing as Professor: Laterality in Posing Orientation for Portraits of Scientists," found that even the direction in which a person faces in their faculty portrait could convey a more "scientific" appearance.[48] Being interested in how people look and display themselves is human and timeless, as is working to maneuver the system.

In thinking about who is and is not considered a "librarian," a lack of privilege conflicts with choice regarding one's ability to ignore stereotypes and others' perceptions. Numerous bloggers have taken on these issues, and considering dress as being one avenue in which we write our identities and they are read by others, these examples look to clothing. Being able to not concern oneself with this reading or writing is a privilege, and *Feministing* blogger Juliana Britto Schwartz examines how people of color (particularly women) are required to assimilate into Western, white culture when dressing for work. She says, "For [women of color] who face judgments around being tacky or aggressive, their clothing must do everything possible to counteract those stereotypes."[49] Cat Smith explains, in considering abled and disabled bodies, that "what passes for a self-aware rejection of fashion on one person will be seen in a completely different way on another body" and that fashion can be used as "a way of challenging ableist assumptions of disabled people's place in the world."[50] In this quote she is referring to Eddie Ndopu's account of presenting himself as a "black queer crip," as he identifies himself:

> Clothes are deeply imbued with the insidiousness of power relations when attached to the bodies wearing them. A hoodie carries the threat of violence when it clads the bodies of young black and brown male-identified and masculine of center people. Wearing the niqab and/or burka catalyzes the white saviour industrial complex to step in and declare euro-western conceptions of womanhood as the universal benchmark of gender based equality, denying Muslim women their agency. In my case, sweats and clothes labeled "frumpy" engender pity. And that is why I refuse to wear them in public.[51]

For those not part of dominant culture groups, identity often needs to be hidden or negotiated in order to assimilate.

When considering white privilege specifically, Peggy McIntosh describes this as "whites are taught to think of their lives as a morally neutral, normative, and average, also ideal, so that when we work to benefit others, this is seen as work which will allow 'them' to be more like 'us.'"[52] In a study on appearance management and border construction to disassociate oneself from certain groups, Anthony Freitas et al., found study participants echo Ndopu's sentiment. The study's authors explain that "several African American males reported the need to be cautious about being mistaken for gang members [and] Asian American students often expressed the desire to appear different from recent immigrants."[53] For marginalized groups, demonstrating who one is *not* through self-presentation can be just as urgent as demonstrating who one *is*.

The urgency of group association or disassociation for humane treatment is very real. Tressie McMillan Cottom, looking at how poor people get ridiculed for spending beyond what is assumed to be their means on status symbol items to disassociate themselves from a lower socioeconomic class, writes, "Belonging to one group at the right time can mean the difference between unemployment and employment, a good job as opposed to a bad job, housing or a shelter, and so on…. [Appearing] presentable as a sufficient condition for gainful, dignified work or successful social interactions is a privilege."[54] Kristin Iverson explains that the concept of *normcore** and lack of concern over identity "is just a case of powerful people flaunting their power by willingly ceding it …and the truth is that some people don't need to worry about their identities because their status is secure."[55] Body size is another stigmatization polarized by privilege. Melissa McEwan argues, "For fat women, being stylish isn't a luxury…. Fat women have all kinds of narratives about sloppiness, laziness, dirtiness to overcome. Sometimes [high-heeled shoes] are a crucial part of looking 'put together' in a way that sufficiently convinces people that we care about ourselves, that manages to counteract pervasive cultural narratives that fat people don't care about ourselves."[56]

It is not only fat women, as McEwan notes, but all women with marginalized bodies who "may strongly relate to the idea of having to be 'put together' in order to be treated as human beings."[57] There are many other groups that do not have the privilege of not caring about fashion or self-presentation. The elderly—again, women in particular—is one example, as aging comes with a loss of power. From this, M. Elise Radina et al., in studying the Red Hat Society, note that "not surprisingly, women experience higher degrees of negative stereotyping and stigma as they age than their male contemporaries."[58] The Red Hat Society uses clothing and presentation-of-self to reclaim power and lessen stigma.† And of course trans* individuals encounter a great deal of stigma attached to their identity. And whether transitioned or in considering gender/queer issues, Mimi Thi Nguyen questions gender presentation, particularly for those whose

---

* *Normcore* is a new nonfashion fashion movement and neologism where the ideal is to appear unfashionable and unconcerned with presentation in order to have greater human connections; see the K-Hole Trend Report under "Youth Mode" at http://khole.net.

† According to its website, the Red Hat Society "has become the international society dedicated to reshaping the way women approaching 50 and beyond are viewed in today's culture," see http://redhatsociety.com/press/letter-to-the-media.

clothing options might not comfortably house or reflect their gender(s) or body type: "For whom is 'self-expression' through clothes or style difficult, unavailable, or even undesirable? What *other* gender presentations, sexual identities, and embodied states can point us suggestively toward alternative ways of inhabiting our clothes and the uncertain stories they tell?"[59] Presentation of self should not have to dictate an either/or existence, particularly so for those not in positions of privilege.

Librarian perspectives on identity and presentation also echo broader concerns with privilege. Chris Bourg, self-identifying as butch, reflects on the improbability of one-size-fits-all wardrobe advice and points out, in considering others' expectations for identity and dress, that "part of being different is always wondering."[60] Cecily Walker, a librarian also writing on identity and intersectionality in librarianship, states, "We can have conversations about purple hair and tattoos and whether they don't represent a professional image, but we shouldn't have them without drawing parallels between these superficial differences and the (in some case) immutable differences that we are born with, or that are central to our identity."[61]

Walker's statement demonstrates the need to recognize these issues, especially when we are working to increase diversity. As Minh-Ha T. Pham makes clear in *Ms. Magazine*, "Fashion, like so many other things associated primarily with women, may be dismissed as trivial, but it shapes how we're read by others, especially on the levels of gender, class, and race. In turn, how we're read determines how we are treated, especially in the workforce."[62]

Through this reflection and understanding how presentation-of-self and clothing choice are impacted by identity and privilege, we pointedly argue that although "not caring" or "not worrying" about (the librarian) stereotype would certainly be ideal, it is not possible for many individuals to do so. Being antifashion can influence a state of "false neutrality," which causes harm through what Dean Spade explains as "foreclos[ing] people's abilities to expose the workings of f*cked up systems on their bodies as they see fit."[63] It can rob us of agency.

Considering how to improve perceptions of librarians, it is important to first examine how and why these perceptions are formed. When there is an unknown, it is common to use heuristics to fill in the blanks, and once these impressions are made, it can be very difficult to reverse them. It is nearly impossible for one to enter a completely unknown situation without expectations or some form of stereotype. Library users who have seen librarians presented in popular culture or who have had impactful experiences in their own lives will depend on heuristics to inform their understanding of a new situation or a new person: the library and librarian in question.

Social psychology professors and researchers Richard E. Nisbett and Lee Ross have explained the "representativeness heuristic" as a means by which individuals explain the unknown; when pertaining to groups of people, a "goodness-of-fit" schema is subconsciously used to relate recognized traits to established categories.[64] When a known stereotype is available, this is what can be used to substitute for lack of understanding. For users who avoid the library, their idea of librarians will be based on what they already know. Whether this is as harmless as assuming librarians wear a lot of cardigans or the more detrimental idea that librarians are irrelevant or even both, previous impressions will carry weight. Once established, these impressions can be inexorable, proving difficult to reverse and particularly so when considering the impact of self-fulfilling prophecies. Sociologist Robert Merton explains this as "a *false* definition of the situation [that evokes] a new behavior which makes the originally false conception come true."[65] Merton notes this as a cause of forced behaviors resulting from stereotyped groups too consciously attempting to not fit their assigned stereotypes.[66]

In the recent decade, blogs have become a popular venue for explorations of the topics of presentation and fashion. Beyond the innumerable sartorial photo blogs, there are also many photo blogs focusing on people who are deemed striking, sometimes for their fashion but often for much more. The blog *Humans of New York* (*HONY*) is a significant example from which many other "Humans of *" blogs have sprung.[67] Further, *HONY* creator and photographer Brandon Stanton also captures poignant statements from his subjects, breaking down barriers of image and stereotype as viewers get a peek beyond the pose. Engaging the public to break down these types of barriers is crucial not just for librarianship but on a much broader scale as well.

An example from librarianship would be the aforementioned publicly viewable Internet policing of how other librarians look: in an effort to avoid certain stereotypes remaining in the spotlight, this instead highlights infighting and essentially the act of shushing (each other) on a grander scale, enforcing what the public might have wrongly assumed to be traits of librarians initially. Robert Rosenthal and Lenore Jacobson, in their highly influential study, *Pygmalion in the Classroom*, discuss motivation for prophecy fulfillment.[68] Counterintuitively, when expectations (even negative or harmful ones) are in place and the reverse occurs (even if the reverse has a beneficial outcome), it causes some form of physical, emotional, or psychic pain. Hence, met expectations lead to satisfaction. In relation to evolutionary advantage, Rosenthal and Jacobson note, "Man has a vested interest in his predictive accuracy."[69] Therefore, we argue that focusing only on response through positive messages and information about what librarians do will essentially fall on deaf ears for those relying on heuristics to inform their interest in libraries. To break free from self-fulfilling prophecies that are a result of stereotypes, Merton advises that "only when the original assumption is questioned and a new definition of the situation introduced, does the consequent flow of events give the lie to the assumption. Only then does the belief no longer father the reality."[70] He makes it clear that self-examination, challenge, and change go hand in hand, and we consequently maintain that self-study is essential in improving the status and perception of librarians.

Stereotypes, in conjunction with heuristics, can additionally be integrated into knowledge structures through thin slicing, or person-perception. This area of research comes from the social sciences where *thin slicing* refers to making judgments from first impressions based on nonverbal behavior in a very short span of time. Nalini Ambady notes in "The Perils of Pondering: Intuition and Thin Slice Judgments" that "the literature on nonverbal behavior suggests that evaluative judgments based solely on nonverbal cues are biologically based and occur automatically, outside awareness, without drawing on conscious, cognitive processing resources."[71] This demonstrates that we make snap judgments of each other before a person might even have a chance to speak, and because these evaluative judgments are automatic and instant, they rely on preexisting knowledge structures (heuristics, stereotypes) to help us quickly assume how to understand another person or group of people. Therefore, we argue that how we are perceived through how we look, or are assumed to look, is not irrelevant and does in fact play a role in our resulting determined value.

Mimi Thi Nguyen, from the blog *Threadbared* and an associate professor of gender and women's studies and Asian American studies, expresses that "the stories we create around persons from their clothes often say more about us, and about the larger social, political, economic discourses and practices that inform our world-views both consciously and unconsciously, than about the persons we are looking at."[72] In considering how we present ourselves and how our values are espoused through presentation, realistically or stereotypically, it is worth understanding how we are actually perceived by the public and what these perceptions mean, whether the basis is looks, values, abilities, or all of the above. Only then can we determine how to reverse these stereotypes, as it will be difficult to defeat the persistent imagery fueling these perceptions without a unified and repetitive front.[*]

As many of the chapters in this volume elucidate and expand upon, there are a variety of librarian stereotypes, each of which does its own work on the public perception of information work, whether for positive or negative. Traditional stereotypes include the dichotomies of stuffy and/

---

[*] Patrick Sweeney, serving on EveryLibrary's board of directors, points out that numerous literature on effective campaigning stresses the importance of repetition in imagery and messaging; see http://pcsweeney.com/2014/02/12/the-slate-article-campaign-math-and-why-that-article-doesnt-matter.

or effeminate man and the spinster prude or highly sexual woman. These images are well ingrained in the public consciousness and are the context we navigate while we work to present ourselves and the value of our work. As Erving Goffman, discussed briefly earlier, wrote in *The Presentation of Self in Everyday Life*, "When an actor takes on an established social role, usually he finds that a particular front has already been established for it."[73] Goffman spoke in terms of how individuals fit into roles and into groups, but the concept carries over to attempts to break free of these established images.

On the flip side of this issue, the original intent of a message can be easy to miss if taken out of context and through one's personal frame of reference. This of course can apply to messaging regarding the value of librarians. Thus, in establishing new images, old images must be reengaged for reference to point out how the new image is different. Jacques Derrida wrote, "Every sign, linguistic or nonlinguistic …can be cited, put between quotation marks; in so doing it can break with every given context, engendering an infinity of new contexts in a manner which is absolutely illimitable."[74] To follow Derrida, we can imagine how librarians' attempts to fight stereotypes can be taken out of their intended context and fed right back into their construction or any multitude of new contexts unintended. One therefore cannot ignore the public perception of libraries and information professions when working to convey their value. Knowing how the audience—whether the public, fellow librarians, trustees with funding, or administrators with power over the future of a library—will encounter the message should strongly influence how it is framed. Working from within the context of stereotype returns us to the Radfords' analysis of how to counter stereotypes in "Librarians and Party Girls." Citing Stuart Hall, they argue that we can reverse stereotypes and substitute positive images in the media to challenge negative images.[75] The Radfords suggest that to reverse the stereotype "would involve media images of librarians as the reverse of their stereotypical images, that is, as young, cool, and hip."[76]

It would be nearly impossible to write about librarian stereotypes and skip over the new addition to our menagerie of images: being "hip." Most notably in 2007, *The New York Times* (*NYT*) published the article "A Hipper Crowd of Shushers" to highlight librarian image with the backdrop of social events and activist work in New York City.[77] But is being reimagined as hipsters truly beneficial to the status of the profession, and does this persona align with the portrayal the Radfords described? This *NYT* article continues to receive unencouraging reactions in LIS online forums, even seven years later. The term *hipster* has taken on an even more negative connotation within the last decade, where many prefer to maintain distance from the descriptor. The 2010 n+1 publication *What Was the Hipster? A Sociological Investigation* revealed derisive definitions and reactions, including Rob Horning pondering, "Or is the hipster a kind of permanent cultural middleman in hyper-mediated late capitalism, selling out alternative sources of social power developed by outsider groups[?]"[78] This is appropriate considering that some iterations of hipsterdom have appropriated other cultures to serve the needs of upper-middle class whites.* The negative responses to the *NYT* article could be attributed to disdain for the notion of a hipster. However, when considering the Radfords' perspective, a more accurate reason for distancing might be that this stereotyping works to divide librarians by exclusionary tactics, demonstrating that a select few are hip, rather than librarianship as a profession. Much of hipster hatred comes from an "us versus them" dichotomy, and so this type of portrayal can have the opposite effect from what was intended.

Additionally, we are at a point where the term *hipster* has become essentially nullified, no longer having meaning because it is describing an age range rather than a delineated subculture.[79] It may also simply be an issue of generational change in librarianship. There have been countless books, articles, video segments, and portrayals in other popular media about how millennials are an awful generation, characterized by hipness. This cer-

---

* For example, see NPR's coverage of Urban Outfitters being sued for appropriating the Navajo Nation trademark: www.npr.org/2012/04/05/150062611/navajo-nation-sues-urban-outfitters-over-trademark.

tainly is not a new type of characterization; Gen X slackers and boomer hippies were similarly discussed as they each entered the workforce. Yet purposeful invocation of hipster imagery for libraries might serve a more innocuous use in an effort to appeal to harder-to-reach library users of this demographic. One reason librarians have more recently been associated with the hipster stereotype may be due to an attempt to increase appeal to the 20- to 30-year-old crowd libraries are hoping to serve.[†] And it is in this type of scenario that the Radfords' call to align librarianship (as opposed to a select few librarians) with the hipster image might indeed carry out a shift in perceptions. Regardless, with these more recent connotations of "hip," it is good to be cautious in what this signifier might represent.

A more pressing concern with the association between librarians and hipness, particularly within the diversity-starved field of LIS, is that the current, popular notion of a hipster often excludes persons of color and those of lower socioeconomic status as well as anyone else not fitting a youthful, able, cisgender existence.[‡] This narrow assumption of what a hipster is defines one-who-is-hip in the 21st century through stereotype. The exclusivity of this stereotype, not to mention the other negative traits associated with it, is detrimental to working for increased diversity within librarianship and our users. This is a recurring problem with all of the librarian stereotypes: they show internally within the field and externally to the public that librarians either "are" or "are supposed to be" a certain way, reflective of dominant culture norms. In parallel, this sends a message about what librarians "should" look like and brings us further into the semiotics of dress and other sociological perspectives on presentation.

Those not fitting into the majority demographic should not need to alter themselves or their presentation-of-self for greater inclusion in librarianship; expecting such alterations is in fact a barrier to increasing diversity. Similarly, in focusing on who gets left out of being assumed to

---

† See Chicago Public Library's "Not What You Think" campaign: www.prlog.org/10139260-its-not-what-you-think-chicago-public-library-launches-new-awareness-campaign.html.

‡ And other demographics that might not be as visible or could address intersectionality.

be an information worker because they *do not* fit the stereotypes, we also need to be careful of excluding by force those who *do* fit the stereotypes. In policing ourselves for how we should not look, we create hostility and further librarianship's problematic self-esteem issues, which does an additional disservice to us internally and in the eyes of the public. We argue that it would be more effective to be positive and supportive of each other, thereby turning the focus to self-examination for an understanding of how to replace negative, stereotypical images and their restrictions with positive, realistic images to the public.

In self-examination, we may also find the root of many librarians' visceral reactions to seemingly unending discussions of librarian stereotypes and public representation; these reactions may be strongly tied to individuals' senses of identity and individualism. In "Shattering the Myth of Separate Worlds: Negotiating Nonwork Identities at Work," Lakshmi Ramarajan and Erin Reid, professors at Harvard Business School and Boston University respectively, explore how the decline of career stability and other influences "are now blurring the distinctions between work and nonwork life domains such that many workers, their organizations, and their occupations must now renegotiate the relationship between work and nonwork identities."[80] If work and nonwork identities are more intertwined, as Ramarajan and Reid argue, then any representation of a librarian, positive or negative, stereotypical or not, becomes a representation not just of one's career (and therefore work identity) but also potentially a representation of who a person sees as oneself at one's core.

Ramarajan and Reid's discussion of the merging of work and nonwork identities appears then to be especially appropriate to apply in the case of librarianship's tempestuous job market.[81] When a person lands a professional-level position, notably after a period of unemployment or underemployment, they may be particularly enthusiastic about claiming their work identity. If they then are confronted with messages that say they must conform to someone else's conception of that work identity, it can be seen as an attack on their sense of self. So in the information professions, we are navigating particularly tricky ground between both work and nonwork identities and identities and image. Even librarians who do not see their nonwork identity as strongly tied to their careers may still find discomfort in discussions of what their work image should and should not be. Stereotypes co-opt an individual's agency in their presentation-of-self, and in an already unstable time, being reminded of a lack of control is threatening and evokes more uncertainty.

But much like spoken and written language, clothing and appearance communicate different messages in different contexts. Though we cannot necessarily control the contexts in which we present ourselves, we can be aware of them and encounter them on our own terms.* Librarians who would argue that how they look is unimportant and that what they do is what communicates their value are not necessarily wrong in their ideology, but the context matters as do the conscious choices we make in how we encounter our contexts. In *Ideology: An Introduction*, literary theorist Terry Eagleton explains ideology in much the same manner: "Ideology is a manner of 'discourse' rather than 'language,' [and] exactly the same piece of language may be ideological in one context and not in another; ideology is a function of the relation of an utterance to its social context."[82] For example, if librarians visiting a cat shelter proclaim that they love cats, few would find it to be an ideological statement. On the other hand, if they said that they love cats while introducing themselves at a library event, it would carry a different weight. Embracing a stereotype to make it your own can signal validation of stereotypes to others. And on the reverse side of the same matter, the Radfords address librarians who position themselves as unique via monikers such as "Leather Librarian" or "Renegade Librarian," stating, "It remains to be seen if these images will succeed in their challenge to the stereotypes, for in a sense they serve to reinforce the

---

* See *Fierce Fashion Futures* on Tumblr as an example of approaching fashion through activism: "Fashion is media and politics at the same time. Fashion is life and art at the same time. Every day we communicate something about who we are, who we want and what kind of world we want with our clothes and our bodies," Fierce Fashion Futures, "About Us," http://fiercefashionfutures.tumblr.com/about.

stereotype by proclaiming, in essence, 'we are librarians, but we are the exceptions to the stereotype.'"[83] Posing as individually in opposition to a stereotype can reinforce it for the rest of the group.

Further, no matter one's ideology regarding librarian image and how one situates oneself within it, by being engaged in information professions (and one might argue, in humanity), we are inherently entangled in the issues of presentation and representation. In their article "Enclothed Cognition," Hajo Adam and Adam Galinsky address the ways in which clothing influences people, finding that it has an impact both on those whom one encounters as well as on the wearer's own behavior.[84] But it is not just the appearance of an item of clothing that affects the wearer and the observer. Adam and Galinsky experimented in giving the same white lab coat to subjects and describing it varyingly as a "painter's coat" or a "doctor's coat" to different effect. "Participants who wore a supposed doctor's coat and participants who wore a supposed painter's coat were in fact wearing the same coat and had the same physical experience, yet, their performance on an attention-related task differed depending on the coat's symbolic meaning."[85] Extrapolating to the information professions, how we are presented has an effect on the work we do and what people expect of us; the respect we afford ourselves and that users afford us and the subsequent expectations on all sides are strongly affected by what "coat" we wear. Of course, there are no easy answers, and it was in contemplating all of these aspects of the librarian stereotype and its effects that we arrived at the idea for this book and sought out a broad range of chapter topics to tackle many of the issues from a variety of angles.

This book's chapters present a wide range of research genres and foci, attempting, in breaking down librarian stereotypes, to not fall victim itself to any stereotype of "information science literature." We have made an effort to include pieces that both focus on specific instances of librarian-presentation such as tattooed librarians and librarians in pornographic novels as well as broader discussions of issues in the occupation, calls for change, and suggestions of how to work toward that change. Each reader will likely spot gaps in our scope—as every reader has their own perspectives and interests. The ways in which our occupation is portrayed by others and by ourselves and our professional organizations are myriad; what do people expect from librarians and what do we want them to expect? Correspondingly, the ways in which librarianship is not portrayed are equally of interest and concern; what or who is missing in the image of librarianship? This book is intended to promote the conversation on librarianship today, its history, and its future, encouraging study of the many facets of the public face of the occupation and its institutions—how it is perceived and how we are actively affecting it. There are two important questions that we encourage everyone to ask again and again and to ask in different ways to grow the discourse to include each reader's personal concerns: How are we and others perpetuating the profession? And how does this impact the libraries and librarianship of the future?

In this themed volume, you will find a wealth of views and a wide range of ideas and approaches to looking at the issues surrounding stereotyping in information work. We have organized the order of the chapters to provide flow and some scaffolding in concepts. Readers began their journey with James V. Carmichael Jr.'s foreword, "Embracing the Melancholy: How the Author Renounced Moloch and the Conga Line for Sweet Conversations on Paper, to the Air of 'Second Hand Rose.'" Since his entrance into the field as a librarian and continuing as a faculty member at the University of North Carolina at Chapel Hill School of Information and Library Science, James has provided poignant research on librarian stereotypes, examining implications regarding gender and LGBTQ issues in librarianship. His contributions to the field in these areas of study are known for high-impact articles beginning in the 1990s such as "The Male Librarian and the Feminine Image: A Survey of Stereotype, Status, and Gender Perceptions" and "The Gay Librarian: A Comparative Analysis of Attitudes towards Professional Gender Issues."[86] A number of our authors cite James's research, and we feel it has come full circle to have his work, written 20 years ago, still be so relevant today, and he continues to provide highly insightful and important research to the field.

With this first chapter, we have framed the context from which the rest of our chapters emerge. In chapter 2, "Academic Librarian Self-Image in Lore: How Shared Stories Convey and Define our Sense of Professional Identity," Sarah Steiner and Julie Jones construct a folklore analysis of the tales librarians tell regarding work, demonstrating the resultant impact on self-perspective and what it means to be an information professional. In chapter 3, Gretchen Keer and Andrew Carlos examine why librarians have historically been obsessed with stereotypes and explore what might have propelled perception anxiety to this level with "The Stereotype Stereotype: Our Obsession with Librarian Representation." Ayanna Gaines follows in chapter 4 with "That's Women's Work: Pink-Collar Professions, Gender, and the Librarian Stereotype" and takes an in-depth look at the struggle for pay equity and status of feminized professions, providing context for librarianship by comparing it with fields encountering similar obstacles. In chapter 5, "From Sensuous to Sexy: The Librarian in Post-Censorship Print Pornography," David Squires addresses the evolution of the "sexy librarian" stereotype and its impact on libraries and their users through an analysis of pornographic novels.

In chapter 6, "Rainbow Warriors: Stories of Archivist Activism and the Queer Record," Terry Baxter examines the transformation of archives and activists through the co-emergence of queer archives and archivist activism. Chapter 7, "Unpacking Identity: Racial, Ethnic, and Professional Identity and Academic Librarians of Color," is Isabel Gonzalez-Smith, Juleah Swanson, and Azusa Tanaka's investigation of perceptions of librarians of color within librarianship, looking to self-study and implications for expanding racial and ethnic diversity in the library workforce. Dorothy Gambrell pairs her artistry with Amanda Brennan for chapter 8, "Librarians and Felines: A History of Defying the 'Cat Lady' Stereotype," a graphic rendering of the mingled stereotypes of librarians and cat aficionados. With chapter 9, "Between Barbarism and Civilization: Librarians, Tattoos, and Social Imaginaries," Erin Pappas explores tattoos and the body of the librarian through an anthro-linguistic analysis of how librarians talk about their tattoos and how these permanent art forms become a site in which the profession's anxieties play out. With chapter 10, "At the Corner of Personality and Competencies: Exploring Professional Personas for Librarians," Lauren Pressley, Jenny Dale, and Lynda Kellam look into assumed and real personas of librarians, linking personality with professional abilities and expectations. Chapter 11, "Student Perceptions of Academic Librarians: The Influence of Pop Culture and Past Experience," is Melissa Langridge, Christine Riggi, and Allison Schultz's examination of student perceptions of librarians based on exposure to popular media and previous interaction with libraries. The chapters are rounded off with Annie Pho and J. Turner Masland's chapter 12, "The Revolution Will Not Be Stereotyped: Changing Perceptions through Diversity," discussing librarianship's complicated history between public perceptions and diversity; they offer actionable suggestions on how to improve both users' relationships with librarians and libraries' efforts for greater diversity. And last, K. R. Roberto, noted cataloger and coauthor of *Revolting Librarians Redux: Radical Librarians Speak Out*, looks to the future of librarianship with challenges and opportunities ahead in his afterword.[87]

This book aims to capture images of both the general state of affairs for information work and its presentation, as well as multiple microcosms of presentation within the world of librarianship, and to explore these particular topics in greater detail. There is much work to be done to reconfigure both librarian stereotypes and the conditions that perpetuate them. Rather than offering a conclusive statement, or an encapsulation of all of the aspects of the value of librarianship and the issues we face as individuals and as a community, we hope that this book reignites the discussion and launches us into productive conversation and action.

Notes

1. Miriam Rigby, "Social Networking 0.0: Cultivating Casual Collaboration," *College and Research Libraries News* 71, no. 1 (2010): 14–15; Miriam Rigby and John Russell, *Sudden Selector's Guide to Anthropology Resources* (Chicago: American Library Association, forthcoming).

2. Nicole Pagowsky et al., "Style and Stereotypes: Perceptions of Librarians" (panel presentation, American Library Association Annual Conference, Anaheim, CA, June 25, 2012); Nicole Pagowsky et al., "Style and Stereotypes: Perceptions of Librarians" (webinar presentation, American Library Association TechSource and Library BoingBoing, September 27, 2012).

3. Roland Barthes, *The Language of Fashion* (London: Bloomsbury Academic, 2006), 107.

4. Malcolm Barnard, *Fashion as Communication* (New York: Routledge, 1996), 42.

5. Ray Tevis and Brenda Tevis, *The Image of Librarians in Cinema, 1917–1999* (Jefferson, NC: McFarland, 2005).

6. Ruth Kneale, *You Don't Look Like a Librarian* (Medford, NJ: Information Today, 2009).

7. William C. Welburn, Janice Welburn, and Beth McNeil, *Advocacy, Outreach and the Nation's Academic Libraries* (Chicago: Association of College and Research Libraries, 2010).

8. Lauren Comito, Aliqae Geraci, and Christian Zabriskie, *Grassroots Library Advocacy* (Chicago: American Library Association, 2012).

9. K. R. Roberto and Jessamyn West, *Revolting Librarians Redux* (Jefferson, NC: McFarland, 2003).

10. Hans Prins, Wilco de Gier, and Russell Bowden, *The Image of the Library and Information Profession* (Munich: K. G. Saur, 1995); Mary Jane Scherdin, *Discovering Librarians* (Chicago: Association of College and Research Libraries, 1994).

11. Pauline Wilson, *Stereotype and Status* (Westport, CT: Greenwood, 1982); Kathleen de la Peña McCook, *The Status of Women in Librarianship* (New York: Neal-Schuman, 1983).

12. Gayatri Chakravorty Spivak, *The Spivak Reader*, ed. Donna Landry and Gerald M. MacLean (New York: Routledge, 1996), 27.

13. Tracey Green, "Images and Perceptions as Barriers to Use of Library Staff and Services," *New Library World* 95, no. 1117 (1994): 19–24.

14. Abigail Luthmann, "Librarians, Professionalism and Image: Stereotype and Reality," *Library Review* 56, no. 9 (2007): 773–80.

15. "Project Information Literacy: A Large Scale Study about Early Adults and Their Research Habits," Project Information Literacy, last modified March 5, 2014, http://projectinfolit.org; "Ethnographic Research in Illinois Academic Libraries," ERIAL Project, accessed April 2, 2014, www.erialproject.org.

16. Constance A. Mellon, "Attitudes: The Forgotten Dimension in Library Instruction," *Library Journal* 113, no. 14 (1988): 137–39.

17. Gary P. Radford, "Flaubert, Foucault, and the Bibliotheque Fantastique: Toward a Postmodern Epistemology for Library Science," *Library Trends* 46, no. 4 (1998): 618.

18. Ibid., 620

19. Marie L. Radford, "Encountering Virtual Users: A Qualitative Investigation of Interpersonal Communication in Chat Reference," *Journal of the American Society for Information Science and Technology* 57, no. 8 (2006): 1046–59.

20. Terrence W. Epperson and Alan Zemel, "Reports, Requests, and Recipient Design: The Management of Patron Queries in Online Reference Chats," *Journal of the American Society for Information Science and Technology* 59, no. 14 (2008): 2268–83.

21. Erving Goffman, *Frame Analysis* (Cambridge, MA: Harvard University Press, 1974), 573–74.
22. Mary Land, "Librarians' Image and Users' Attitudes to Reference Interviews," *Canadian Library Journal* 45, no. 1 (1988): 15–20.
23. Ibid., 18.
24. Cathy De Rosa and Jenny Johnson, *From Awareness to Funding* (Dublin, OH: OCLC, 2008), https://oclc.org/content/dam/oclc/reports/funding/fullreport.pdf.
25. "EveryLibrary: Building Voter Support for Libraries," EveryLibrary, accessed April 5, 2014, http://everylibrary.org.
26. James V. Carmichael Jr., "The Gay Librarian: A Comparative Analysis of Attitudes towards Professional Gender Issues," *Journal of Homosexuality* 30, no. 2 (1996): 14.
27. Marie L. Radford and Gary P. Radford, "Librarians and Party Girls: Cultural Studies and the Meaning of the Librarian," *Library Quarterly* 73, no. 1 (2003): 59.
28. "Improving Salaries and Status of Library Workers," American Library Association–Allied Professional Association, last modified 2012, http://ala-apa.org/improving-salariesstatus.
29. Melissa Lamont, "Gender, Technology, and Libraries," *Information Technology and Libraries* 28, no. 3 (2009): 141, http://ejournals.bc.edu/ojs/index.php/ital/article/view/3221/2834
30. Ibid.
31. Marie L. Radford and Gary P. Radford, "Power, Knowledge, and Fear: Feminism, Foucault, and the Stereotype of the Female Librarian," *Library Quarterly* 67, no. 3 (1997): 262.
32. Ibid.
33. Ibid., 263
34. "Improving Salaries and Status."
35. Audre Lorde, "The Master's Tools Will Never Dismantle the Master's House," in *Sister Outsider*, ed. Audre Lorde (Berkeley, CA: Crossing Press, 2007), 112.
36. See Eli Pariser, The Filter Bubble, last modified March 26, 2012, www.thefilterbubble.com.
37. See *Sartorial Sidelines*, http://sartorialsidelines.blogspot.com; *She Could Be a Pharmer in Those Clothes*, http://shecouldbeapharmer.blogspot.com; *The Fashionable Esq.*, http://thefashionableesq.blogspot.com.
38. Carole McGranahan et al., "Conference Chic, or, How to Dress Like an Anthropologist," *Savage Minds* (blog), November 20, 2013, http://savageminds.org/2013/11/20/conference-chic-or-how-to-dress-like-an-anthropologist.
39. Jason B. Jones, "The Academic Wardrobe: Getting Dressed," *Chronicle of Higher Education Profhacker* (blog), February 3, 2010, http://chronicle.com/blogs/profhacker/the-academic-wardrobe-getting-dressed/22952; James M. Lang, "Looking like a Professor," *Chronicle of Higher Education,* July 27, 2005, http://chronicle.com/article/Looking-Like-a-Professor/45035; Kerry Soper, "RateMyProfessor'sAppearance.com," *Chronicle of Higher Education,* September 12, 2010, http://chronicle.com/article/RateMyProfessorsAppearance-com/124336.
40. Female Science Professor, "Wearing Me Out," *Chronicle of Higher Education,* October 1, 2012, http://chronicle.com/article/Wearing-Me-Out/134740.
41. Maria Schine Stewart, "Those Really Smart Clothes," *Inside Higher Ed,* August 15, 2012, www.insidehighered.com/advice/2012/08/15/find-your-own-fashion-sense-classroom-essay; Jessica Quillin, "The Well-Dressed Academic," *Inside Higher Ed,* June 10, 2011, www.insidehighered.com/advice/entrepreneurship/quillin_advice_column_on_dressing_for_success; Nate Kreuter, "Why I (Usually) Wear a Tie," *Inside Higher Ed,* October 24, 2011, www.insidehighered.com/advice/2011/10/24/essay-value-professors-wearing-ties-or-equivalent.

42. "Class Acts" (slide show), *New York Times Magazine*, September 16, 2008, www.nytimes.com/slideshow/2008/09/16/magazine/20080921-STYLE_index.html.
43. Tanisha R. Ford, "Haute Couture in the 'Ivory Tower,'" *Racialicious* (blog), August 8, 2012, www.racialicious.com/2012/08/08/haute-couture-in-the-ivory-tower.
44. Nalini Ambady and Robert Rosenthal, "Half a Minute: Predicting Teacher Evaluations from Thin Slices of Nonverbal Behavior and Physical Attractiveness," *Journal of Personality and Social Psychology* 64, no. 3 (1993): 431.
45. K. David Roach, "Effects of Graduate Teaching Assistant Attire on Student Learning, Misbehaviors, and Ratings of Instruction," *Communication Quarterly* 45, no. 3 (1997): 125–41.
46. Jennifer L. Bonnet and Benjamin McAlexander, "First Impressions and the Reference Encounter: The Influence of Affect and Clothing on Librarian Approachability," *Journal of Academic Librarianship* 39, no. 4 (2013): 335–46.
47. Chia-Jung Tsay, "Sight over Sound in the Judgment of Music Performance," *Proceedings of the National Academy of Sciences* 110, no. 36 (2013): 14580–85.
48. Carel ten Cate, "Posing as Professor: Laterality in Posing Orientation for Portraits of Scientists," *Journal of Nonverbal Behavior* 26, no. 3 (2002): 175–92.
49. Juliana Britto Schwartz, "Learning to Dress 'Professionally' in a White Man's World," *Feministing* (blog), March 4, 2014, http://feministing.com/2014/03/04/learning-to-dress-professionally-in-a-white-mans-world.
50. Cat Smith, "Normcore Is Bullsh*t," *The Stylecon* (blog), March 3, 2014, www.thestylecon.com/2014/03/03/normcore-bullsht.
51. Eddie Ndopu, "A Black Crip's Perspective on Fashion and Embodied Resistance," *The Feminist Wire* (blog), February 26, 2013, http://thefeministwire.com/2013/02/a-black-crips-perspective-on-fashion-and-embodied-resistance.
52. Peggy McIntosh, "White Privilege: Unpacking the Invisible Knapsack," *Independent School* 49, no. 2 (1990): 31–36, http://people.westminstercollege.edu/faculty/jsibbett/readings/White_Privilege.pdf.
53. Anthony Freitas et al., "Appearance Management as Border Construction: Least Favorite Clothing, Group Distancing, and Identity Not!" *Sociological Inquiry* 67, no. 3 (1997): 332.
54. Tressie McMillan Cottom, "The Logic of Stupid Poor People," *tressiemc* (blog), October 29, 2013, http://tressiemc.com/2013/10/29/the-logic-of-stupid-poor-people.
55. Kristin Iverson, "On Normcore: Why Only Beautiful People Can Get Away with Dressing Ugly," *Brooklyn Magazine*, February 28, 2014, www.bkmag.com/2014/02/28/on-normcore-why-only-beautiful-people-can-get-away-with-dressing-ugly.
56. Melissa McEwan, "Here We Go Again," *shakesville* (blog), December 9, 2013, www.shakesville.com/2013/12/here-we-go-again.html.
57. Ibid.
58. M. Elise Radina et al., "'Give Me a Boa and Some Bling!' Red Hat Society Members Commanding Visibility in the Public Sphere," in *Embodied Resistance*, ed. Chris Bobel and Samantha Kwan (Nashville, TN: Vanderbilt University Press, 2011), 67–77.
59. Mimi Thi Nguyen, "Gender/Queer: 'The Oldest Queer Girl Story in the Book,'" *Threadbared* (blog), February 2, 2010, http://iheartthreadbared.wordpress.com/2010/02/02/genderqueer-the-oldest-queer-girl-story-in-the-book.
60. Chris Bourg, "What Does Suit Up Mean for This Butch?" *Feral Librarian* (blog), March 17, 2012, http://chrisbourg.wordpress.com/2012/03/17/suitup_butch.
61. Cecily Walker, "On Privilege, Intersectionality, and the Librarian Image," *Cecily Walker* (blog), December 20, 2013, http://cecily.info/2013/12/20/on-privilege-intersectionality-and-the-librarian-image.

62. Minh-Ha T. Pham, "If the Clothes Fit: A Feminist Takes on Fashion," *Ms. Magazine,* January 17, 2012, http://msmagazine.com/blog/2012/01/17/if-the-clothes-fit-a-feminist-takes-on-fashion.

63. Dean Spade, "Dress to Kill, Fight to Win," *Listen Translate Translate Record (LTTR) Journal* 1 (2002): 15, www.lttr.org/journal/1/dress-to-kill-fight-to-win.

64. Richard E. Nisbett and Lee Ross, *Human Inference* (Englewood Cliffs, NJ: Prentice-Hall, 1980), 17–42.

65. Robert K. Merton, "The Self-Fulfilling Prophecy," *Antioch Review* 8, no. 2 (1948): 195.

66. Ibid., 197.

67. Brandon Stanton, *Humans of New York,* www.humansofnewyork.com.

68. Robert Rosenthal and Lenore Jacobson, *Pygmalion in the Classroom* (New York: Holt, Rinehart and Winston, 1968).

69. Ibid., 9.

70. Merton, "Self-Fulfilling Prophecy," 197.

71. Nalini Ambady, "The Perils of Pondering: Intuition and Thin Slice Judgments," *Psychological Inquiry* 21, no. 4 (2010): 271.

72. Mimi Thi Nguyen, "Teaching: Brief Notes on the Unreliable Stories Clothes Tell," *Threadbared* (blog), September 15, 2009, http://iheartthreadbared.wordpress.com/2009/09/15/teaching-brief-notes-on-the-unreliable-stories-clothes-tell.

73. Erving Goffman, *The Presentation of Self in Everyday Life* (1959; repr., Garden City, NY: Anchor, 1990), 27.

74. Jacques Derrida, *Limited Inc.* (Evanston, IL: Northwestern University Press, 1988), 12.

75. Stuart Hall, ed., *Representation: Cultural Representations and Signifying Practices* (Thousand Oaks, CA: Sage Publications, 1997); Radford and Radford, "Librarians and Party Girls," 67.

76. Radford and Radford, "Librarians and Party Girls," 67.

77. Kara Jesella, "A Hipper Crowd of Shushers," *The New York Times,* July 8, 2007, www.nytimes.com/2007/07/08/fashion/08librarian.html.

78. Rob Horning, "The Death of the Hipster," in *What Was the Hipster?* eds. Mark Grief, Kathleen Ross, and Dayna Tortorici (New York: n+1 Foundation, 2010), 79.

79. Dan Ozzi, "Please, God, Let 2014 Be the Year We Retire the Word 'Hipster,'" *Noisey,* January 3, 2014, http://noisey.vice.com/en_au/blog/please-god-let-2014-be-the-year-we-retire-the-word-hipster.

80. Lakshmi Ramarajan and Erin Reid, "Shattering the Myth of Separate Worlds: Negotiating Nonwork Identities at Work," *Academy of Management Review* 38, no. 4 (2013): 621.

81. Ibid., 623.

82. Terry Eagleton, *Ideology* (London: Verso, 1991), 9.

83. Radford and Radford, "Librarians and Party Girls," 68.

84. Hajo Adam and Adam D. Galinsky, "Enclothed Cognition," *Journal of Experimental Social Psychology* 48, no. 4 (2012): 918–25.

85. Ibid., 922.

86. James V. Carmichael Jr., "The Male Librarian and the Feminine Image: A Survey of Stereotype, Status, and Gender Perceptions," *Library and Information Science Research* 14, no. 4 (1992): 411–46; Carmichael, "The Gay Librarian."

87. Roberto and West, *Revolting Librarians Redux.*

Bibliography

ACRL Assessment Committee. "Value of Academic Libraries Toolkit." Association of College and Research Libraries, October 2010. www.ala.org/acrl/issues/value/valueofacademiclibrariestoolkit.

Adam, Hajo, and Adam D. Galinsky. "Enclothed Cognition." *Journal of Experimental Social Psychology* 48, no. 4 (2012): 918–25.

Ambady, Nalini. "The Perils of Pondering: Intuition and Thin Slice Judgments." *Psychological Inquiry* 21, no. 4 (2010): 271–78.

Ambady, Nalini, and Robert Rosenthal. "Half a Minute: Predicting Teacher Evaluations from Thin Slices of Nonverbal Behavior and Physical Attractiveness." *Journal of Personality and Social Psychology* 64, no. 3 (1993): 431–41.

American Library Association–Allied Professional Association. "Improving Salaries and Status of Library Workers." American Library Association–Allied Professional Association, last modified 2012. http://ala-apa.org/improving-salariesstatus.

Barnard, Malcolm. *Fashion as Communication*. New York: Routledge, 1996.

Barthes, Roland. *The Language of Fashion*. London: Bloomsbury Academic, 2006.

Bonnet, Jennifer L., and Benjamin McAlexander. "First Impressions and the Reference Encounter: The Influence of Affect and Clothing on Librarian Approachability." *Journal of Academic Librarianship* 39, no. 4 (2013): 335–46.

Bourg, Chris. "What Does Suit Up Mean for This Butch?" *Feral Librarian* (blog), March 17, 2012. http://chrisbourg.wordpress.com/2012/03/17/suitup_butch.

Carmichael, James V., Jr. "The Gay Librarian: A Comparative Analysis of Attitudes towards Professional Gender Issues." *Journal of Homosexuality* 30, no. 2 (1996): 11–57.

———. "The Male Librarian and the Feminine Image: A Survey of Stereotype, Status, and Gender Perceptions." *Library and Information Science Research* 14, no. 4 (1992): 411–46.

Chrastka, John. "Library Campaigns and Ballot Measures." EveryLibrary presentation slides posted July 5, 2013, www.slideshare.net/EveryLibrary/library-campaigns-and-ballot-measures.

Comito, Lauren, Aliqae Geraci, and Christian Zabriskie. *Grassroots Library Advocacy*. Chicago: American Library Association, 2012.

Cottom, Tressie McMillan. "The Logic of Stupid Poor People." *tressiemc* (blog), October 29, 2013. http://tressiemc.com/2013/10/29/the-logic-of-stupid-poor-people.

de la Peña McCook, Kathleen. *The Status of Women in Librarianship: Historical, Sociological, and Economic Issues*. New York: Neal-Schuman, 1983.

De Rosa, Cathy, and Jenny Johnson. *From Awareness to Funding: A Study of Library Support in America: A Report to the OCLC Membership*. Dublin, OH: OCLC, 2008. https://oclc.org/content/dam/oclc/reports/funding/fullreport.pdf.

Derrida, Jacques. *Limited Inc*. Evanston, IL: Northwestern University Press, 1988.

Eagleton, Terry. *Ideology: An Introduction*. London: Verso, 1991.

Epperson, Terrence W., and Alan Zemel. "Reports, Requests, and Recipient Design: The Management of Patron Queries in Online Reference Chats." *Journal of the American Society for Information Science and Technology* 59, no. 14 (2008): 2268–83.

ERIAL Project. "Ethnographic Research in Illinois Academic Libraries." Accessed April 2, 2014. www.erialproject.org.

EveryLibrary. "EveryLibrary: Building Voter Support for Libraries." Accessed April 5, 2014. http://everylibrary.org.

Female Science Professor. "Wearing Me Out." *Chronicle of Higher Education,* October 1, 2012. http://chronicle.com/article/Wearing-Me-Out/134740.

Fierce Fashion Futures. "About Us." *Fierce Fashion Futures*, last modified February 21, 2013.

http://fiercefashionfutures.tumblr.com/about.

Ford, Tanisha R. "Haute Couture in the 'Ivory Tower.'" *Racialicious* (blog), August 8, 2012. www. racialicious.com/2012/08/08/haute-couture-in-the-ivory-tower.

Freitas, Anthony, Susan Kaiser, Davis Joan Chandler, Davis Carol Hall, Jung-Won Kim, and Tania Hammidi. "Appearance Management as Border Construction: Least Favorite Clothing, Group Distancing, and Identity Not!" *Sociological Inquiry* 67, no. 3 (1997): 323–35.

Goffman, Erving. *Frame Analysis*. Cambridge, MA: Harvard University Press, 1974.

———. *The Presentation of Self in Everyday Life*. Garden City, NY: Anchor, 1990. First published 1959 by Anchor.

Green, Tracey. "Images and Perceptions as Barriers to Use of Library Staff and Services." *New Library World* 95, no. 1117 (1994): 19–24.

Horning, Rob. "The Death of the Hipster." In *What Was the Hipster? A Sociological Investigation*, edited by Mark Grief, Kathleen Ross, and Dayna Tortorici, 78–84. New York: n+1 Foundation, 2010.

Jaeger, Paul T., John Carlo Bertot, Christine M. Kodama, Sarah M. Katz, and Elizabeth J. DeCoster. "Describing and Measuring the Value of Public Libraries: The Growth of the Internet and the Evolution of Library Value." *First Monday* 16, no. 11 (2011). doi:10.5210/fm.v16i11.3765.

Jesella, Kara. "A Hipper Crowd of Shushers." *New York Times*, July 8, 2007. www.nytimes.com/2007/07/08/fashion/08librarian.html.

Jones, Jason B. "The Academic Wardrobe: Getting Dressed." *Chronicle of Higher Education Prof-hacker* (blog), February 3, 2010. http://chronicle.com/blogs/profhacker/the-academic-wardrobe-getting-dressed/22952.

Juliana Britto Schwartz. "Learning to Dress 'Professionally' in a White Man's World." *Feministing* (blog), March 4, 2014. http://feministing.com/2014/03/04/learning-to-dress-profession-ally-in-a-white-mans-world.

Kneale, Ruth. *You Don't Look Like a Librarian: Shattering Stereotypes and Creating Positive New Images in the Internet Age*. Medford, NJ: Information Today, 2009.

Iverson, Kristin. "On Normcore: Why Only Beautiful People Can Get Away with Dressing Ugly." *Brooklyn Magazine*, February 28, 2014. www.bkmag.com/2014/02/28/on-normcore-why-only-beautiful-people-can-get-away-with-dressing-ugly.

Lamont, Melissa. "Gender, Technology, and Libraries." *Information Technology and Librar-ies* 28, no. 3 (2009): 137–42, http://ejournals.bc.edu/ojs/index.php/ital/article/view/3221/2834.

Land, Mary. "Librarians' Image and Users' Attitudes to Reference Interviews." *Canadian Library Journal* 45, no. 1 (1988): 15–20.

Lang, James M. "Looking Like a Professor." *Chronicle of Higher Education*, July 27, 2005. http://chronicle.com/article/Looking-Like-a-Professor/45035.

Lorde, Audre. "The Master's Tools Will Never Dismantle the Master's House." In *Sister Outsider: Essays and Speeches*, edited by Audre Lorde, 110–13. Berkeley, CA: Crossing Press, 2007.

Luthmann, Abigail. "Librarians, Professionalism and Image: Stereotype and Reality." *Library Review* 56, no. 9 (2007): 773–80.

McEwan, Melissa. "Here We Go Again." *shakesville* (blog), December 9, 2013. www.shakesville.com/2013/12/here-we-go-again.html.

McGranahan, Carole, Kate Fischer, Rachel Fleming, Willi Lempert, and Marnie Thomson. "Con-ference Chic, or, How to Dress Like an Anthropologist." *Savage Minds* (blog), November 20, 2013. http://savageminds.org/2013/11/20/conference-chic-or-how-to-dress-like-an-anthropologist.

McIntosh, Peggy. "White Privilege, Unpacking the Invisible Knapsack." *Independent School* 49, no. 2 (1989): 31–36, http://people.westminstercollege.edu/faculty/jsibbett/readings/White_Privilege.pdf.

Mellon, Constance A. "Attitudes: The Forgotten Dimension in Library Instruction." *Library Journal* 113, no. 14 (1988): 137–39.

Merton, Robert K. "The Self-Fulfilling Prophecy." *Antioch Review* 8, no. 2 (1948): 193–210.

Ndopu, Eddie. "A Black Crip's Perspective on Fashion and Embodied Resistance." *The Feminist Wire* (blog), February 26, 2013. http://thefeministwire.com/2013/02/a-black-crips-perspective-on-fashion-and-embodied-resistance.

Nguyen, Mimi Thi. "Gender/Queer: 'The Oldest Queer Girl Story in the Book.'" *Threadbared* (blog), February 2, 2010. http://iheartthreadbared.wordpress.com/2010/02/02/gender-queer-the-oldest-queer-girl-story-in-the-book.

———. "Teaching: Brief Notes on the Unreliable Stories Clothes Tell." *Threadbared* (blog), September 15, 2009. http://iheartthreadbared.wordpress.com/2009/09/15/teaching-brief-notes-on-the-unreliable-stories-clothes-tell.

Nisbett, Richard E., and Lee Ross. *Human Inference: Strategies and Shortcomings of Social Judgment.* Englewood Cliffs, NJ: Prentice-Hall, 1980.

Ozzi, Dan. "Please, God, Let 2014 Be the Year We Retire the Word 'Hipster.'" *Noisey*, January 3, 2014. http://noisey.vice.com/en_au/blog/please-god-let-2014-be-the-year-we-retire-the-word-hipster.

Pagowsky, Nicole. *Librarian Wardrobe* (blog). 2014, http://librarianwardrobe.com.

Pagowsky, Nicole, Miriam Rigby, Jenny Benevento, Allie Flanary, and K. R. Roberto, "Style and Stereotypes: Perceptions of Librarians." Panel presentation at the American Library Association Annual Conference, Anaheim, CA, June 25, 2012.

Pagowsky, Nicole, Miriam Rigby, Jenny Benevento, Dale McNeill, and K. R. Roberto, "Style and Stereotypes: Perceptions of Librarians." Webinar presentation hosted by American Library Association TechSource and Library BoingBoing, September 27, 2012.

Pariser, Eli. The Filter Bubble. Last modified March 26, 2012. www.thefilterbubble.com.

Pham, Minh-Ha T. "If the Clothes Fit: A Feminist Takes on Fashion." *Ms. Magazine,* January 17, 2012. http://msmagazine.com/blog/2012/01/17/if-the-clothes-fit-a-feminist-takes-on-fashion.

Prins, Hans, Wilco de Gier, and Russell Bowden. *The Image of the Library and Information Profession: How We See Ourselves: An Investigation: A Report of an Empirical Study Undertaken on Behalf of IFLA's Round Table for the Management of Library Associations.* Munich: K. G. Saur, 1995.

Project Information Literacy. "Project Information Literacy: A Large Scale Study About Early Adults and Their Research Habits." Last modified March 5, 2014. http://projectinfolit.org.

Radford, Gary P. "Flaubert, Foucault, and the Bibliotheque Fantastique: Toward a Postmodern Epistemology for Library Science." *Library Trends* 46, no. 4 (1998): 616–34.

Radford, Marie L. "Encountering Virtual Users: A Qualitative Investigation of Interpersonal Communication in Chat Reference." *Journal of the American Society for Information Science and Technology* 57, no. 8 (2006): 1046–59.

Radford, Marie L., and Gary P. Radford. "Librarians and Party Girls: Cultural Studies and the Meaning of the Librarian." *Library Quarterly* 73, no. 1 (2003): 54–69.

———. "Power, Knowledge, and Fear: Feminism, Foucault, and the Stereotype of the Female Librarian." *Library Quarterly* 67, no. 3 (1997): 250–66.

Radina, M. Elise, Lydia K. Manning, Marybeth C. Stalp, and Annette Lynch. "'Give Me a Boa and Some Bling!' Red Hat Society Members Commanding Visibility in the Public Sphere." In

Embodied Resistance: Challenging the Norms, Breaking the Rules, edited by Chris Bobel and Samantha Kwan, 67–77. Nashville, TN: Vanderbilt University Press, 2011.

Ramarajan, Lakshmi, and Erin Reid. "Shattering the Myth of Separate Worlds: Negotiating Non-work Identities at Work." *Academy of Management Review* 38, no. 4 (2013): 621–44.

Rigby, Miriam. "Social Networking 0.0: Cultivating Casual Collaboration." *College and Research Libraries News* 71, no. 1 (2010): 14–15.

Rigby, Miriam, and John Russell. *Sudden Selector's Guide to Anthropology Resources*. Chicago: American Library Association, forthcoming.

Roach, K. David. "Effects of Graduate Teaching Assistant Attire on Student Learning, Misbehaviors, and Ratings of Instruction." *Communication Quarterly* 45, no. 3 (1997): 125–41.

Roberto, K. R., and Jessamyn West. *Revolting Librarians Redux: Radical Librarians Speak Out*. Jefferson, NC: McFarland, 2003.

Rosenthal, Robert, and Lenore Jacobson. *Pygmalion in the Classroom: Teacher Expectation and Pupils' Intellectual Development*. New York: Holt, Rinehart and Winston, 1968.

Scherdin, Mary Jane. *Discovering Librarians: Profiles of a Profession*. Chicago: Association of College and Research Libraries, 1994.

Smith, Cat. "Normcore is Bullsh*t." *The Stylecon* (blog), March 3, 2014. www.thestylecon.com/2014/03/03/normcore-bullsht.

Soper, Kerry. "RateMyProfessor'sAppearance.com." *Chronicle of Higher Education,* September 12, 2010. http://chronicle.com/article/RateMyProfessorsAppearancecom/124336.

Spade, Dean. "Dress to Kill, Fight to Win." *Listen Translate Translate Record (LTTR) Journal* 1 (2002): 15. www.lttr.org/journal/1/dress-to-kill-fight-to-win.

Spivak, Gayatri Chakravorty. *The Spivak Reader: Selected Works of Gayatri Chakravorty Spivak*. Edited by Donna Landry and Gerald M. MacLean. New York: Routledge, 1996.

Stanton, Brandon. *Humans of New York* (blog). www.humansofnewyork.com.

ten Cate, Carel. "Posing as Professor: Laterality in Posing Orientation for Portraits of Scientists." *Journal of Nonverbal Behavior* 26, no. 3 (2002): 175–92.

Tevis, Ray, and Brenda Tevis. *The Image of Librarians in Cinema, 1917–1999*. Jefferson, NC: McFarland, 2005.

Tsay, Chia-Jung. "Sight over Sound in the Judgment of Music Performance." *Proceedings of the National Academy of Sciences* 110, no. 36 (2013): 14580–85.

Walker, Cecily. "On Privilege, Intersectionality, and the Librarian Image." *Cecily Walker* (blog), December 20, 2013. http://cecily.info/2013/12/20/on-privilege-intersectionality-and-the-librarian-image.

Welburn, William C., Janice Welburn, and Beth McNeil. *Advocacy, Outreach and the Nation's Academic Libraries: A Call for Action*. Chicago: Association of College and Research Libraries, 2010.

Wilson, Pauline. *Stereotype and Status: Librarians in the United States*. Westport, CT: Greenwood, 1982.

CHAPTER 2

Academic Librarian Self-Image in Lore

How Shared Stories Convey and Define our Sense of Professional Identity

Sarah K. Steiner and Julie Jones

Introduction

At one point or another, we have all shared stories, jokes, and maybe even gossip with our colleagues at work. The desire to connect verbally is a unifying characteristic of humans from all cultures and backgrounds. We interact with each other regularly, and through these informal interactions, we establish cultural norms, shared values, and a sense of group identity. Sometimes we converse just to be polite, about things like the weather, our pets, or our weekend activities, but in many cases, the things that we say can be meaningfully analyzed in terms of subtextual messages. Like the members of any group, academic librarians communicate concepts that they find significant via cautionary tales, depictions of heroic or shrewd librarians, and jokes about problems that we see in the profession. The stories that academic librarians find worthy of repetition provide direct insight into our self-perceptions and into the image we would like to extend to the public. The recollections and stories of 31 academic librarians and library science students form the basis for this study of themes in librarian informal communication, with additional support from librarian-generated content on the open Web.

The formal term for much of the aforementioned shared information is *folklore*. Folklore studies, known as *folkloristics*, consider the informal communication and belief systems of communities, also known as *folk groups*. Folk groups (and folklore) can spring from geographic proximity, shared interests, familial ties, shared professions, or shared interests.[1] Though we don't often refer to it by its formal name, most of us encounter folklore daily. We repeat or repost urban legend e-mails about tricky criminals or Facebook privacy scandals, we avoid walking under ladders or going out on Friday the 13th, and we laugh at jokes heard around the water cooler. Stories, legends, jokes, superstitions, rituals, and traditions are all types of folklore. Folklore is such an ingrained part of the human experience that we often do not notice it, but it occurs across all cultures. Folklorist Alan Dundes notes that the primary aim of the folklorist is to ask "fundamental questions as to why a given item of folklore was created in the first place, or why it continues to be told or performed."[2] Via these questions, analysts can glean much about a folk group's respective fears, ideals, and values. Folklore scholar Robin Croft succinctly summarizes the import of folklore in our culture: "The oral tradition has long been studied by social psychologists and cultural anthropologists for the insights it can provide: folklore both mirrors and shapes the anxieties, fears, hopes and understandings of societies and of groups within it."[3] According to eminent folklorists Robert A. Georges and Michael Owen Jones, "Phenomena become folklore because other *individuals besides their creators* find them meaningful and subsequently *behave in ways that enable them to generate those phenomena anew*" (emphasis added).[4] Often, the source of folk stories is said to be "a friend of a friend,"[5] and librarian folklore is no exception; the veracity of the claims is insignificant because factuality is not the point of folklore. The point is the transmission of the underlying message, and, secondarily, the general entertainment of the listener or reader.

Researchers have explored the folklore and superstitions of a variety of professions, and there is a fairly sizable body of work related specifically to the folklore of academic institutions. Most notable are the works *Piled Higher and Deeper: The Folklore of Campus Life* by Simon J. Bronner and *The Folklore of Academe* by J. Barre Toelken.[6] In these two works, Bronner and Toelken explore some of the most common student and faculty folk themes in institutions of higher education (including the pervasive

"15-minute rule" applied by students left waiting for a late professor, hazing rituals, and traditional drinking games). Though the folklore of college students and teaching faculty has been observed and documented, little attention has been paid by publishing writers to the folklore of academic library workers, and no one has addressed how the folklore of librarians speaks to our desired and perceived self-image. The most relevant previous study was conducted by Stacey Hathaway-Bell for *American Libraries*, wherein Hathaway-Bell focuses on urban legends, a particular type of folklore, in public and academic libraries.[7]

The collection of folklore obtained for this study reveals the shared beliefs and values of academic librarians as a folk group. The lore illuminates a handful of striking trends: attention to our core values of access, education and learning, the public good, professionalism, and patient service;* desire to be taken seriously as professionals; concern over the continued viability of the profession in the face of rapid technological and cultural changes; fears about behaving inappropriately or violating cultural norms in the workplace; and concern over the general dangers and trials inherent in public service. The lore of librarians evidences a desire to preserve information access for everyone, but the necessity of working with diverse populations requires a clear and specific skill set. Often, aspects of that skill set are passed along through word-of-mouth (or social media) lore rather than via formal training manual. When considered together, the themes of these stories say a lot about the holistic "librarian image" that we perceive and want to cultivate.

Research Methods and Editorial Note

Respondents were recruited via a variety of methods between 2010 and 2013. Some were approached via snowball sampling because they were known to have previously shared or created jokes, narratives, or other folklore. Those individuals suggested others who might make good interviewees. The authors also contacted four electronic mailing lists for master's students in library and information science to recruit current students, in order

---

* All of these values match up to the American Library Association's Core Values of Librarianship, which is available on the ALA website: www.ala.org/advocacy/intfreedom/statementspols/corevalues.

to get a feel for how newcomers are being indoctrinated by current members of the profession. Most interviews were conducted orally, either in person or via Skype, but some were conducted via e-mail. Respondents were asked to answer a series of semi-structured questions about their indoctrination experiences, stories or jokes that they had heard or repeated, and legends from their libraries. Respondents often did not answer all of the questions because they reported having no related stories to share, and the questionnaire was fluid to help respondents feel comfortable speaking about a variety of topics. Librarians and library science students from 19 unique colleges and universities were interviewed. In some cases, several individuals from the same institution were interviewed to trace how stories grow and change through repetition to better deliver didactic or cautionary messages.

To preserve readability in spoken interview transcript excerpts, the authors have removed nonessential instances of "filler" words such as *like*, *um*, and *ah*. In instances where sections were omitted from the taped interview, the omission is marked as [section omitted]. Editorial comments have been enclosed in brackets. The names and institutions of respondents have been eliminated and replaced with generic placeholders in brackets.

The 31 transcripts and additional web content included in this study were analyzed via a system of theme identification and categorization: the primary categories explored were indoctrination tales, jokes, games, cautionary tales, hero tales, patron-nicknaming conventions, and behavior-governing stories. (In some cases, a single anecdote fit more than one of these categories. In those cases, the dominant category was chosen for organizational clarity.) This paper focuses on those tales, jokes, legends and the web content that emphasize librarian concerns over self and public perception of the profession and of library spaces. Each section includes an explanation of the type of folklore, illustrative quotes, and an analysis of trends and potential meanings. Due to space limitations, not all quotes could be included, so many are summarized and reported in aggregate.

Indoctrination Tales and Jokes

At some point, every one of us was new to the field of librarianship. Our early days in a new profession are often marked by collegially shared folk stories, and these stories are often remarkably similar regardless of library type or location. Many librarians will talk animatedly about how they were prepared for work in a new library with tales of the most colorful regular patrons or with wry commentary on the types of questions they should expect to receive. These stories are used to welcome and prepare newcomers by bracing them for the potential perils of working with patrons. In many cases, they also communicate institutional norms of acceptable librarian responses and behavior. Since these stories are heard in an important professional transition point, they are often strong memories.

One of the more common message themes imparted to new librarians relates to the types of questions asked at the reference desk—specifically, the prevalence of overly simple or impossibly difficult queries. Librarians repeat customary warnings that most questions will be directional in nature or that patrons will unwittingly present misinformation as fact. In some variations, students quickly become bored or irate when the librarian cannot meet all requests immediately. One interviewee had this to say:

> Patrons often ask questions such as, "I'm looking for a book—I don't know the title, but it's got a blue cover. No, I don't know the author either." Sometimes they'd have a very, very vague description of its contents, or sometimes they'd know vaguely what section of the library or shelf they think they last saw it in, possibly years ago…. I've actually been asked variations of this question in the past. I've also seen it in a video about librarian careers made in the 1940s, I think. [section omitted] I always feel like there's a bit of affection mixed in with the frustration when librarians joke about this—it does seem to indicate that the patron has an almost supernatural confidence in us, to expect us to find what they need with so little information!

> Second, of course the classic librarian joke is about how much time we spend dealing with staplers. Pointing out where they are, fixing them, refilling them…. "I got a master's degree for this?" is the usual tone of these. And I'd say a variation is how much time we spend with printers, or pointing out where the bathrooms are. —Respondent 1

Another respondent stated

> Students are either too intimidated or too lazy to come to the reference desk. Instead they will message the librarian through the chat tool even though they are within sight of the reference desk. Students are not willing to try alternative research methods, such as looking at print indexes, starting with a reference source, locating a bibliography on their topic, etc., even if that research method would be easier to use than keyword searching. Students want to be able to cross search all of the library holdings just like Google [when asked reference interview questions].".... The student looks clearly perturbed. You have apparently proven yourself to be worthless in answering what the student perceives to be a simple question. —Respondent 4

Tales and anecdotes like these prepare new professionals and highlight the fears of the speaker. As noted by both respondents, they often reflect sadness regarding the decline of traditional reference questions and a sense of pride that librarians are often able to solve difficult questions even with insufficient information. This kind of story has a clear practical application, but also highlights two concerns:

- that librarians are perceived only as purveyors of basic information, and

- that we are viewed as increasingly irrelevant in the age of easy Google searching.

A different respondent made this relevant comment:

> Yes, the questions have become rather simplified, and I feel it's reflective of well … of No Child Left Behind, and just the closure of school libraries. So, as a result, you know, a lot of these kids who I see—and I've been doing this as an academic librarian for a little over eight years now—I just see them not able to formulate any questions and I think the availability of Google makes them approach whatever they come across in their un-

dergraduate classes and in some cases even graduate classes and … so their questions subsequently become very simple.
—Respondent 30

Another common indoctrination story thread covers norms for handling needy patrons. Every interviewee who was asked about their interactions with patrons had stories about time-consuming individuals, and most of these patrons had been given simple monikers that librarians used among themselves. In many cases, respondents noted that the monikers were widely known among most public services staff. Several respondents expressed guilt about having assigned names to certain patrons, but felt that the names were sometimes necessary for communicating about problem patrons with other library employees.

The following set of quotations came from three different librarians who worked, at the time of the interviews, at the same institution. All of them were familiar with a single time-consuming individual to whom they referred as "Baby Bird." No one could pinpoint the genesis of the name.

"Baby Bird" was the nickname given to an elderly, mild mannered intellectual fellow. [section omitted] I still see him in the library. He'll come and say "Hello [Jane]." He was given the name because he always wanted you to do his searches. No matter how many times you showed him how to use [the catalog] or whatever database he was using, he would, I think, pretend not to remember how to use it. —Respondent 23

* * *

Well, he was Baby Bird before I even got there, so he's been Baby Bird for over eight years. And he was, I was told that he was Baby Bird because whenever he'd come up to the desk, people felt like they had to feed him by hand essentially, the answers—that he was just trying to get you to do his work for him, and that you'd tell him to do something and then he'd come back the next day or a little while later and ask the same question, which is kind of unfair, since he doesn't speak English as a first language, and probably eight years ago that was probably even more pronounced. —Respondent 5

* * *

The other patron that I can think of [section omitted] was Baby Bird. And this was when I worked here about ten years ago [2001]. I don't know how many people referred to him by this nickname, but one librarian mentioned him by nickname or used this nickname in reference to this patron, and in my mind anyway, it immediately caught on because it seemed very apt. This was an older gentleman who would come up to the reference desk regularly, and he would ask for help with very very basic library searching processes, and he was a regular user of the library, in fact, still is. [section omitted] We called him this because he would come to the reference desk and ask for some very basic search help, and he was always very polite and very grateful but completely baffled and seemed completely helpless by—with the process of doing research. [section omitted] After a certain amount of time and when you know you and your colleagues have shown this person how to do the same thing over and over again, it becomes more tempting to be a little bit judgmental about it, I guess. That's why I do feel a little bad about the nickname, but it just seems too apt because it really felt like he was playing up the helplessness a great deal in order to get people to do his work for him, and that was my very uncharitable impression of him after a time. —Respondent 1

None of the interviewees expressed ire with "Baby Bird," though some had a tone of affectionate mild frustration. Rather, they found that his regular appearances at the reference desk necessitated some clear way to reference him as an individual. The concept of the needy patron appeared in many more stories. These patron descriptions are, in one way, simple anecdotes, but they also highlight our concern that our time as helpers is sometimes taken advantage of and that we have little recourse to avoid those patrons who monopolize more than their fair share of time either out of laziness or a lack of understanding of libraries. When repeated, tales like these serve to solidify our self-identity as patient (and sometimes long-suffering) helpers of more difficult individuals.

Some people also spoke about having been indoctrinated with stories from the "old days," or with stories or jokes about ineffective managers. In this example, both of those concepts are present:

> Another librarian here [section omitted] talks about the culture of this library before like, say 1990. And it was very rigid in the sense that it was almost like how lawyers need to account for their time in 15 minute blocks. He said that you would have to do the same thing back in the '70s and '80s under this dean…. I don't know how true that is, but I've heard it from a couple different people that it was a very rigid, a very … there wasn't a lot of autonomy, and I think he described it almost as big brother-ish. I've heard that phrase from a couple of people about the olden days. And interestingly, I heard that at [another university where I was employed] about a former dean as well, so it may be a cultural shift that's happened over time in libraries, just the accounting for your day to day activity and the way it's done, that seems to be something that's changed and that people talk about. —Respondent 3

In this story, the "old days" are spoken of as a time of oppression. This story could be entirely factual, or it could be a sort of tall tale, wherein the facts have been "exaggerated to the limits of credibility or beyond in order to reveal emotional truths, to awaken [the] audience, to exorcise fears, to define and bind a social group."[8] Either way, in this scenario, the story informs newer hires that they now have improved freedom at work, at least in some ways. In situations wherein a work environment has become toxic or otherwise dysfunctional, library employees may find that their "old days" folklore highlights idyllic elements of the past, rather than negative ones.

Many readers may recognize another theme from the story about rigid time accounting—the theme that librarians' roles as professionals or faculty members are regularly under attack and that librarians must defend their autonomy. Librarians' faculty status is a hotly contested topic in academic libraries, so perceived attempts to diminish the prestige of librarianship through micromanagement is generally viewed as undesirable.

The theme of oppressive management was reflected in another story from a librarian who currently serves as a teaching faculty member for a master of library science program. She described having heard complaints about creative oppression from a large number of her students:

> Students think library directors don't encourage thinking outside the box—that they don't want creativity. They sometimes feel discouraged from already having worked in libraries, and it's not one or two students—my students say every semester that they're bothered by administration. There seems to be a disconnect there. —Respondent 14

The pervasive concern regarding professional stifling of academic librarians by management is also reflected in jokes online. The following two lightbulb jokes have been shared repeatedly on librarian-hosted sites on the Internet. Each highlights mild scorn regarding managers' unwillingness to deviate from documented procedure and the perception that they are likely to overplan for even the simplest of tasks. Both jokes carry the message that management is stifling and red-tape-heavy and that academic libraries tend to complete work (or, perhaps, not complete it) via an overabundance of committees.

> Q. How many library system managers does it take to change a lightbulb?
>
> A. All of them, as the manual was lost in the last move (or flood).
>
> * * *
>
> Q. How many library managers does it take to change a lightbulb?
>
> A. At least one committee and a lightbulb strategy focus meeting and plan.

The same concern over a perceived reduction in the professional status of librarians appears in a third variation of the lightbulb joke.

> Q: How many academic librarians does it take to change a lightbulb?

> A: Just five. One changes the lightbulb while the other four form a committee and write a letter of protest to the Dean, because after all, changing lightbulbs IS NOT professional work!

The prevalence of jokes and stories like these shows that librarians continue to feel significant concern over their professional identity, but the joke delivery mode implies that the self-mockery is affectionate in tone. Lightbulb jokes have been described as "a whimsical meditation on the ways Americans make social decisions and get things done,"[9] and these examples are no exception. Folklorist Judith Kerman notes that they began largely as taunts of groups that the joke teller viewed as outsiders, but, as is the case with these jokes, they grew more commonly to poke fun at the teller's own professional, social, or ethnic groups.[10]

Cautionary and Hero Tales

Another custom in the folklore of many groups is the cautionary tale, and librarians share them in abundance. Cautionary tales are similar to indoctrination tales in that they are a type of informal training and community-building exercise, but they include an added element of danger or warning. The point of these stories is to help the listener to feel prepared and protected against frightening events or individuals, or alternatively, to spur action by inspiring fear or anger. In some cases, cautionary tales conclude with an inspiring heroic response from a library employee who saves the day with assertiveness, sleuthing skills, or a cool head and a quick wit.

As public servants, librarians deal with a wide variety of patrons, so it is inevitable that some of those patrons will pose a physical threat or be generally disruptive. Library workers often recall and pass along informal tales of eccentric individuals and potentially harmful behaviors to alert others to the potential perils of working with the public. In some cases these stories die out, but in other cases they grow, change, and become widely known not just in the library where they took place, but in other libraries and institutions. This mutation and continuation is a classic feature of folklore.

Here is one example from a library science student, who heard it from a fellow student during a class discussion:

> We were talking about library policies, and how it's important to have your policies written down—and not just written down, but make sure that they actually are pretty airtight in terms of what they dictate regarding behavior. Because ... and I don't know if this was a public library or an academic library. We were talking about that, and one of my classmates was actually telling a story about how [section omitted] they had a policy that dictated that you must wear a shirt and shoes. And so, they had a patron come in wearing a shirt and shoes and nothing else. And he got upset when they said you have to leave, and I think there was, I mean, the story I heard was there was a lawsuit involved eventually. So that sort of became an example of, you know, you need to be really clear in your policies. —Respondent 12

This story presents a clear didactic message about careful preparedness. It fosters a sense of mild paranoia that policies must be in place and must be very carefully written. When considered with the jokes about committees and micromanagement, it also demonstrates the amusing push and pull created by librarians' feeling of obligation to red tape. Many people complain about committees and policies, but they persist in most institutions.

Another recurrent theme in librarian cautionary tales relates to the patron who creates routine disturbances. In most of these instances, the patron creates a mild or serious nuisance for either the library's employees or patrons. The severity is higher than in cases like "Baby Bird's," where no one is harmed or unnerved. As in indoctrination tales regarding patrons, in each case, problematic individuals have been assigned simple, descriptive names that help library employees relate warnings about that person to each other when the person's real name is unknown.

There is the story of Body Parts Man. Body Parts Man, which I hear that he still does this, calls into reference and asks for the specific weights of human organs. Once, a friend of mine had an encounter with Body Parts Man and after she was able to answer how much a human eyeball weighs, he asked her if she thought that HER eyeball would weigh that much if it wasn't in her head anymore. —Respondent 17

* * *

There used to be this really heavyset guy who I would call The Leaner, because if there was a woman sitting across from him he would sort of sit—and this guy was like 300 pounds—he'd just sort of be going like this [leaning]. —Respondent 5

* * *

The Egg Man … was actually very nice, not a problem patron. However, he was fairly pale, large, bald, and rounded. Pretty much looked like an egg. The library where I worked at the time had a couple of larger public computer labs, and three private carrels with PCs. He always signed up for a private carrel, and he was rather aromatic, so patrons who came after him would complain bitterly about the smell in the carrel and force us to hose it down with deodorizer. Since he was such a nice person, I always suspected that he signed up for the carrel, to not subject everyone in the large labs to the smell. —Respondent 17

* * *

I actually don't know anyone that saw The Shoe Violator, but a library GA [graduate assistant] relayed this story to me from a library faculty member. Apparently, students (female) on the study floors of the library used to just take off their shoes while they studied. Some of these students would apparently just wander off into the stacks to look for more books and just leave their shoes. The Shoe Violator would apparently steal girls' shoes and they were found later, having been "used" for his weird foot fetish fantasies. —Respondent 13

* * *

I have one story about a couple in a study room.... I did get this second hand from a previous colleague. The story was that the study rooms in this library had closed doors, I mean, opaque doors, and didn't have windows, as far as I can recall, or they may have had very small windows, but they didn't have glass walls, so there was a great deal of privacy in the study room. And there was apparently a couple that was being very vocally amorous in one of the study rooms and one of my colleagues had to go knock on the door and interrupt them, and they were embarrassed and left the library. —Respondent 1

Stories like these form a point of reference for employees, but they also facilitate bonding between service point staffers who must work with the same problematic patron (or with other similar patrons at other libraries).

In some cautionary tales, the interviewee describes how a librarian took charge and resolved the situation in heroic fashion—these stories contain elements of the traditional folkloric hero tale. In library hero tales, our image as helpers and solvers of problems is emphasized, and listeners presumably take away the message that they too can effect positive change in their libraries through attentiveness, action, and assertiveness. When library patrons share stories of assault (physical or sensory) in libraries, the underlying message is that one must be careful, even in spaces that are perceived as safe. This is a regularly recurrent theme in urban legends.

One especially relevant hero tale relates the story of a library employee who was terminated due to erratic behavior and, in response, ran through the building threatening the safety of others and threatening to take his own life. Two employees of the same library reported on this event (Story 1 and 2). In the first version, the point of the story is the event itself, which is a simple anecdote or cautionary tale. In the second version, the story has evolved to include a much more dramatic hero element, where a brave librarian saves the day.

Story 1
They eventually talked him [the angry employee] down and got it all sorted. [section omitted.] But later on, about two years later, my old boss who was involved in all this heard somebody at a conference talking about it. It's like "have you heard that crazy story about that crazy guy who went insane and was knocking books down and then took himself hostage?" And so she heard it as a legendary story, and she had experienced it. —Respondent 5

* * *

Story 2
In subsequent years the story morphed considerably so that one day, going into the break lounge to get my lunch out, I overheard a variation of the story in which [an employee] had wrestled the young man to the ground and disarmed him, although he wasn't named—some unknown heroic librarian had apparently wrestled the young man to the ground. I have no idea if the story is still told—I suspect that it is—but I was there and I can tell you there was no bodily contact between any librarians and the young man. —Respondent 8

This story is, like much folklore, dynamic in nature and has evolved to better deliver an inspirational message about librarian bravery and heroism.

Another common thread in academic librarians' indoctrination/cautionary tales covers our interactions with the homeless. The following stories, shared by five individuals at the same institution, demonstrate how a single incident can spawn years of discussion when it strikes a cultural nerve. The accuracy and origins of the story line are unclear, but it had been oft-repeated and was widely known. Respondents reported first hearing about the event(s) in the 1990s or early 2000s, so at the time of the interviews, the details had been in circulation for well over a decade.

I don't know if this is at [university] or if it was someplace else, but I think that there's some folk tale, um ... some student that would just live off Ramen noodles and lived up in the ceiling. That's all I know really, is that there's somebody that lived in the ceiling tiles, and that maybe somebody pushed open one and was able to see that there's this box of Ramen, or something like that. There was food left up there, and so that's what made people wonder about it, but that would have been before my time too, 'cause I really think I would have sought that one out if it had happened while I was there. — Respondent 4

* * *

All I know is that I've heard coworkers talk about people sleeping or hiding in an attic I didn't even know we had. This was so long ago, but someone may have said the police found someone up there at one point. How they would get up there in the first place is a mystery to me. —Respondent 27

* * *

Apparently at some point there had been a foreign student who had lost his funding, or housing, and had essentially moved into the library. (I want to say he was Chinese or at least from Asia, but that could be faulty memory.) He avoided the security guards at closing time by hiding, and was stashing his stuff—clothing, toothbrush, etc.—in the ceiling tiles of one of the men's rooms. —Respondent 1

* * *

There was supposedly a guy who lived on the Library 9th floor. He was supposedly a student from China who couldn't afford housing. [section omitted] The story was that this student from China came by and couldn't afford housing, so while he was here doin' graduate work he lived on the 9th floor and everybody just sorta looked the other way. [section omitted] [This happened] Just sometime in the past. [section omitted] I've heard that one so often and so long that I couldn't pinpoint a person where that had come from. —Respondent 5

* * *

When I first came to work here in 2005, I was warned to always check the ceiling tiles in the bathrooms as I went into the stalls, because homeless people lived up in the ceilings and had been caught peeping on the girls in the bathrooms. The person who told me said that everyone in the building knew about this issue because ceiling tiles had been found askew, and because packages of ramen noodles and other food had been found up there. I still checked those tiles for the first few months I was here. —Respondent 26

This case is particularly interesting because it shows how stories like this one change gradually over time to better deliver a cautionary, image-related, or educational message. The story evolved from a general anecdote into a pointed cautionary tale wherein our helplessness to stop the invasion of our libraries by the homeless is stressed—for Respondent 26, the point of the retelling was to protect her from the potential for workplace assault. Every individual interviewed from this institution knew about the homeless person or people who had allegedly lived in the ceiling, and it had become a cultural touchstone.

Respondents from several other academic libraries had similar tales about homeless people finding shelter in library stairwells, closets, or ceilings. The indication is that this is a concern in many institutions.

There was a rumor that a homeless man was able to reside in the ceiling of the library for a few weeks before anyone realized that he was there. —Respondent 13

* * *

I did once hear that there was a homeless man living in a rarely used stairwell behind the department I currently work in. He had set up fairly extensive housekeeping there before he was discovered and evicted. I've never established if this was true or not. —Respondent 17

* * *

We did twice have a guy living in an electrical closet in the library, making the staff think they had a ghost until he was discovered (before the renovations when more door locks were added). —Respondent 22

In the first and second scenarios above, the librarians openly expressed unsurety about the veracity of the stories, but repeated them anyway. In all three stories, the tellers' sense of security was restored by library employees who were able to take action by finding and ejecting the unlawful tenants. So, rather than these tales being solely cautionary in nature, they are also hero tales, wherein the librarian or university employee is presented as solving a serious problem in the building. (Though they are not included for space reasons, thematically similar tales about patrons who engage in loud or public sexual relations in the library came up repeatedly. In many cases, these liaisons were noted as being disrespectful of other patrons, and the librarian had to step in to protect the other patrons and restore order.)

Another notable cautionary trend relates to our fear that libraries and librarians are perceived as obsolete or behind the times. In some cases, we chastise ourselves for failing to keep up with the changes in the world. This lightbulb joke highlights the theme:

Q: How many academic librarians does it take to change a lightbulb?

A: CHANGE?!?!?!

In at least one case, the concept of the library as an out-of-date institution is reflected not only in the stories of librarians, but in the folklore of the wider world: the infamous story of the library with the sinking foundation has become legend at many universities and is repeated by librarians, faculty, and students alike. According to the story, Library X is reportedly sinking into the ground because builders failed to take into account the weight of the books when building or because of some other structural deficiency. One librarian reported hearing this story:

> The main library tower at [University Library] is sinking 1 inch every year because when the architects designed the library, they didn't take into account the weight of the books, so the foundation couldn't support it. Of course, this is not only false, but is a fairly common one across other academic libraries. [The university's] main library is sitting on top of a sheet of limestone, so it's not going anywhere. —Respondent 21

The legend of the sinking library is documented on the popular urban legend documentation site Snopes.com. Their site says

> I have heard from several different people claiming that their alma mater (or someone else's) built a library but did not factor in the weight of the books. After the building was completed and the books were added, the building began to sink. Now, the university can only put books on every other floor, or something like that.[11]

Stacey Hathaway-Bell also found evidence of this legend in her article, "Satan's Shelving: Urban Library Legends." She says of her own experience, "Legends of sinking libraries are widely disseminated and often believed by patrons and librarians alike. I distinctly remember hearing about a sinking library at least once during library school and I had no reason to disbelieve the tale because it is plausible."[12]

The Snopes essay on the topic notes that "though a few libraries have experienced settling problems, none of them was the result of an addlebrained architect who left out the key calculation regarding the weight of the library's holdings…. So far, the 'weight of the books' explanation has failed to hold up about any library it's been told about (and the list is almost endless)."[13]

While this story does not make a direct statement about library obsolescence, the tie-in is clear: the library sinks slowly but inexorably under the weight of its archaic, heavy paper books. The "experts" who planned the library made a fundamental strategic error, and it's too late to correct it. If only the library would catch up and purchase more electronic content, perhaps this problem could be solved—but that does not happen in any of the legends. The library simply sinks and molders.

Concern over the public's general perception of the import of librarians appeared in a few other ways in the interviews. Some individuals expressed their concern pointedly:

> It seems the general public has a skeptical view of how important libraries are in our society. When a doctor of mine found out I was working in a library, his comment was "How sweet. You know, those aren't going to be around for much longer." And people sometimes look puzzled when I say I am getting a degree in library science. It could be the term "library science" which is puzzling, but it could also be they think "why go into something that antiquated." —Respondent 16

Another individual commented that a family member teased his decision to pursue a master of library science degree:

> I've had someone demean the value of my master's degree before. My sister said she didn't understand why I got a Master's degree to learn how to shelve books. She was trying to be funny, but it kinda hurt my feelings at the time. —Respondent 31

The open Web is also rife with librarian-written blog posts, articles, and debates about the continued relevance of libraries and librarians. Anecdotally, most librarians seem to believe that libraries are not obsolete (though they may need to adapt and change with the world), but these interviews and web posts show that librarians harbor concern that the public, university/college officials, and lawmakers will find libraries irrelevant and dated. Many respondents indicated a sense of sadness or frustration that our students and the public do not perceive libraries as relevant and that library spaces are disrespected or even damaged by a small percentage of patrons and librarians. Libraries around the world are combating fears of our pending demise through a variety of creative means, but our sense of concern about the image of libraries has not yet been fully assuaged.

Behavior-Governing Stories

Through lore, librarians establish their own heroes—brave individuals who handle problem patrons or manage physical threats caused by patrons or other employees—but they also tell tales of individuals who fail to uphold the professional group image. Often, the exploits of poorly behaved librarians are discussed among colleagues, and these discussions create a normative standard for behavior. They serve as professional cautionary tales that help us to determine what is and is not appropriate. Some of the interviewees shared stories like these, which focused on unacceptable dress, unsuitable break-time activities (or break length), and a public failure of temper control:

> This particular library assistant is what we'd fondly call a character. She often wore unusual or inappropriate clothes to work, and one of her more outlandish outfits was a swimsuit, cover-up, and flip flops. This was during the time when flip flops were typically only worn to the beach or pool. Sometimes, she'd wear a swimsuit and beach towel wrapped around her waist. During lunch breaks, she'd sun herself on the quad. —Respondent 19

* * *

> I used to hear that there was a reference librarian who [section omitted] would fall asleep under the table [in one of the library's classrooms] as a way to take a break from the day. So you might go in there to use it and all of a sudden you see these just two legs stickin' out from under the table. —Respondent 5

* * *

> I remember shortly after I started my first professional reference job that I noticed that a particular librarian worked on the

reference desk but never taught any bibliographic instruction sessions. I asked around and was told by several people that she had been removed from her teaching duties after she "freaked out" in the middle of a session. Apparently a student had been rude and then questioned her authority and she ended up yelling profanities at the student. I don't think that the story ever left our library (since it would reflect poorly on the whole library), but everyone there knew what had happened. I never confirmed the exact details of the story, but the message was clear—no matter how much students push your buttons, don't lose your cool! —Respondent 31

In these cases, repetition of cautionary behavior tales gives peers a chance to distance themselves from and, hopefully, prevent such behaviors in newcomers. Distancing via incredulity and in some cases mockery is common of any folk group, but in libraries, individuals who behave in questionable ways may meet with an especially strong response. Since librarians are concerned not only with their image, but with the future of the institution of libraries, they may worry that a librarian who seems to have no work or who is unfriendly will further damage our perceived relevance.

Conclusion

Librarian folklore shows what we strive for, what concerns we share, and what we find most important in our work lives. More than just providing interesting anecdotes, folklore analysis can lead to improved professional and psychological insight and improved interpersonal communication. Librarians' informal shared stories illuminate our fears and concerns, and they underpin and deepen our sense of professional self. The folklore collected in this study shows that librarians place a high value on their role as protectors. Librarian folktales consistently highlight librarians' efforts to protect information access, fairness, quality service, the future of libraries, and the physical and emotional safety of patrons. This study also gives us a more human basis for declarations that appear in formalized vision statements and policies. For example, librarian folklore reflects a clear congruence with the values formally outlined in the American Library Association's "Core Values of Librarianship": access, confidentiality/privacy, democracy, diversity, education and lifelong learning, intellectual freedom, the public good, professionalism, service, and social responsibility.[14]

Ultimately, while we may talk and joke about ourselves and occasionally about the people we serve, these utterances do not generally reflect mockery, but rather a sense of affection and caring. Folklore studies like this one are often conducted for analysis by folklorists, but the findings can also be used by the group's members to gain a better sense of their professional zeitgeist and communication modes and, ultimately, to assess the deeper messages that are carried in both idle and professional talk. Folk stories can strengthen the bond between librarians everywhere, and create a stronger sense of community.

Notes

1. Jan Harold Brunvand, *The Study of American Folklore*, 4th ed. (New York: Norton, 1998).
2. Alan Dundes, foreword to *Folklore and Psychoanalysis*, by Paulo de Carvalho-Neto (Coral Gables, FL: University of Miami Press, 1968), 9.
3. Robin Croft, "Folklore, Families and Fear: Exploring the Influence of the Oral Tradition on Consumer Decision-Making," *Journal of Marketing Management* 22, no. 9/10 (November 2006): 1053.
4. Robert A. Georges and Michael Owen Jones, *Folkloristics* (Bloomington: Indiana University Press, 1995), 231.
5. Linda S. Watts, *Encyclopedia of American Folklore* (New York: Facts on File, 2007), 423.
6. Simon J. Bronner, *Piled Higher and Deeper* (Little Rock, AR: August House, 1990); J. Barre Toelken, *The Folklore of Academe*, in Brunvand, *Study of American Folklore*.
7. Stacy Hathaway-Bell, "Satan's Shelving: Urban Library Legends," *American Libraries* 29, no. 7 (1998): 44–49.
8. Carolyn S. Brown, *The Tall Tale in American Folklore and Literature* (Knoxville: University of Tennessee Press, 1987), 2.
9. Judith Kerman, "The Light-Bulb Jokes: Americans Look at Social Action Processes," *Journal of American Folklore* 93, no. 370 (October–December 1980): 455, www.jstor.org/stable/539876.
10. Ibid.
11. "That Sinking Feeling," Snopes.com, last modified June 23, 2011, www.snopes.com/college/halls/sinking.asp
12. Hathaway-Bell, "Satan's Shelving," 45.
13. "That Sinking Feeling."
14. "Core Values of Librarianship," American Library Association, adopted June 29, 2004, www.ala.org/advocacy/intfreedom/statementspols/corevalues.

Bibliography

American Library Association. "Core Values of Librarianship." Adopted June 29, 2004. www.ala.org/advocacy/intfreedom/statementspols/corevalues.

Bronner, Simon J. *Piled Higher and Deeper: The Folklore of Campus Life.* Little Rock, AR: August House, 1990.

Brown, Carolyn S. *The Tall Tale in American Folklore and Literature.* Knoxville: University of Tennessee Press, 1987.

Brunvand, Jan Harold. *The Study of American Folklore: An Introduction,* 4th ed. New York: Norton, 1998.

Croft, Robin. "Folklore, Families and Fear: Exploring the Influence of the Oral Tradition on Consumer Decision-Making." *Journal of Marketing Management* 22, no. 9/10 (November 2006): 1053–76.

Dundes, Alan. Foreword to *Folklore and Psychoanalysis,* by Paulo de Carvalho-Neto. Coral Gables, FL: University of Miami Press, 1968.

Georges, Robert A., and Michael Owen Jones. *Folkloristics: An Introduction.* Bloomington: Indiana University Press, 1995.

Hathaway-Bell, Stacey. "Satan's Shelving: Urban Library Legends." *American Libraries* 29, no. 7 (1998): 44–49.

Kerman, Judith B. "The Light-Bulb Jokes: Americans Look at Social Action Processes." *Journal of American Folklore* 93, no. 370 (October–December 1980): 454–58, www.jstor.org/stable/539876.

Snopes.com. "That Sinking Feeling." Last modified June 23, 2011. www.snopes.com/college/halls/sinking.asp.

Toelken, J. Barre. *The Folklore of Academe.* In Brunvand, *The Study of American Folklore,* 317–37.

Watts, Linda S. *Encyclopedia of American Folklore.* New York: Facts on File, 2007.

CHAPTER 3

The Stereotype Stereotype

Our Obsession with Librarian Representation

Gretchen Keer and Andrew Carlos

There is a healthy record of librarian stereotypes as the subject of scholarly and trade literature in library science. As far back as the early 1900s, librarians have observed and commented on public perceptions of libraries and librarians.[1] Over the last 10 to 15 years, this interest in librarian stereotypes (especially those concerning fashion, sexuality, and subcultural membership) has only increased. But why are we, as individual librarians and as a profession, so deeply interested in, invested in, and driven to change librarian stereotypes?

In this chapter, we explore whether this interest is productive and whether or not public perception of librarians is malleable. We suggest that librarianship must engage in robust theoretical exploration to rehabilitate our dysfunctional relationship with librarian stereotypes. And we posit that, if the question of stereotypes is one worth answering, the answers lie in understanding the history of stereotypes in our profession and also in looking outside the profession to larger social conditions.

We cannot separate our understanding of library stereotypes from the history of librarianship that influenced their development in the first place. Librarians are not explicitly responsible for the creation and perpetuation of negative stereotypes at their own expense, but neither are they fully removed from the cultural milieu that gave birth to those stereotypes. Our review of library science–based literature around librarian stereotypes has led us to note that both the development of those stereotypes and the sustained interest in them came from two root causes: the history of the development of librarianship as a profession, and the negotiation of gender, race, class, and sexuality within library organizations.

To get a clearer picture of how librarian stereotypes are situated within the larger social fabric, we have consulted literature in library science, sociology, psychology, education, and popular culture.

Stereotypes

Before we can analyze the origins of and our sustained interest in librarian stereotypes, and in order to understand how they work, we must first understand what stereotypes are. For the purposes of this chapter, *stereotype* refers to a cultural shortcut that conveys simplistic assumptions about librarians as a group or about individual librarians as a result of their profession. Stereotypes are developed by consensus in that they make sense within the cultural context of their creation. They communicate information about assumed personality traits (fussiness, organization, intellectualism, seriousness, humorlessness, sexual repression, permissiveness or deviance, professional competency, technological virtuosity, and more) that can be read in both positive and negative lights. However, the word *stereotype* carries with it a negative connotation and marks the target of the stereotype as occupying contested social territory.[2]

Although this chapter is particularly interested in those stereotypes that have been classified in the literature as "negative" ones, even positive-seeming stereotypes can have negative effects. In fact, because they seem harmless on the surface, they are more damaging and more difficult to resist.[3] *Stereotype threat,* identified in the late 1990s by Claude Steele, is the anxiety experienced by people from marginalized groups when they find themselves in situations that are associated with some stereotype about their group.[4] Stereotype threat negatively affects the performance of people under its influence, in large part because of the energy and effort it takes to actively resist the stereotype. The stereotypes that create this kind of anxiety range from the obviously negative (women are bad at math) to the ostensibly positive (African American men are good at basketball).

Stereotype threat has been framed as both an individual psychological experience and an experience shared by members of marginalized groups. Librarians in general, being a group of people who train for and pursue a particular type of employment, are not an oppressed minority. However, librarianship has been considered a subculture, and contemporary librarians often identify personally with their jobs.[5] As a result, professional stereotyping can have an added layer of personal insult. Librarianship is also a feminized profession, and those who labor in feminized professions are afflicted with the same disadvantages that affect individual women in the working world at large.* Further, individual librarians have overlapping cultural memberships that may render them vulnerable to stereotype threat. The stereotypes that exist about librarians are not purely about the occupation of "librarian," but invoke the raced, gendered, and classed nature of librarians as individuals.

Librarian Stereotypes

There are numerous librarian stereotypes, with the most recognizable being the middle-aged, bun-wearing, comfortably shod, shushing librarian (which Nancy Pearl has notably and humorously attempted to reclaim with an action figure).[6] Other popular contemporary librarian stereotypes include the sexy librarian, the superhero librarian, and the hipster or tattooed librarian.[7] These stereotypes are all characterized predominantly as feminine, white women. Newer librarian stereotypes, particularly those proffered by librarians themselves, tend to be depicted as younger white women.† The original librarian stereotype, which was superseded by the introduction of his prudish sister, was that of the fussy (white) male curmudgeon.[8] Some librarians have attempted to reclaim these stereotypes, and others have written numerous articles describing and decrying these stereotypes, as well as demanding or offering alternative images of librarians.‡

---

* In their 2005 *Journal of Personality and Social Psychology* article, "Exposure to Benevolent Sexism and Complementary Gender Stereotypes: Consequences for Specific and Diffuse Forms of System Justification," John T. Jost and Aaron C. Kay point out that "in cases of gender-based stereotyping, attitudes toward the disadvantaged group of women are very often favorable in content and yet prejudicial in their consequences."

† Although in some cases (as with the AskALibrarian.org "We Are Librarians" logos) there is a male version; see http://info.askalibrarian.org/marketing/logos.

‡ See Gale's "Are You a Librarian Superhero?" contest (https://www.facebook.com/pages/Are-You-a-Librarian-Superhero/177946468912677) and blogs such as *This Is What a Librarian Looks Like* (http://lookslikelibraryscience.com).

Offering alternative librarian imagery, however, can be tricky. It is true that, as the profession and its surrounding social conditions have evolved, public perception of librarianship has shifted. This observation is borne out by research in social psychology on cultural stereotypes and positioning theory.[9] Sociologists Luk van Langenhove and Rom Harré present a theory in which each participant in a cultural conversation (of which the experiences of stereotyping or being stereotyped are examples) occupies a specific social position. They offer two options for changing stereotypes: to offer a new representation to replace the stereotype, or to change the rules of the conversation that created the stereotype to begin with. If the new representation is introduced purely as a one-for-one replacement, or if the person or group offering the new representation is in the position of what Langenhove and Harré call a "convincer," this approach will fail. Offering up new, "positive" stereotypes to supplant the old, less flattering ones is an example of taking the convincer approach. Instead, the conversation itself needs to be changed.[10]

The ways in which individual librarians and the library profession at large have attempted to change the conversation have been hit or miss. While many articles, books, and blog posts address librarian stereotypes in thoughtful ways, some of these interactions are dysfunctional and counterproductive. In some cases, librarians have used stereotypes to police each other.* In other cases, we have used an incomplete theoretical structure to attempt to combat stereotypes without first relating them to larger social inequalities or to cultural conversations.† Some librarians have attempted to use a reclamation strategy to rehabilitate the public image of our field. However, we have largely fallen into the common pitfall that

---

* See our discussion later in this chapter of gender-predicting personality tests.

† The following two examples describe works that acknowledge inequity-based perceptions that underpin one or more librarian stereotypes but then fail to interrogate the stereotype back to broader social inequities. In *The Assertive Librarian* (Oryx Press, 1984, 14), Janette S. Caputo cites the results of studies employing gender-predicting personality tests (themselves laden with assumptions and stereotypes) as evidence that librarians do in fact possess the stereotypical traits associated with them. *Librarians and the Awakening from Innocence* (G. K. Hall., 1989) includes a chapter called "Respect for Librarians and Librarian Self-Respect" in which the author, Herbert S. White, argues, "if librarianship is to change its outside perceptions it must first change its self-perceptions" (170).

faces most such projects: addressing the symptom without fully articulating the problem.

Many articles describe how popular culture sees the librarian. A number of those articles employ the very stereotypes they seek to redress. One of the very few critical examinations of the underpinnings of such portrayals is Gary and Marie Radford's use of Michel Foucault's discourse of fear+ as a way of "speaking about the library and the librarian that transcends any specific image or portrayal."[11] In fact, they argue that the discourse of fear is what makes these images possible and fuels the public's ambivalence about librarians.[12] Their application of theory in the pursuit of a holistic understanding of librarian stereotypes stands out for its lack of self-conscious anxiety.

Not all ambivalence or complaint about librarians results in stereotyping, however. What librarians might dismiss as a stereotype might actually be an informed critique by an experienced super-user. Umberto Eco, for instance, created a librarian villain in his novel *The Name of the Rose*. Taken at face value, one might conclude that Eco is rehashing the trope of the cranky, unhelpful librarian and taking it to the extreme of a librarian who kills to maintain control over the information in his care. However, Jeffrey Garrett points out that Eco was a scholar with vast experience of libraries (and their frustrations) worldwide. He asserts that Eco "confronts librarianship not as some dis-embodied notion of 'service,' not as an ideal that we all believe ourselves striving for, but as an assemblage of real persons performing real work in real institutions, all of which acquire through time an inertia of their own."[13] In this case, the stereotype is a warning that "librarians … may fall victim to the same temptations that other mortals might."[14] The reminder that librarians are real people doing real work is easily passed over in favor of more glamorous observations, but it is vital to the question of librarian stereotypes.

Librarians' firmly held ethics, our beliefs about information and access, and even our understanding of appropriate professional behavior are all situated in the time in which we live. Today's librarians, especially public librarians, struggle to balance the public's desire for best-selling fic-

---

+ Where the "discourse of fear" is how we talk about power and control.

tion, for example, with our belief that an informed citizenry should read widely. Library historian Dee Garrison points out that there was a similar tension between the gentility-obsessed library leadership of the antebellum period and the urban workers whom the librarians aimed to serve.[15] Librarians of that time felt that the library was as important as schools and hospitals, but the labor force disagreed. Librarians believed that they could facilitate moral uplift by guiding their patronage toward "good" books and away from popular media, and they lamented the fact that the working classes did not use the library. When asked, urban workers were adamant that what they needed was not more guidance from librarians but rather more leisure time (by way of weekends) to pursue self-education through library services. Then, as now, issues of economy and justice were primary concerns of ordinary citizens. The relevance of library services to those concerns continue to play a huge role in the efficacy of library services, and also in the perception of librarians by the public.

Librarians, of course, are aware of this tension. However, our response has typically been to correct the public's misunderstanding of our role. It is commonly believed that library users will routinely neglect librarians as professional sources of knowledge if they continue to be unaware of librarians' skills.[16] Adding to this sense of anxiety about public perception and librarianship, as well as to anxieties about the future of education in general and higher education in particular, is the fact that we are now in a period of extreme uncertainty. Political reactions to economic upheaval over the last five years have meant an upswing in the trend toward austerity and privatization, pitting government-supported services against each other in competition for funding.

Additionally, popular culture can also send mixed signals about librarians. Stereotypical portrayals of librarians in popular culture reflect to librarians that they inhabit a degraded social status. On the other hand, highly respected authors and other creative people will often, when asked, sing the praises of libraries and librarians who influenced their education and development as artists and thinkers. Cory Doctorow is one outspoken library supporter who said, "Public libraries have always been places where skilled information professionals assisted the general public with the eternal quest to understand the world."[17] Indeed, when the topic of this chapter was described to them, several non-librarians expressed surprise that librarians put any stock whatsoever in librarian stereotypes perpetuated by television shows and movies.

In this contradictory climate, we see the value of having an overwhelmingly positive image of librarianship in the minds of the public. For example, Shaheen Majid and Azim Haider argue that it is not enough to have a high-tech library filled with technologically proficient librarians. You have to have a public that knows and understands this to really change the way the public sees the librarian.[18] In their estimation, it is this acknowledgement that raises the value of the library, as well as encourages others to join the profession. This perspective underpins the current trend toward "self-branding" and other marketing efforts in librarianship. If one looks at the history of librarian stereotypes, however, it becomes clear that fostering goodwill through self-promotion is not the whole story.

Librarianship as a Profession

Librarian stereotypes can be traced, in part, to cultural anxieties about the emergence of the professions. One of the central arguments in library history over the last 60 years has been whether or not librarianship is, can be, or should be a profession and, if it is a profession, whether or not librarianship succeeds at the professionalization project. A survey of the literature unearths titles such as, "The Librarian: From Occupation to Profession?" *The Maturity of Librarianship as a Profession*, "Librarianship Is a Discipline," "Criteria for Improving the Professional Status of Librarianship," "Librarianship, Professionalism, and Social Change," "The Professionalization of Librarianship," "Ambiguous Authority and Aborted Ambition: Gender, Professionalism, and the Rise and Fall of the Welfare State," "Professional Status of Librarianship Revisited," *The Evolution of Librarianship into a Profession*, "Gender, Power, and the Dangerous Pursuit of Professionalism," "'Louder Please': Using Historical Research to Foster Professional Identity in LIS Students," and "Is Librarianship a Profession?"[19] This large body of literature on the history of library professionalization began to proliferate when social scientists became interested in the sociology of the professions in the 1960s. It includes ruminations on how librarianship might become a profession, whether or not librarianship should be a profession, and, more recently, questioning the foregone conclusion that librarianship is a profession. The most critical analyses of the professionalization of librarianship have come from feminist historians, who point out the unquestioning devaluation of women's work in such a project.[*]

To unpack the concern over professionalism, we must first consider what professionalism is. Definitions abound, but most agree that the professions have privileged knowledge, provide a service rather than a product, and have a code of ethics that guides their decisions.[20] Writing as a library consultant in 1980, Dale E. Shaffer argues that any occupation may become a profession if it follows a set of carefully defined criteria.[21] Shaffer provides these criteria based on a reported survey of over 220 articles, which he sadly does not cite. However, other authors follow this same line of reasoning, couching their recommendations for how to become a professional in terms of individual social and occupational success, as well as touting the benefits of professionalization for librarianship in general.[†]

Doctors, lawyers, and businessmen are considered the first professionals. However, Shaffer points out that the word *profession* originally referred to the vow taken by a monk. He argues that "the oldest profession is priesthood, which claims the professed knowledge, power, and ability to intercede between ordinary men or things and beings extraordinary or divine."[22] This vision of a professional as a man of God would probably have appealed very strongly to the earliest American librarians.

Librarianship emerged in its modern form during a time of rapid change in American society, as the Victorian era was coming to a close and a new and youthful urban attitude was taking precedence over more traditional community-based values. The burgeoning field of librarianship was swept up in this change, which was largely coming from the overwhelming success of the capitalist business model. Early American librarians almost

---

[*] See our discussion later in this chapter of the negotiation of class, gender, and sexuality in library organizations.

[†] See titles such as Janette S. Caputo's The Assertive Librarian (Oryx, 1984) and Marcia J. Nauratil's *The Alienated Librarian* (Praeger, 1989), both of which offer tips on how to avoid stress, set good boundaries, and thrive in a professional environment.

exclusively came from New England gentility or, by virtue of their educational background and politics, became accepted as part of that class. They believed in the possibilities of moral uplift for the poor and uneducated and saw themselves as the perfect missionaries for the job. By the mid-1870s, however, American society was turning away from the educated class as a beacon of moral and economic authority. Instead, "as business and politics became more openly aligned after the Civil War, the gentry were … displaced from power and prestige."[23] The sons of educated men began turning to individualistic pursuits, and those who followed more communal paths were seen as old-fashioned.

At the same time, after the American Civil War, a new ideal of masculinity was emerging: the "Self-Made Man." Bryan Rindfleisch describes how the Self-Made Man was at odds with the old masculine ideal, the Patriarch, on a number of raced and classed levels.[24] Although the Patriarch's strongest foothold was in the south, he, like library leaders during the late 1800s, was steeped in cultural values that valued a "non-laboring livelihood" as "the emblem of one's elite status."[25] Old guard library leaders were something of a hybrid version of this archetype since they indeed labored for a living, but they revered the elite status the Patriarch represents.

As gentility was abandoned by young men, it became more identified both with old-fashioned values and with femininity. Women were looked to as keepers of the culture, and they took that responsibility seriously. However, as genteel society became almost entirely embodied by the "lady," the genteel lady became "a new social type—a curious transitional blend of feminist and domestic queen."[26] These upper- and middle-class women, like their male counterparts, were grappling with competing gender ideals and blending them into a hybrid. So, as librarianship resisted the hypermasculine modern consumerist culture, it also became a natural harbor for the newly adventurous modern woman.

Melvil Dewey was a prime example of the Self-Made Man, and as such he linked professional status with power and influence. He applied business tactics, such as efficiency and entrepreneurship, to his work as a library innovator. Dewey was driven to professionalize librarianship, and he was able to convince his colleagues to pursue this path because his plan "promised to provide, in the proper proportions, a new power base and entry route for the new middle class, romantic reform in the service of national rationalization and bureaucratization, an amelioration of class conflict, moral values for a disordered society, an outlet for the changing needs of women, and an acceptance of the force of mass culture in an urbanized nation."[27] In librarianship, this drive toward rationalization and efficiency resulted in the founding in 1876 of the American Library Association and, in 1887, of the School of Library Economy at Columbia College.[28]

However, this new entrepreneurial ideology was not embraced by the majority of library leaders until the 1890s, and in the meantime the old guard did not go down without a fight. As American librarianship was burgeoning into a profession, the very things that had defined the erudite, educated librarian began to fall out of favor, and modernization dimmed the genteel class's preeminence as the arbiters of cultural correctness. During this time, librarianship was in full-throttle moral-uplift mode, battling the tides of labor unrest and popular fiction.[29] This tension between an idealized vision of educated gentility and the relentless push of capitalist modernization, and between the Self-Made Man and his suffragist sister, can still be felt in debates within librarianship today over censorship, the preeminence of technology, information access, and social activism.

Librarianship tends to be a very public-facing occupation, both on the job and off the job. People recognize librarians throughout their community and engage them in conversation. This creates a sticking point for librarians. At what point in their day can they take off the mask of professionalism that they are wearing? This extends beyond physical space. Consider the situation in which librarians become acquainted with their patrons through social media. Does the idea of professionalism extend to this realm as well?

With the rise of various information and communication technologies, librarians now have access to a venue for discussion that is speedier and more frequently updated than either the postal service or conferences, as well as one that allows for intercultural communication, not just among different varieties of librarianship, but across diverse geographical locations. Examples include various Tumblrs depicting library stereotypes,

Facebook groups of all types of librarians having discussion about the profession, and online newsletters being shared with the public. The openness of these communication mediums brings up an interesting issue with professionalism.

Contemporary librarians find themselves reflecting at on the same questions that have dogged our field since its earliest days: Is librarianship a profession?[30] If so, what does that mean? What does it mean that librarianship is a feminized profession? How can we as a profession resist gendered societal pressures to be passive and nurturing at the expense of respect and compensation? Is the lack of respect afforded to librarians simply due to the decline of professionalism (and its attendant power) in general? Or are librarians themselves somehow responsible for the lack of respect afforded them? Are stereotypes a way for our culture to work out its ambivalence about the status of librarians? It is true that people tend to respect their doctors, lawyers, professors, and clergy even if they do not always understand them but do not respect librarians in the same way?

And if, as Brenton Faber argues, "professionalism is a social movement predicated on knowledge control, social elitism, and economic power," do librarians really want to be considered professionals?[31] Does, in fact, "professionalism" work in direct contradiction to stated librarian ethics? And, conversely, do our professional ethics actually work against our professional status? The work of librarianship revolves around providing access to information, following the belief that an informed citizenry makes a robust democracy, while the hallmark of professionalism is undoubtedly gatekeeping.

Ultimately, librarians' opinions about librarianship as a profession and the public's opinions on the topic are in agreement on the most salient point. Based on the numerous articles in the library literature that grapple with the status of librarianship[32] and question librarianship as a profession,[33] as well as the prevalence of blog posts and articles in the popular media that explore librarian stereotypes, we can conclude that, despite being beloved by a number of prominent and not-so-prominent individuals, librarianship as we know it is often treated in popular culture as a low-status profession or not a profession at all.

Negotiation of Class, Gender, and Sexuality in Organizations

Whether or not we agree that librarianship is a profession, it is commonly described, like teaching and nursing, as a feminized occupation. This designation has been used to explain, and sometimes excuse, a range of inequalities and difficulties faced by the profession since the term began to be popular in the 1970s.[34] Writing as a new librarian in 1977, Bayles makes the following observation: "One thing that immediately struck me … is our total lack of power and self-respect as a profession."[35] This perception is also reflected in the ways feminized professions have been portrayed in the literature. For example, while predominantly male professions are simply called "professions," early literature identified the female-dominated occupations as "semi-professions."[36] The struggle of white-collar women to be recognized as legitimate members of the workforce and to expand societal definitions of "women's work" is reflected in the sexualized (or desexualized) stereotypes that are now affiliated with librarianship.

Librarianship was not always a female-dominated occupation. Middle-class white women in the United States began entering "genteel" professions such as librarianship only in the late 19th century. It was much later that women of other races and ethnicities were given entry into the profession. The earliest librarians in America were educated white men from established families in New England. Many of them had fathers who worked as clergy or professors. Early male librarians were also career changers, which contributed to the stereotype of librarians as "men who failed at something else." As clerks tasked with babysitting books, male librarians were seen as passive, fussy, and custodial.

When (white) women began entering the profession in the 1880s, the librarian stereotype took on a new dimension. As the male librarian stereotype became more pronounced, there arose a new female librarian stereotype. By 1900, the passive, submissive, and plain librarian stereotype we recognize today had emerged. She was so prevalent that one librarian joked that "he had heard so much about this lady, he was 'growing rather fond of the old girl.'"[37] Women were hired to take over the less desirable aspects of librarianship and were paid low wages because they had no leverage. Library administrators endeavored to hire women because they were better educated than men attracted to the profession and were unable to demand comparable wages.[38]

Women themselves were invested in upholding an ideal of Victorian genteel virtue as a way of rationalizing their entry into the previously male-only domain of white-collar work. Garrison points out, "It is not surprising that [women], like males, defended their class interests. They upheld the sanctity of the family, of the capitalist economy with its formula of hard work and delayed sensual gratification, of Protestant nativism, of parental discipline, and of their nurturing, expressive functions—for these were the ideals that had traditionally given meaning to their lives."[39] These are ideals that fit easily into what became the feminized (also called helping) professions.

By the end of the 1920s, white women did indeed come to dominate librarianship. In fact, in 1930 librarianship was 90 percent female.[40] In response, librarians tied themselves in knots trying to rationalize that fact. For instance, from the 1960s through the late 1970s, gender-predicting personality tests were administered as entrance requirements for both library school admission and employment. The tests, such as the California Psychological Inventory (CPI) Femininity Scale, asked subjects to answer True or False to such statements as "I want to be an important person in the community" (the correct feminine answer being False) and "I am somewhat afraid of the dark" (True).[41] The feminine answer to "I think I would like the work of a librarian" was, of course, True. The more "feminine" answers the applicant gave, the more positively they were rated.[42]

These practices were meant to give a scientific rationale for hiring decisions, but the logic was flawed: if librarianship is female-dominated, then all librarians (regardless of gender) will be, indeed must be, feminine-minded. Female and male librarians alike have been caught up in the resulting gender-role stereotypes. Female librarians were automatically sexually repressed spinsters because it was impossible for our culture to acknowledge an educated, intelligent woman with a healthy relationship to sexuality. Male librarians had to be gay because it was impossible to fathom a heterosexual (which is here conflated with masculine) man who would willingly do "women's work."[43] These stereotypes persist, despite advances in civil rights, because these cultural assumptions and inequalities still exist.

The trend in librarianship has been to counter the ill effects of being a feminized occupation with a strong dose of professionalism. Librarian and scholar James Carmichael in particular draws our attention to the feminist critique that "professionalism has too often been modeled on preexisting masculinized institutional structures."[44] Other scholars argue that because "bureaucratic management—abstract, rational, objective, instrumental and controlling—has been essentially masculine in the way it has been implemented and theorized ... a case might be made, therefore, for viewing the library profession ... as masculine in nature."[45] Thus librarianship resists easy categorization as either a "feminine" or a "masculine" pursuit while being claimed (and sometimes denigrated) as both.

To round out the discussion of gender and librarianship, some research has been done to examine the experiences of men who become librarians. In particular, Carmichael explores the feminine stereotype of male librarians in "The Male Librarian and the Feminine Image: A Survey of Stereotype, Status, and Gender Perceptions."[46] In a survey sent to nearly 700 male librarians, Carmichael attempted to discern certain views of the professional from a male perspective. In asking about possible male stereotypes, Carmichael received some expected results that further reinforce the stereotype of the gay male librarian and of the dowdy male librarian, both of which rely on a stereotype of feminine (or emasculated) men. The survey results, however, provide a male-dominated, heteronormative view of librarianship. Underlying the respondents' discussion of the gay male stereotype is a fear of being assumed to be gay or too feminine by being in a feminine profession. Ten years later, Paul S. Piper and Barbara E. Collamer re-created Carmichael's survey and found that male librarians are relatively comfortable in the field and moreover do not see it as a 'woman's profession.'[47]

This relative comfort may be due to a number of gender-related social changes in the intervening years. Garrison makes the point that the early male librarian was "caught in a paradox. Catering to the feminine increased his identification with what many regarded as the weaker sex. On the other hand, since women were his chief allies, to exalt womanhood was to enhance his own declining status and authority."[48] An improvement in the status of women overall has provided male gender roles with more flexibility as well.

By the 1950s, librarianship was in what some call its Golden Age. Federal support was booming and libraries were relied on more and more to supplement public schooling.[49] According to Suzanne Hildenbrand, however, "a review of the library literature of the period reveals contradictory trends: a gradual accumulation of data documenting the second-class place of women in the profession and the growth of a library history oblivious to that place."[50] Library literature both noted and ignored the fact that women, who made up the majority of the library profession by this point, were hired more often at part time rates as well as paid less and promoted less often than men. These statistics began to be addressed when there was an upswing in feminist perspectives in librarianship in the 1960s and 70s, including several history projects designed to unearth the overlooked contributions of women to the profession.[51]

Reviewing the history of librarianship and librarian stereotypes helps us to remember that libraries reside fully within current cultural climates. Garrison reminds us that, "like the school, the library tend[s] to be [as] progressive as society, in fostering civil liberties and political representation, and to be [as] oppressive as the economic system, in maintaining inequality of income and opportunity by a division of the citizens along lines of class, race, and sex."[52] This division can be further seen in discussions on sexuality within librarianship, or rather the lack of discussion when it comes to sexuality.

Many articles present a heteronormative view of sexuality, disregarding the possibility of other gender and sexual expressions, in the surveys and research being conducted.[53] In each of these articles, no questions were raised regarding LGBT issues or stereotypes related to librarianship. This lack of representation can be seen through a quick browse through LISTA, revealing a lack of references related to LGBT issues in the profession; those references that do mention LGBT issues focus mainly on collection development and LGBT patrons.

According to Carmichael, the study of LGBT library professionals has been conducted mainly by those outside the field.[54] As a group, librarians have historically allowed others to define their image and their self-worth, reacting both positively and negatively to images seen throughout the media.[55] By allowing outside media and outside scholars to define who we are as a profession, we lose agency in creating our images and, to a greater extent, the stereotypes that arise about our profession. Recent projects, such as the Litwin Books Series on Gender and Sexuality in Information Studies and others, aim to take ownership of the discussion surrounding LGBT issues in librarianship.

When we address library stereotypes at face value without taking into account the broader social realities that not only make them possible but also reinforce their potency, we put ourselves in a quixotic situation. This is when new (and equally damaging) stereotypes are invented, sometimes by librarians themselves, to supplant the old.

Conclusion

Our exploration of librarian stereotypes led us to delve into American library history, the history of the sociology of professions, the psychology of stereotypes, and the evolution of American gender roles. Through this exploration we have found that stereotypes, including professional stereotypes, are symptomatic of systemic inequality. They cannot be neutralized by an approach that avoids critically engaging with those systems. Nor can they be subverted by merely turning them on their head.

Popular culture will not be dissuaded from perpetuating negative stereotypes simply because librarians insist they are not true. After all, contemporary librarians are still living with the legacy of the earliest librarians who objected to fiction on moral grounds, and popular culture has a long history of mocking that which opposes it. As societal roles for women and other marginalized groups have changed, librarianship has also changed, but at a much more conservative pace.

Because larger structural inequalities such as sexism, racism, and classism are at work in the creation and perpetuation of popular narratives about librarians, improving the psychological well-being of individual librarians is not the solution to the problem of librarian stereotypes. It is important to acknowledge that stereotype threat is at work within librarianship because of the raced, classed, and gendered reality of individual librarians' lives.

We conclude that the most effective way to combat the negative effects of librarian stereotypes is to work diligently toward social justice for marginalized groups. Furthermore, creating alternative imagery to supplant objectionable stereotypes in fact makes the situation worse. Ultimately, public perception of librarianship can and will change, but if we wish to have some influence over it, we must both stop spending so much energy on policing our coolness factor and put more energy into being a profession that stands for fairness and equality among all people.

Notes

1. Hellen R. Keller, "The Old-Fashioned Virtues versus the Ideal Librarian," *Library Journal* 34, no. 7 (1909): 295–98.
2. Luk Van Langenhove and Rom Harré, "Cultural Stereotypes and Positioning Theory," *Journal for the Theory of Social Behavior* 24, no. 4 (1994): 360. doi:10.1111/j.1468-5914.1994. tb00260.x.
3. Aaron C. Kay, et al., "The Insidious (and Ironic) Effects of Positive Stereotypes," *Journal of Experimental Social Psychology* 49, no. 2 (2013): 287–91.
4. Claude Steele, *Whistling Vivaldi* (New York: Norton, 1999).
5. Laura Miller, "The Self-Image of the Library Profession," *International Library Review* 21 (1989): 141–55.
6. Leonard Kniffel, "Open Letter to Nancy Pearl," *American Libraries* 39, no. 4 (2003): 34.
7. Kathrin Dodds, "Advertising the Librarian Image: Stereotypical Depictions of Librarians in Advertising" (paper, PCA-ACA Annual Conference, New Orleans, LA, April 8, 2009), www. academia.edu/226036/Advertising_the_Librarian_Image_Stereotypical_depictions_of_ librarians_in_advertising.
8. Dee Garrison, *Apostles of Culture* (New York: Free Press, 1979), 13.
9. Langenhove and Harré, "Cultural Stereotypes," 369.
10. Langenhove and Harré, "Cultural Stereotypes," 370.
11. Gary P. Radford and Marie L. Radford, "Libraries, Librarians, and the Discourse of Fear," *Library Quarterly* 71, no. 3 (2011): 299.
12. Ibid., 300.
13. Jeffrey Garrett, "Missing Eco: On Reading 'The Name of the Rose' as Library Criticism," *Library Quarterly* 61, no. 4 (1991): 386.
14. Ibid.
15. Dee Garrison, *Apostles of Culture* (New York: Free Press, 1979), 49.
16. Maura Seale, "Old Maids, Policeman [*sic*], and Social Rejects," *Electronic Journal of Academic and Special Librarianship* 9, no. 1 (2008), http://southernlibrarianship.icaap.org/content/ v09n01/seale_m01.html.

17. Cory Doctorow, "Libraries, Hackspaces, and E-waste: How Libraries Can Be the Hub of a Young Maker Revolution," *Raincoast Books Blog*, February 24, 2013, www.raincoast.com/blog/details/guest-post-cory-doctorow-for-freedom-to-read-week.

18. Shaheen Majid and Azim Haider, "Image Problem Even Haunts Hi-Tech Libraries: Stereotypes Associated with Library and Information Professionals in Singapore," *Aslib Proceedings* 60, no. 3 (2008): 229–41. doi:10.1108/00012530810879105.

19. William J. Goode, "The Librarian: From Occupation to Profession?" *Library Quarterly* 31, no. 4 (1961): 306–320; Dale E. Shaffer, *The Maturity of Librarianship as a Profession* (Metuchen, NJ: Scarecrow, 1968); Sandy Bayles, "Librarianship Is a Discipline," *Library Journal* 102, no. 15 (1977): 1715–17; Dale E. Shaffer, *Criteria for Improving the Professional Status of Librarianship*, ERIC publication no. ED 188626 (self-published paper, 1980); William F. Birdsall, "Librarianship, Professionalism, and Social Change," *Library Journal* 107, no. 3 (1982): 223–226; Michael F. Winter, "The Professionalization of Librarianship," *Occasional Papers/University of Illinois Graduate School of Library and Information Science*, vol. 160 (Urbana: University of Illinois, 1983); Suzanne Hildenbrand, "Ambiguous Authority and Aborted Ambition: Gender, Professionalism, and the Rise and Fall of the Welfare State," *Library Trends* 34, no. 2 (1985): 185–98; Elsie Stephens, "Professional Status of Librarianship Revisited," *Journal of Library Administration* 7, no. 1 (1986): 7–12; Monica Anne Coffey, *The Evolution of Librarianship into a Profession*, (Saint Louis, MO: Saint Louis University Press, 1990); Roma M. Harris, "Gender, Power, and the Dangerous Pursuit of Professionalism," *American Libraries* 24, no. 9 (1993): 874–876; Jean L. Preer, "'Louder Please': Using Historical Research to Foster Professional Identity in LIS Students," *Libraries and the Cultural Record* 41, no. 4 (2006): 487–96; David Lonergan, "Is Librarianship a Profession?" *Community and Junior College Librarians* 15, no. 2 (2009): 119–22.

20. Brenton Faber, "Professional Identities," *Journal of Business and Technical Communications* 16, no. 3 (2002): 308; Jim Elmborg, "Literacies, Narratives, and Adult Learning in Libraries," *New Directions for Adult and Continuing Education*, no. 127 (2010): 72–73, doi:10.1002/ace.382.

21. Shaffer, "Criteria for Improving," 1.

22. Ibid., 7.

23. Garrison, *Apostles of Culture*, 13.

24. Bryan C. Rindfleisch, "'What It Means to Be a Man': Contested Masculinity in the Early Republic and Antebellum America," *History Compass* 10, no. 11 (2012): 852–65, 10.1111/hic3.12005.

25. Ibid., 853–54.

26. Garrison, *Apostles of Culture*, 12.

27. Ibid., 169.

28. Coffey, *Evolution of Librarianship*, 1.

29. Garrison, *Apostles of Culture*, 9.

30. Lonergan, "Is Librarianship a Profession?"

31. Faber, "Professional Identities," 332.

32. For example, Shaffer, *Maturity of Librarianship*.

33. For example, Lonergan, "Is Librarianship a Profession?"

34. Kathleen Weibel, "Toward a Feminist Profession," *Library Journal* 101, no. 1 (1976): 263–67; Dee Garrison, "The Tender Technicians: The Feminization of Public Librarianship, 1876–1905," *Journal of Academic Librarianship* 3, no. 1 (1977): 10–19.

35. Bayles, "Librarianship Is a Discipline," 1715.

36. See titles such as Amitai Etzioni's *The Semi-Professions and Their Organization* (New York: Free Press, 1969).

37. Garrison, *Apostles of Culture*, 194.
38. Ibid., 168.
39. Ibid., 185.
40. Christine Williams, "Daring to Find Our Names: The Search for Lesbigay Library History," in *A Lesbigay Gender Perplex*, ed. James V. Carmichael Jr. (Westport, CT: Greenwood, 1998), 37.
41. Jody Newmyer, "The Image Problem of the Librarian: Femininity and Social Control," *Journal of Library History (1974–1987)* 11, no. 1 (1976): 56.
42. Ibid., 55.
43. Williams, "Daring to Find Our Names," 37, 41.
44. James V. Carmichael Jr., "The Male Librarian and the Feminine Image: A Survey of Stereotype, Status, and Gender Perceptions," *Library and Information Science Research* 14, no. 4 (1992): 412.
45. Alistair Black, "Man and Boy: Modifying Masculinities in Public Librarianship, 1850-1950." In *Gendering Library History*, eds. Evelyn Kerslake and Nickianne Moody (Liverpool: Liverpool John Moores University Press, 2000), 210.
46. Carmichael, "The Male Librarian."
47. Paul S. Piper and Barbara E. Collamer, "Male Librarians: Men in a Feminized Profession," *Journal of Academic Librarianship* 27, no. 5 (2001): 410.
48. Garrison, *Apostles of Culture*, 12.
49. Suzanne Hildenbrand, "Library Feminism and Library Women's History: Activism and Scholarship, Equity and Culture," *Libraries and Culture* 35, no. 1 (2000): 52.
50. Ibid.
51. Hildenbrand, "Library Feminism and Library Women's History," 53; Herman Greenberg, "Sex Discrimination against Women in Libraries," in *Women in Librarianship*, ed. Margaret Myers and Mayra Scarborough, 49-62 (New Brunswick, NJ: Rutgers University Press, 1975); Debra Gold Hansen, Karen F. Gracy, and Sheri D. Irvin, "At the Pleasure of the Board: Women Librarians and the Los Angeles Public Library," *Libraries and Culture* 34, no. 4 (Fall 1999): 311–46.
52. Garrison, *Apostles of Culture*, 62.
53. Majid and Haider, "Image Problem Even Haunts Hi-Tech Libraries"; Dodds, "Advertising the Librarian Image"; Ramirose Ilene Attebury, "Perceptions of a Profession: Librarians and Stereotypes in Online Videos," *Library Philosophy and Practice*, 2010: 1–22; Seale, "Old Maids, Policeman [*sic*], and Social Rejects."
54. Carmichael, "The Male Librarian."
55. Abigail Luthmann, "Librarians, Professionalism and Image: Stereotype and Reality," *Library Review* 56, no. 9 (October 16, 2007): 773–80, doi:10.1108/00242530710831211.

Bibliography

Attebury, Ramirose Ilene. "Perceptions of a Profession: Librarians and Stereotypes in Online Videos." *Library Philosophy and Practice*, 2010: 1–22.

Bayles, Sandy. "Librarianship Is a Discipline." *Library Journal* 102, no. 15 (1977): 1715–17.

Birdsall, William F. "Librarianship, Professionalism, and Social Change." *Library Journal* 107, no. 3 (1982): 223–26.

Black, Alistair. "Man and Boy: Modifying Masculinities in Public Librarianship, 1850-1950." In *Gendering Library History*, edited by Evelyn Kerslake and Nickianne Moody, 209-20. Liverpool: Liverpool John Moores University Press, 2000.

Caputo, Janette S. *The Assertive Librarian*. Phoenix, AZ: Oryx Press, 1984.

Carmichael, James V., Jr. "The Male Librarian and the Feminine Image: A Survey of Stereotype, Status, and Gender Perceptions." *Library and Information Science Research* 14, no. 4 (1992): 411–46.

Coffey, Monica Anne. *The Evolution of Librarianship into a Profession*. Saint Louis, MO: Saint Louis University Press, 1990.

Doctorow, Cory. "Libraries, Hackspaces, and E-waste: How Libraries Can Be the Hub of a Young Maker Revolution." *Raincoast Books Blog*, February 24, 2013. www.raincoast.com/blog/details/guest-post-cory-doctorow-for-freedom-to-read-week.

Dodds, Kathrin. "Advertising the Librarian Image: Stereotypical Depictions of Librarians in Advertising." Paper, PCA-ACA Annual Conference, New Orleans, LA, April 8, 2009. www.academia.edu/226036/Advertising_the_Librarian_Image_Stereotypical_depictions_of_librarians_in_advertising.

Elmborg, Jim. "Literacies, Narratives, and Adult Learning in Libraries." *New Directions for Adult and Continuing Education* no. 127 (2010): 67–76. doi:10.1002/ace.382.

Etzioni, Amitai. *The Semi-Professions and Their Organization: Teachers, Nurses, Social Workers*. New York: Free Press, 1969.

Faber, Brenton. "Professional Identities." *Journal of Business and Technical Communication* 16, no. 3 (2002): 306–37.

Garrett, Jeffrey. "Missing Eco: On Reading 'The Name of the Rose' as Library Criticism." *Library Quarterly* 61, no. 4 (1991): 373–88.

Garrison, Dee. *Apostles of Culture: The Public Librarian and American Society, 1876–1920*. New York: Free Press, 1979.

———. "The Tender Technicians: The Feminization of Public Librarianship, 1876–1905." *Journal of Academic Librarianship* 3, no. 1 (1977): 10–19.

Goode, William J. "The Librarian: From Occupation to Profession?" *Library Quarterly* 31, no. 4 (1961): 306–20.

Hansen, Debra Gold, Karen F. Gracy, and Sheri D. Irvin. "At the Pleasure of the Board: Women Librarians and the Los Angeles Public Library." *Libraries and Culture* 34, no. 4 (Fall 1999): 311–46.

Harris, Roma M. "Gender, Power, and the Dangerous Pursuit of Professionalism." *American Libraries* 24, no. 9 (1993): 874–876.

Hildenbrand, Suzanne. "Ambiguous Authority and Aborted Ambition: Gender, Professionalism, and the Rise and Fall of the Welfare State." *Library Trends* 34, no. 2 (1985): 185–98.

———. "Library Feminism and Library Women's History: Activism and Scholarship, Equity and Culture." *Libraries and Culture* 35, no. 1 (2000): 51–65.

Jost, John T., and Aaron C. Kay. "Exposure to Benevolent Sexism and Complementary Gender Stereotypes: Consequences for Specific and Diffuse Forms of System Justification." *Journal of Personality and Social Psychology* 88, no. 3 (March 2005): 498–509. doi:10.1037/0022-3514.88.3.498.

Kay, Aaron C. Martin V. Day, Mark P. Zanna, and A. David Nussbaum. "The Insidious (and Ironic) Effects of Positive Stereotypes." *Journal of Experimental Social Psychology* 49, no. 2 (2013): 287–91.

Keller, Helen R. "The Old-Fashioned Virtues versus the Ideal Librarian." *Library Journal* 34, no. 7 (2009): 295–98.

Langenhove, Luk Van, and Rom Harré. "Cultural Stereotypes and Positioning Theory." *Journal for the Theory of Social Behaviour* 24, no. 4 (1994): 359–72. doi:10.1111/j.1468-5914.1994.tb00260.x.

Lonergan, David. "Is Librarianship a Profession?" *Community and Junior College Libraries* 15, no. 2 (2009): 119–22.

Luthmann, Abigail. "Librarians, Professionalism and Image: Stereotype and Reality." *Library Review* 56, no. 9 (October 16, 2007): 773–80. doi:10.1108/00242530710831211.

Majid, Shaheen, and Azim Haider. "Image Problem Even Haunts Hi-Tech Libraries: Stereotypes Associated with Library and Information Professionals in Singapore." *Aslib Proceedings* 60, no. 3 (2008): 229–41. doi:10.1108/00012530810879105.

Miller, Laura. "The Self-Image of the Library Profession." *International Library Review* 21, no. 2 (1989): 141–55.

Myers, Margaret, and Mayra Scarborough, eds. *Women in Librarianship: Melvil's Rib Symposium.* New Brunswick, NJ: Rutgers University Press, 1975.

Nauratil, Marcia J. *The Alienated Librarian.* New Directions in Information Management no. 20. New York: Greenwood, 1989.

Newmyer, Jody. "The Image Problem of the Librarian: Femininity and Social Control." *Journal of Library History (1974–1987)* 11, no. 1 (1976): 44–67.

Piper, Paul S., and Barbara E. Collamer. "Male Librarians: Men in a Feminized Profession." *Journal of Academic Librarianship* 27, no. 5 (2001): 406–11.

Preer, Jean L. "'Louder Please': Using Historical Research to Foster Professional Identity in LIS Students." *Libraries and the Cultural Record* 41, no. 4 (2006): 487–96.

Radford, Gary P., and Marie L. Radford. "Libraries, Librarians, and the Discourse of Fear." *Library Quarterly* 71, no. 3 (2001): 299–329.

Rindfleisch, Bryan C. "'What It Means to Be a Man': Contested Masculinity in the Early Republic and Antebellum America." *History Compass* 10, no. 11 (2012): 852–65. doi:10.1111/hic3.12005.

Seale, Maura. "Old Maids, Policeman [*sic*], and Social Rejects." *Electronic Journal of Academic and Special Librarianship* 9, no. 1 (2008). http://southernlibrarianship.icaap.org/content/v09n01/seale_m01.html.

Shaffer, Dale E. *Criteria for Improving the Professional Status of Librarianship.* ERIC publication no. ED 188626. Self-published paper, 1980.

———. *The Maturity of Librarianship as a Profession.* Metuchen, NJ: Scarecrow Press, 1968.

Steele, Claude. *Whistling Vivaldi: How Stereotypes Affect Us and What We Can Do.* New York: Norton, 1999.

Stephens, Elsie. "Professional Status of Librarianship Revisited." *Journal of Library Administration* 7, no. 1 (1986): 7–12.

Weibel, Kathleen. "Toward a Feminist Profession." *Library Journal* 101, no. 1 (1976): 263–67.

White, Herbert S. *Librarians and the Awakening from Innocence: A Collection of Papers.* Boston: G. K. Hall, 1989.

Williams, Christine. "Daring to Find Our Names: The Search for Lesbigay Library History." In *A Lesbigay Gender Perplex: Sexual Stereotyping and Professional Ambiguity in Librarianship,* edited by James V. Carmichael Jr., 37–46. Westport, CT: Greenwood, 1998.

Winter, Michael F. "The Professionalization of Librarianship." *Occasional Papers/University of Illinois Graduate School of Library and Information Science,* vol. 160. Urbana: University of Illinois, 1983.

CHAPTER 4

That's Women's Work

Pink-Collar Professions, Gender, and the Librarian Stereotype

Ayanna Gaines

"Who Do You Want to Be in Bed?" asks Valerie Frankel. In her article of that title in *Self* magazine, she explores the idea that women have two identities: their public persona and their private sexual personality. Although there seems to be a range of sexual personas, "Women do tend to fall into two subcategories: (1) Naughty Librarians, or women who are shy in public and assertive in private, and (2) Powerhouse Paulines [who are bold publicly but mild-mannered sexually]."[1] Frankel's article does several things simultaneously: it not only reinforces the traditional stereotype of the librarian as shy, unassertive, and nonsexual, but it also puts forth the hypersexualized secondary stereotype of the Sexy Librarian, the librarian whose sexuality is bubbling just beneath the surface.

Librarianship, teaching, and nursing are all highly feminized professions. These professions, along with other so-called "pink-collar" jobs, have historically been dominated by women. "Pink-collar" jobs are now defined as those jobs dominated by women, and are considered to bring with them less social status and pay than other jobs [requiring comparable education].[2] Even though these fields require professional education, many people still hold stereotyped views of those who work in them. These stereotypes result in recruiting difficulties and loss of status, among other complications. Librarianship's status as a feminized profession is what leads to the persistence of its negative and demoralizing stereotypes. The negative librarian stereotypes present themselves not only in the way that librarians are perceived physically, but also in the understanding (or lack thereof) of the work of the librarian. This lack of understanding, along with the resulting devaluing of the profession, stems from the assumption that library work is "women's work" and is therefore not as worthy as other types of work. The assumption that there is "women's work" at all furthers the gendering of work activities. The main problem is not that there are negative stereotypes of librarians, but rather that these negative stereotypes stem from hackneyed ideas of what women are and what women do. To confront these stereotypes and their implications, what may be needed is a radical change in the way that society views work.

The issue of the librarian stereotype is not a new one—in its 1876 inaugural issue, *Library Journal* published an article on the profession wherein the editor, Melvil Dewey, stated that the librarian was considered "a mouser in musty books," and that the profession should move beyond this image.[3] The 1982 book *Stereotype and Status: Librarians in the United States* by Pauline Wilson looks at documents dating as far back as the 1920s, in which librarians react to their professional stereotype.[4] The librarian stereotype has been well described by the professional literature. Luthmann defines the most common stereotype: "an older, single, white woman, generally accoutered with one or more of the following: cardigan, pearls, tweed skirt, hair in a bun, and spectacles perched on the nose."[5] Radford and Radford go further and ascribe to the stereotype such attributes as "an obsession with order, sexual repression, matronly appearance, dowdy dress, fussiness, dour facial expressions, and monosyllabic speech."[6] Seale, however, believes there are four stereotypes in addition to the old maid stereotype: the policeman librarian, the librarian as parody, the inept librarian, and the hero/ine librarian.[7] Attebury adds three more categories to these five: the sexy librarian, the psycho librarian, and the fun and positive librarian.[8] These last three can be safely considered subcategories, offshoots of their parent stereotypes. The sexy librarian, in particular, is a reinterpretation of the old maid and can be read either as the end result of the release of the repressed sexuality of the old maid librarian, or as a hypersexualized styling of the old maid librarian.

Despite the existence of a separate policeman stereotype, Attebury notes how the police-like enforcer characteristic creeps into the common librarian stereotype. She draws on Radford and Radford's discussion on Foucault to explain how this plays into the gender aspect of the stereotype: "Portraying the library as an institutional symbol and enforcer of a venerable system of cultural knowledge and power, the authors claim that the negative trappings of female librarianship serve to mitigate the awesomeness of the system. That is, true, 'the female librarian is presented as fearsome, but beneath the stern exterior, there is nothing to fear; there is only a woman.'"[9]

In addition, female librarians also serve as warnings about the power of the library system, showing what happens when one becomes controlled by its rules. Women become less than themselves, losing their humanity, their empathy, their sexuality.[10] It's a frightening enough prospect that some librarians try to avoid the stereotype at all costs. They go to extremes to prove their humanity and their sexuality.

Librarians themselves may be responsible for the sexy librarian stereotype, as a way of denying that they are different from anyone else, according to Wilson.[11] The sexy librarian has become attractive in multiple ways and has gained traction as its own stereotype. Attebury studied videos created by librarians and nonlibrarians alike for their use of the librarian stereotypes.[12] She grouped videos into eight categories: Old Maid, Policeman, Parody, Inept, Hero/ine, Fun/Positive, Sexy, and Psycho. The majority of nonlibrarian videos featured negative stereotypes; 93 percent of those videos featured either the Policeman, the Old Maid, or the Inept Librarian stereotype.* Eighteen percent of videos presented the Sexy Librarian.[13] The Sexy Librarian is so popular with the public that there is a review by Candi Strecker of pornographic novels featuring librarians available on the website ChipRowe.com,[14] and several vendors sell Sexy Librarian costumes all year round, including Sears.com (which sells two).†

While some, such as Luthmann, argue that the librarian stereotype is produced more by librarians themselves than by the media, such images do exist in the wild.[15] They appear in the mass media, in commercials, in

---

* Some videos contain more than one stereotype, so percentages do not add up to 100 percent.

† Sears.com search results page for "sexy librarian" (accessed May 13, 2013) included two costumes; see www.sears.com/search=sexy%20librarian.

television shows, as Halloween costumes, in movies. They even inhabit YouTube videos, which, Attebury notes, are crucial in the construction and distribution of culture.[16] Mass media produces stereotypes, according to Seale (citing Stuart Hall): "These representations are not insignificant or unimportant. . . . The mass media 'produce . . . representations of the social world, images, descriptions, explanations and frames for understanding how the world is and why it works as it is said and shown to work.'"[17]

Yet problems arise when stereotypes become our only lens through which we interpret actions and people and make decisions. When the stereotypes become pervasive—and become the reason that people choose not to pursue a certain career, or voters choose to not support a library referendum—then there is a distinct problem with the stereotype. When these stereotypes foster an attitude that only women can be librarians, then these stereotypes can be harmful.

In the Victorian era, librarianship, like elementary school teaching and nursing, was a woman-dominated profession, seen as appropriate for unmarried women. In librarianship, unmarried women were able to flourish and provide "the atmosphere of a middle-class home with good and morally uplifting books, to rescue the masses from moral and intellectual poverty."[18] The increase in the number of educational opportunities for women in the latter half of the 19th century coincided with the uptick in open positions for educated women, especially in teaching and librarianship.[19] During the last part of the 1800s, women were recruited as teachers, librarians, and nurses because they were viewed as "cheap, educated labor."[20] Librarianship was seen as an easy transition for women from the domestic realm to that of the working world.

In 1870, approximately 80 percent of all library employees were male, but by 1900, approximately 80 percent of all library employees were female.[21] At Columbia College in 1887, there were three men in Melvil Dewey's first class of 20. Passet believes this is due to the fact that men in librarianship at that time could obtain positions in administration based on experience and other educational credentials without needing Dewey's degree. She also posits that the library school curriculum was seen as "mechanical—preparing people for subordinate positions—rather than intellectual in substance."[22] In addition, promotional literature published in that era about the field promoted librarianship as being suitable for women, stating that "women as a class far surpass men"; as for the meager salaries that librarianship would pay, women were "infinitely better than equivalent salaries will produce of the other sex."[23] Today, the profession continues to be heavily dominated by women. Of the 118,666 credentialed librarians surveyed in 2009–2010, 98,273, or 82.8 percent, were women.[24]

Roma Harris believes that the librarian stereotype is "bound up in general sex role stereotypes."[25] She quotes Garrison in saying that "the dominant image [of librarianship] is that of 'genteel traditionalism, ineffectual males and shushing spinsters.'"[26] The stereotype of the female librarian, as we have seen and as is reinforced by this quote, is intermingled with stereotypes of women, and of single women in particular. The dominant image of the librarian is of a dour woman who wants to maintain order among her books. Even the male librarians do not come off any better; they are "ineffectual," as if being in a woman's profession has somehow made them less capable. The overall effect is not flattering to women's work or to women in general. It begs the question: Must a woman be a spinster, or a man ineffectual, to be a librarian? Or does the work simply have that effect on one employed in the profession?

Majid and Haider's study further demonstrates how entrenched the gender stereotype of the librarian profession has proven to be. They administered a questionnaire to patrons at three academic libraries and three public libraries in Singapore, asking about perceptions of librarians. Out of 214 respondents, 57.9 percent felt that only women could be librarians, while 38.3 percent felt the profession was suitable for both genders.[27] The idea that librarians could be male is still alien to people; the library still seems to be the dominion of women.

In addition to the gender stereotype, there is also a pervasive stereotype about the job of the librarian. Majid and Haider make note of Hernon and Pastine's 1977 study at the University of Nebraska that looked at the role of academic librarians; the perception of librarians was of the common stereotype, "a little old lady behind the desk, checking out or shelving books, filing cards, and keeping the library in order."[28] With regard to the role that academic librarians play within the larger organization, Majid and Haider cite a 1987 study that finds that, while faculty think that librarians are useful, they do not perceive them as having any responsibilities other than a service role within the institution—that is, not having any management, research, or teaching responsibilities. In addition, they were not seen as contributing to the greater educational system.[29] Majid and Haider observe that Bowden was able to link the poor image of librarians with their resulting low status; Bowden went even further to state that there was little understanding of the scope of responsibility of the librarian and that the poor reputation of librarianship was a result of the feminization of the profession.[30] The pink-collar aspect of the profession was considered responsible for how little it was esteemed. Again, the idea that librarianship is somehow "women's work" damages the profession. We see society's perception that the work that women do is not as respected, and how this perception, in turn, reflects women's reduced status in society's eyes.

If one were to look at the obituaries of librarians published in the *New York Times*, one would get a very different image of the profession. Dilevko and Gottlieb's scholarship, which looked at the portrayal of librarians in these obituaries, found that 63.4 percent were of men, and a large percentage of these obituaries were of academic librarians.[31] Rather than being painted as the stereotypical "shy, sheltered, dour, or dowdy individuals," librarians are instead portrayed as engaged in large-scale endeavors such as "international outreach" and "consciousness-raising."[32] Overall, one can derive from descriptions in the obituaries that librarianship is "a glamorous profession that offers individuals a fulfilling, exciting, worldly, and eventful career."[33] Yet this positive image is predominantly the domain of male librarians, and academics at that. Even allowing for gender, this image is in direct opposition to the "ineffectual male" stereotype that often attaches itself to the image of the male librarian.[34] Further, it cannot be ignored that the negative stereotypes of librarians, the "shelving, stamping, and shushing" that Radford and Radford allude to, are predominantly the sphere of female librarians.[35] Many librarians contribute to "small librarianship" by recommending books, working the reference desk, or interacting with children or the elderly. However, if these acts are remembered at all, it is through the lens of the gendered stereotype, with all its negative connotations.[36] What is made public for the consumption of others in these obituaries is the positive, male-dominated "big librarianship," which is much more glamorous. As Dilevko and Gottleib point out, there seems to be little desire to redefine the profession as consisting of "small and caring acts" that can greatly affect the lives of patrons.[37] Librarianship is, at its core, a caring profession.

Along with teaching and nursing, librarianship is "care work," one of many occupations that provide "a face-to-face service that develops the human capabilities of the recipient," widely defined as health, skills, or cognitive development.[38] Care work often pays less not just because it includes jobs that are predominantly taken care of by women. Instead, assert England, Budig, and Folbre, care work pays less because it involves tasks that are, in people's minds, associated with women and mothering, more so than other "women's work," and thus salaries are capped accordingly. Mothering and nurturing are seen as natural and innate, rather than skills to be cultivated. Likewise, mothers, and those who mother, are expected to provide care, and to do so out of love rather than for monetary compensation. Thus, there is a salary penalty.[39]

Being a caring profession seems to fly in the face of being considered a "true profession." Librarianship has been moving toward the "male model of professionalism," an "expert model," and away from the "service model" of librarianship, the "small librarianship" that values care and service and is more "female-intensive."[40] With the stress on what is seen as more positive, aspects such as information systems and "managerial prowess," there is a resultant neglect of small caring acts that make librarianship so meaningful to the lives of so many.[41] The logic seems to be that it is the old service-based and care-based aspect of librarianship that has resulted in the persistence of the negative female-based librarian stereotypes. It does not seem to enter into the equation that it is, instead, "the systemic devaluation of woman's work" that is the root of the problem.[42]

This tension between "big librarianship" and "small librarianship," between male and female, can also be seen in the rivalry between the paradigm of "librarianship" and "information science." Badovinac and Južnič believe that the "information science" aspect is winning, as it represents progress, science, or male domination.[43] The male aspect of librarianship is often praised or privileged over those forms of librarianship that are considered feminine.

As a result of the desire to professionalize and become more like the male-dominated professions, stratification has developed within the library. Management and technology, positions, which are considered to be the most "masculine," are the most highly prized and valued, while positions in children's services and cataloging are not as highly valued. Harris believes that, in essence, professionalization is being used as an attempt to escape the female soul of the profession.[44]

There is movement to divorce some of the feminine connotations from the profession. In some circles, the term *librarian* is being replaced with *information professional* as *librarian* is linked too closely with women and is thus viewed in a negative light.[45] This emphasis on the word *professional* also reflects librarianship's move toward professionalization.[46] Librarianship is attempting to adopt the characteristics of historically male-dominated professional occupations, such as law and medicine, in order to attain some of the status that these occupations have. Image and prestige are often the concern of professions such as teaching, nursing, and librarianship, occupations that are sometimes referred to as "semi-professions."[47] Semi-professions, as defined by Etzioni, have a shorter training period, a less legitimate status, a less specialized body of knowledge, less of a right to privileged information, and "less autonomy from supervision or societal control than 'the' professions."[48] One may argue that librarianship has become more of a profession. With the growth of the body of scholarship in librarianship, privileged communication is becoming more established.

Another problem stems from the fact that there is much discussion over what is considered a profession: there are no clear criteria.[49] One thing is evident, however: in the eyes of the trait theorists, librarianship and other feminized professions will never be considered full professions,[*] despite having the characteristics that trait theorists attribute to professional occupations, such as a "a unique body of abstract knowledge, a code

---

[*] The trait theory of professionalism is a sociological theory of work whereby professions can be distinguished from each other through the application of set criteria.

of ethics for practitioners, [and] an orientation toward service," because librarianship is seen by others as being clerical or administrative, not professional. There is no acknowledgment of the deeper knowledge of librarianship.[50] Indeed, a movement toward "professionalism," toward the male aspect of other careers, can be seen as a move away from the feminine aspect of librarianship. However, is it to the benefit of librarianship to leave behind the feminine nature of the profession, in the process shedding this aspect of the stereotype that accompanies it? Or is this denying an essential aspect of the very nature of librarianship? There must be a way to professionalize librarianship without denying its past or cutting out its heart.

Gender plays a part in the reduced status and salary of librarianship due to its role as a pink-collar profession. Regardless of attempts to challenge the gender balance of librarianship, it is necessary to examine the role that the librarian stereotype has played in the lives of male librarians. Carmichael's seminal article on the male librarian and the female image includes a review of the literature surrounding the image of librarians.[51] What is revelatory is the image of men that emerges. Male librarians, in spite of their gender, are not exempt from the librarian stereotype. Before the profession became feminized, male librarians had their own reputation, closely linked to issues of gender. Melvil Dewey was described by Amherst College president Julius Seelye as being "a bit of an old maid." [52] One library student was described by a library faculty member to a prospective employer as having "a somewhat effeminate manner."[53] What is worth noting is that these effeminate descriptors were used in a derogatory sense, and often coupled with the anti-intellectual commentary that was common in the 19th century and was usually aimed at librarians and social reformers. Even Ralph Waldo Emerson "warned young male students against becoming 'effeminate gownsmen.'" [54]

Dickinson, citing Newmyer, notes that the stereotype of the librarian tended to lean toward "grim, grouchy, eccentric, and male" prior to 1870, and the librarian was a distinctly bookish man, according to Sable.[55] His tasks involved enforcing loan periods and, with closed stacks, acting as a custodian for the collection, providing select individuals access to texts.[56] The idea of the broken-down man who had failed at other careers was also present in the image of the early librarian. There was perhaps some reason for this image: Passet's examination of male library school students shows that there were a number of older men in attendance, men in search of second careers.[57]

There is a sense of denial inherent in the discussion of male librarians stemming in part from the fact that librarianship is a feminized profession. We see this in the way that male librarians are portrayed as worldly in their obituaries and in the way that any mention of the more feminine aspects of the profession are left out.[58] Yet we see this denial in other instances. Citing Williams's scholarship about male nurses, James Carmichael notes that men in feminine professions, out of fear of being perceived as gay, go out of their way to explain that they are, in fact, not. In addition, male nurses will seek out higher-level administrative positions in an effort to get away from the gay male nurse stereotype.[59] A similar denial may be at work in librarianship. Carmichael has observed that, despite the fact that in librarianship women are predominant, there is still gender stratification.[60] There are more men in administrative positions, and they thus are allotted a certain amount of privilege with regard to their career and educational opportunities. Since 1870, women have made up anywhere from 78.5 percent to 91 percent of the library profession but the percentage of women in administrative positions has been significantly lower.[61] An Association of Research Libraries survey in 2010 found that, while only 17.2 percent of librarians were men, they held 40 percent of the director positions in university libraries.[62]

The stereotype that the men in Carmichael's study were most familiar with was "effeminate, probably gay."[63] Another popular strain of stereotype related to lack of social skills, power, and ambition. The scholar was identified 49 percent of the time, while the know-it-all was acknowledged 23 percent of the time. In open-ended questions, the most noticeable stereotype that developed was the socially inept, unambitious librarian who is a librarian simply because he has failed in other professions. He's poorly dressed, obsessive, and anal-retentive, living to work instead of working to live.[64]

Newmyer, according to Carmichael, has cited several examples of 19th century eccentrics and world-famous former librarians as a way of suggesting that the male stereotype has been seen historically as quirky and somewhat negative.[65] Carmichael further asserts that the gendered stereotyping of librarianship has had a detrimental effect on the psyche of male librarians, according to Carmichael. Because of societal expectations of men to not only compete but to also be the primary financial providers for their families, men in feminized professions will often pursue administrative positions rather than risk disapproval. They separate themselves from those areas in librarianship that are seen as more feminine, such as children's services and cataloging. Interestingly, several subjects in Carmichael's study acknowledged that men were expected to become administrators and were looked upon as "inferior" or "weak" if they chose to do otherwise.[66] In some instances, men opt to remain in their positions; one such librarian chose to stay in children's services (a heavily female-dominated area) and encountered the "glass escalator" throughout his career in the form of pressure to change tracks or to move into administration.[67] The glass escalator moves male workers ever upward, and men may either move along with it or work to stay in place.[68] How does the feminization of the profession affect the stereotype of the male librarian? For one, Newmyer's "grim, grouchy, eccentric, and male" librarian and Sable's bibliophilic man "who lived only for his books"[69] were transformed over time into different entities altogether: the "kindly and sometimes effeminate misfit" and the "weak and non-masculine individuals."[70] As the profession became viewed more as a "woman's job," men in the profession became viewed as those who had failed in more traditionally masculine fields. Librarianship was seen as the last bastion of hope for men. Because of this, and because of the low salaries in librarianship, men often aspired to administrative positions; not only would the compensation be higher, but the intellectual rigor of administration was thought to be more suitably challenging (and more akin to that of male-dominated professions) than positions such as reference, which were considered to be less stimulating.[71]

In the literature, it has been noted how men have reacted to the female nature of the librarian stereotype. Harris notes that Wilson, in her book *Stereotype and Status: Librarians in the United States,* made the comment that in the professional literature, male librarians were quick to put a wall between themselves and the profession by stressing their gender, and thus the fact that the stereotype did not apply to them, to the reader.[72] Harris, quoting McReynolds, also points out that men stressed the similarities of librarianship to male-intensive professions in an attempt to suppress the feminine aspect of librarianship.[73] Wilson goes as far as to quote a study as saying, "The male librarian wants first, before proving himself as a librarian, to prove himself as a male. He does not want to be considered as belonging to the female stereotype."[74] Yet he often encounters stereotypes of himself as "wimpy and asexual."[75]

Despite the presence of the male librarian stereotype, it can be argued that it has more prominence in the minds of librarians than in the popular culture. Dickinson's analysis of James Carmichael Jr.'s famous study is that the effeminate or gay librarian stereotype is more prominent in the librarian profession than out of it.[76] In 1993, Ann O'Brien and Martin Raish, published a filmography of 126 motion pictures featuring librarians; only 11 of those films feature male librarians or library assistants; this seems to point out the prominence of the female librarian stereotype.[77] However, it cannot be ignored that the male librarian characters in the films did have many of the characteristics of the past stereotypes, being either "failed," "meek," or "unpleasant."

In nursing, gender stereotypes are a reality as well. The quintessential mother, the Mother Nature stereotype, lies behind many of nursing's clichés because nursing is so closely linked to women, and women are often thought of as having an instinctive skill to be nurses.[78] In a 1910 article in the *American Journal of Nursing*, Edna Foley wrote about nursing being an ideal profession for college women: "It is a field open only to women. Male nurses are misnomers, save in rare instances, and these only serve as exceptions to prove the rule."[79] In the 21st century, male nurses are still somewhat rare. In 2003, 92.1 percent of all registered nurses in the United States were women.[80] As of 2010, 8.9 percent of the registered nurses in the United States were male, according to the United States Department of Labor.[81]

Gender stereotyping has persisted. On television, the nurse is stereotyped as being either maternal or romantic and not having much in the way of "intellectual abilities."[82] However, the nurse is not always motherly; in 1981, playing on the idea of the sexy nurse, Playboy planned to do a feature on nurses, an action which a group of nurses protested.[83] Male nurses must also contend with the female stereotype; it is often assumed that they are gay, a situation that is similar to the one faced by male librarians.[84] The nursing stereotype can be detrimental to recruitment efforts; Harris quotes Rayner, who noted that British career counselors were telling students that "they can do better than nursing."[85] In addition, the information that school counselors provide students about the profession is often incorrect or not enough for students to base an accurate decision on.[86] The image of nurses can also affect the amount of funding that nurses receive in federal budgets.[87] Rezaei-Adaryani, Salsali, and Mohammadi, summarizing the findings of Ellis and Hartley and of Kearns, concur; the notion that people have of nursing may indeed jeopardize the amount of resources that the profession is assigned.[88] This is similar to the plight in which school librarians find themselves. Often thought of as resembling Marian the Librarian in *The Music Man* despite being busy behind the scenes collaborating with classroom teachers and helping students, school librarians are often seen as easy pickings by legislators looking to make cuts in the budget.[89] As Marie L. Radford states in the blog *Library Garden*, "Thinking of libraries as dusty, unused places (instead of vital community centers) and librarians as unproductive, fussy old biddies who shuffle around the library shushing, stamping, and shelving is useful to the powerful elite who use this ill-informed view as justification to cut already low salaries and benefits for public librarians, fire librarians, reduce hours and close libraries."[90]

Teaching, another feminized profession, is not safe from stereotyping by society. In addition, equating a profession like teaching to care, and care subsequently with being female, punishes the practitioners. Early education is especially female-dominated, and this thinking keeps women in what King, quoted by Weaver-Hightower, calls "the early education sweatshop," and labels those men who choose to pursue careers in this area "unnatural."[91] Men who do pursue the field are subject to commentary and teasing from others; in response, they assert characteristics of masculinity to make up for the supposed ease of the coursework and "cute" factor of some of the projects.[92] In addition, they mark some aspects of the teacher education program as female, and inherently negative, and then distance themselves from those aspects.[93] Sandefur and Moore note how teachers are often portrayed as "insensitive, misguided, victimizing, or incompetent."[94] The negative image of teachers, as witch or wimp, may even act as a deciding factor behind the public's decision to not support public education.[95] In their study of children's picture books, Sandefur and Moore discovered that the predominant image of the teacher is that of a white, non-Hispanic woman. Only 42 percent of the images demonstrated the teacher acting in a competent, sensitive fashion; the majority of the images represented a negative (female) image of teachers.[96] When teachers are portrayed as a positive, albeit unrealistic, influence, as many of them are in Rick Breault's study of teachers in film, then the majority of them are male.[97]

Men in elementary school teaching are affected by gender stereotyping as well. There are few of them to begin with; in 1990, 14.8 percent of elementary teachers were male, down from 16.3 percent in 1980.[98] Only 18.3 percent of elementary and middle school teachers are men, according to the US Bureau of Labor Statistics' 2011 *Current Population Survey,* and only 2.3 percent of kindergarten and preschool teachers are male.[99] Elementary school teaching is a profession that is predominantly female, as the statistics bear out. Those men who go into teaching in this area may find themselves "tracked" into areas that are considered more legitimate for men, such as administration. It is not coincidental that these positions that are considered more appropriate for men are also more prestigious and better paying. The men who decide to follow the path leading to more pay and more prestige encounter the aforementioned "glass escalator."[100] Those male elementary school teachers who decide to forego the glass escalator and stay in the classroom must often fight the suspicion that they are pedophiles.[101]

It is entirely possible that the fact that men are employed in feminized professions, with all the negative connotations and stereotypes therein, is pushing men toward the glass escalator. Society often labels men in these professions as sexual deviants or failures. To escape these stereotypes, men veer toward more "legitimate" tracks in the professions as a matter of self-defense.[102]

Yet more men are entering fields previously dominated by women. Out of the 20 fastest-growing job categories for white college-educated men ages 25–39 from 2000 to 2010, eight of those categories were pink-collar professions. Primary school teachers saw the largest change in men employed, with teachers' aides and miscellaneous teachers following behind. Registered nurses came in ninth.[103] But why is there such high demand for positions wherein men will still have to confront a stereotype that demeans them or challenges their masculinity? Is it the allure of advancement via the glass escalator that is captivating to some? Are men changing their definitions of masculinity? Or is it that men are not as cognizant of the stereotypes until they are in the trenches? This idea that men enter blindly into their chosen professions unaware that they will be pigeonholed into stereotypes is counter to the experiences described in Carmichael's study; 24 percent of men had always been aware of the librarian stereotype, while 25 percent learned of the stereotype before graduate school. This comprises almost half of his sample; contrast this with the 26 percent of men who learned of the librarian stereotype at the workplace.[104] Yet it cannot be due entirely to the promise of promotion either; as has been previously discussed, many men have balked at the idea of being placed on the glass escalator. According to an article from the *New York Times*, men are choosing these careers for the same reasons that have supposedly attracted women to pink-collar careers: "less stress and more time at home."[105] This sentiment carries with it the belittlement that accompanies attitudes about pink-collar work: that it isn't real work, that it isn't taxing or over-stressful. Nurses, teachers, and librarians engage in real work, each with its own stressors. To assume that pink-collar work is easy belittles women as well as men.

Librarianship has felt the negative impact of stereotypical portrayals by the media. The negative stereotype keeps the public from seeing the usefulness of the librarian. Further, if this librarian stereotype is not replaced with a positive image, then the public is left with no idea of what a librarian does at all. The public's perception of librarianship is that it is not necessarily a profession, resulting in reduced status, which can, in turn, inhibit the use and importance of librarians in organizations. If librarians are not respected within their larger institutions and are therefore not put to use, then their status will be further reduced and librarianship further devalued.

One of the more dangerous assumptions about women and work is that gender determines one's competence in one's career—that nature, rather than skill, is the true strength behind the employee. Sandra Bem is quoted by Harris as saying: "Female behavior is interpreted to fit the stereotype of what women are like, and one important aspect of the female stereotype in American society is that females are incompetent except in certain highly stereotyped roles as wife and mother."[106] While this quote relates to the conundrum of the image of nurses, the same factors come into play for libraries. In essence, librarians are defined, and thus stereotyped, by their gender, not by their profession. Librarianship, nursing, teaching, and other female fields are seen as requiring the "natural" attributes of women, but not necessarily intelligence. However, male-dominated professions such as engineering require "competence and great intellectual ability."[107] What is noticeable about some of these stereotypes is the fact that a woman who is employed as a librarian or nurse or teacher is merely incidental because her major, and main, characteristic is that she is female.[108] In some instances it is her innate ability to mother that is the focal point. In other instances, it is her ability to organize, or it could be her sexuality, or lack thereof. Regardless, it is these attributes, rather than her skills or mind, that make her what she is in her profession. The female fields are seen as relying on the natural talents of women rather than on their intellect or technical abilities.[109] Thus, gender becomes the most important aspect of the image of the profession, and thus of the stereotype.

The stereotype of the librarian, in its many forms, persists because it is irrevocably tied to the notion that librarianship is a feminized, or pink-collar, profession. The notion that librarianship is a "woman's job" is so ingrained that we cannot easily separate this idea from the individual performing the job. As a result, the profession is perceived as a semi-profession, and its status and the resulting salaries are reduced. Librarianship also experiences problems in funding and recruitment, as the nature of "women's work" is denigrated.

What is the solution? If the funding, support, respect, and status of libraries and librarians are tied to stereotypes rooted in false notions of gender roles, how can this be rectified? Should librarians continue to culture jam, to refute the stereotype by putting their own spin on it? Should they engage in public relations and write letters or otherwise engage the media when such stereotypes appear? Should they continue professionalizing the field, adopting attributes of more masculine careers such as medicine and law in an effort to gain respect?

What may be needed is a radical shift in the way in which we view work. There are three choices. On the one hand, we may discontinue the use of the concept of "pink-collar." The term itself is old and refers to what was formerly seen as work without prestige or hope for advancement. By assigning this term to professions such as nursing, teaching, and librarianship, we are saying that they, too, are not worthy of prestige and respect. What we mean by "pink-collar" is "feminized professions." As Tennery points out, "pink-collar" classifies the work that women *should* have and belittles that work, as well as the men who choose to perform it.[110] It buys into stereotypes of gender that hurt both men and women.

Tied to this is a second proposition: feminized professions are not valued, perhaps, because women and the work they do are not valued. If we want the work of librarians to be valued, we would need to improve how women are viewed and treated in librarianship and in society.[111] The very core of the problem is not the stereotyping of the professions and the work, but rather the stereotyping of women and the way in which those professional stereotypes gain currency from the gender stereotypes. It may behoove librarianship to join together with the nursing and teaching professions to fight this as a feminist problem, as proposed by Harris.[112]

There is also the fact that more men are pursuing fields where they often face their own battles with stereotypes of feminized professions. Perhaps the small but steady increase of the numbers of men in careers predominantly occupied by women has to do with the fact that men themselves are creating their own definitions of masculinity and are applying those definitions as they see fit. While gender may be socially constructed, not all interpretations of what it means to be masculine or feminine are rooted in gender-role stereotypes.[113] Thus, men who choose to enter fields such as librarianship are redefining masculinity to include characteristics that are commonly seen as being feminine, such as caring for and nurturing others. By claiming these traits as part of their own gender-role definition, they are helping to refute the stereotyping of both genders.

Another proposition is to attempt to resemble those careers that are considered "masculine," such as law and medicine. However, this brings with it the problem of denying an essential aspect of the profession, the fact that it has traditionally been a caring profession. Can the caring aspect be reconciled with full professionalism? And will this cause an evolution of the stereotype of the librarian? Medicine is already seeing a sea change toward compassion and caring. Carolyn and Matthew Bucksbaum have donated $42 million to the University of Chicago to create an institute dedicated to helping improve the doctor-patient relationship.[114] If medicine can embrace compassion, then certainly librarianship's compassion can coincide with the traditional notion of professionalism.

I would like to suggest that a solution rests at the core of how we view gender and mothering in our society. Assuming that only women can "mother" or nurture is denying the real contributions of men, while continuing to propagate harmful stereotypes. Caring is a task that can be carried out by anyone, regardless of gender, and it takes real skill, not just a specific body type. Tackling this problem will change not only how we view librarianship, but how we view all caring professions.

Notes

1. Valerie Frankel, "Who Do You Want to Be in Bed?" *Self* 31 (May 2009): 158.
2. "Pink-Collar Workers," in *Ready Reference: Women's Issues*, vol. 2, ed. Margaret McFadden (Pasadena, CA.: Salem Press, 1997), 667.
3. Melvil Dewey, "The Profession," *American Library Journal* 1 (September 1876–August 1877): 5–6, Google Play, https://play.google.com/store/books/details/the_library_journal?id=0R0DAAAAYAAJ.
4. Pauline Wilson, *Stereotype and Status*, Contributions in Librarianship and Information Science, no. 41 (Westport, CT: Greenwood, 1982), 13.
5. Abigail Luthmann, "Librarians, Professionalism and Image: Stereotype and Reality," *Library Review* 56 (2007): 775, doi:10.1108/00242530710831211.
6. Marie L. Radford and Gary P. Radford, "Librarians and Party Girls: Cultural Studies and the Meaning of the Librarian," *Library Quarterly* 73 (2003): 60.
7. Maura Seale, "Old Maids, Policeman, and Social Rejects: Mass Media Representations and Public Perceptions of Librarians," *Electronic Journal of Academic and Special Librarianship* 9 (2008), http://southernlibrarianship.icaap.org/content/v09n01/seale_m01.html.
8. Ramirose Ilene Attebury, "Perceptions of a Profession: Librarians and Stereotypes in Online Videos," *Library Philosophy and Practice*, paper 433 (October 19, 2010): 5, http://digitalcommons.unl.edu/libphilprac/433.
9. Ibid., 2.
10. Ibid., 2.
11. Wilson, *Stereotype and Status*, as cited in Attebury, "Perceptions of a Profession," 3.
12. Attebury, "Perceptions of a Profession," 4.
13. Ibid., 6.
14. Candi Strecker, "Sex in the Stacks: Librarian Porn Novels Reviewed" ChipRowe.com, 2011, www.chiprowe.com/articles/library.html.
15. Luthmann, "Librarians, Professionalism and Image," 777.
16. Attebury, "Perceptions of a Profession," 4.
17. Stuart Hall, "The Whites of Their Eyes: Racist Ideologies and the Media," in *Gender, Race and Class in Media: A Text-Reader*, 2nd ed., ed. Gail Dines and Jean M. Humez (Thousand Oaks, CA: Sage Publications, 2003), as quoted in Seale, "Old Maids, Policeman, and Social Rejects," 1.
18. Michael Engle, "Remythologizing Work: The Role of Archetypal Images in the Humanization of Librarianship," last modified August 8, 2006, http://ecommons.library.cornell.edu/bitstream/1813/3902/1/archetype.html.
19. Thad E. Dickinson, "Looking at the Male Librarian Stereotype," *The Image and Role of the Librarian*, ed. Wendi Arant and Candace R. Benefiel (Binghamton, NY: Haworth, 2002), 103.
20. Roma M. Harris, *Librarianship* (Norwood, NJ: Ablex, 1992), 14.
21. Joanne E. Passet, "Men in a Feminized Profession: The Male Librarian, 1887–1921," *Libraries and Culture* 28 (1993): 386.
22. Ibid., 387.
23. Ibid., 388.
24. "Table A-1: Number of Credentialed Librarians by Characteristic, 2009–2010," "Diversity Counts," American Library Association, last modified 2013, www.ala.org/offices/sites/ala.org.offices/files/content/diversity/diversitycounts/diversitycountstables2012.pdf.
25. Harris, *Librarianship*, 77.

26. Dee Garrison, *Apostles of Culture: The Public Librarian and American Society, 1876–1920* (New York: Free Press, 1979), 223, as quoted in Harris, *Librarianship*, 77.

27. Shaheen Majid and Azim Haider, "Image Problem Even Haunts Hi-Tech Libraries: Stereotypes Associated with Library and Information Professionals in Singapore," *Aslib Proceedings: New Information Perspectives* 60 (2008): 235, doi:10.1108/00012530810879105.

28. Peter Hernon, and Maureen Pastine, "Student Perception of Academic Librarians," *College and Research Libraries* 38 (1977): 129–39, as cited in Majid and Haider, "Image Problem Even Haunts," 230–31.

29. Gaby Divay, Ada M. Ducas, and Nicole Michaud-Oystryk, "Faculty Perceptions of Librarians at the University of Manitoba," *College and Research Libraries* 48 (1987): 27–35, as cited in Majid and Haider," Image Problem Even Haunts," 231.

30. Russell Bowden, "Introduction," in Russell Bowden and Donald Wijasuriya, eds., *The Status, Reputation, and Image of the Library and Information Profession*, Proceedings of the IFLA Pre-Session Seminar, Delhi, 24–28 August 1992, IFLA Publication 68 (Munich: De Gruyter Saur, 1994), as cited in Majid and Haider, "Image Problem Even Haunts," 231.

31. Juris Dilevko and Lisa Gottleib, "The Portrayal of Librarians in Obituaries at the End of the Twentieth Century," *Library Quarterly* 74 (2004): 171.

32. Ibid., 172–173.

33. Ibid., 174.

34. Garrison, *Apostles of Culture*, 223, as cited in Harris, *Librarianship*, 77.

35. Dilevko and Gottleib, "Portrayal of Librarians," 174.

36. Ibid., 175.

37. Ibid., 176.

38. Paula England, Michelle Budig, and Nancy Folbre, "Wages of Virtue: The Relative Pay of Care Work," *Social Problems* 49 (2002): 455.

39. Ibid., 457.

40. Harris, *Librarianship*, 20, as cited in Dilevko and Gottleib, "Portrayal of Librarians in Obituaries," 176.

41. Dilevko and Gottleib, "Portrayal of Librarians in Obituaries," 176.

42. Ibid.

43. Branka Badovinac and Primož Južnic, "Aspects of Representation of Library and Information Science," *New Library World* 112, no. 7/8 (2011): 294, doi:10.1108/03074801111150431.

44. Harris, *Librarianship*, 1.

45. Amanda Bird, "The Under Representation of Women in a 'Feminized Profession,'" *Dalhousie Journal of Interdisciplinary Management* 3 (2007), http://ojs.library.dal.ca/djim/article/view/2007vol3Bird/41.

46. Harris, *Librarianship*, 1.

47. Ibid., 3.

48. Amitai Etzioni, preface to *The Semi-Professions and Their Organization*, ed. Amitai Etzioni, (New York: Free Press, 1969), v.

49. Harris, *Librarianship*, 5.

50. Ibid., 5–6.

51. James V. Carmichael Jr., "The Male Librarian and the Feminine Image: A Survey of Stereotype, Status, and Gender Perceptions," *Library and Information Science Research* 14 (1992): 411–46

52. Edward G. Holley, *Raking the Historical Coals: The A.L.A. Scrapbook of 1876* (New York: Beta Phi Mu Chapbook 8, 1967), 49, as quoted in Carmichael, "The Male Librarian," 416.

53. Carmichael, "The Male Librarian," 417.

54. Joe L. Dubbert, *A Man's Place: Masculinity in Transition* (Englewood Cliffs, NJ: Prentice-Hall, 1979), 57, as quoted in Carmichael, "The Male Librarian," 416.

55. Jody Newmyer "The Image Problem of the Librarian: Femininity and Social Control," *Journal of Library History* 11 (1976): 44-67, and Arnold P. Sable, "The Sexuality of the Library Profession," *Wilson Library Bulletin* 43 (1969): 748–51, as cited in Dickinson, "Looking at the Male Librarian Stereotype," 98.

56. Dickinson, "Looking at the Male Librarian Stereotype," 99–100.

57. Passet, "Men in a Feminized Profession," 392–393.

58. Dilevko and Gottlieb, "Portrayal of Librarians in Obituaries."

59. Christine. L. Williams, *Gender Differences at Work: Women and Men in Nontraditional Occupations* (Berkeley: University of California Press, 1989), 107-109, as cited in Carmichael, "The Male Librarian," 415.

60. Carmichael, "The Male Librarian."

61. Ibid.

62. Association of Research Libraries, "Annual Salary Survey (2009–10)," www.arl.org/bm~doc/ss09.pdf, as cited in "Fact Sheet 2011: Library Workers: Facts and Figures," Department for Professional Employees, AFL-CIO, http://ala-apa.org/files/2012/03/Library-Workers-2011.pdf.

63. Carmichael, "The Male Librarian," 427.

64. Ibid., 430.

65. Newmyer "Image Problem of the Librarian," as cited in Carmichael, "The Male Librarian."

66. Ibid.

67. Christine L. Williams, "The Glass Escalator: Hidden Advantages for Men in the 'Female' Professions," *Social Problems* 39, no. 3 (1992): 256, www.jstor.org/stable/3096961.

68. Ibid.

69. Newmyer, "Image Problem of the Librarian," and Sable, "Sexuality of the Library Profession," as quoted in Dickinson, "Looking at the Male Librarian Stereotype," 98.

70. Locke J. Morrisey and Donald O. Case, "There Goes My Image: The Perception of Male Librarians by Colleague, Student, and Self," *College and Research Libraries* 49, no. 5 (1988): 454, and Ronald Beaudrie and Robert Grunfeld, "Male Reference Librarians and the Gender Factor," *Reference Librarian* 15, no. 33, (1991): 211–13, as quoted in Dickinson, "Looking at the Male Librarian Stereotype," 104.

71. Dickinson, "Looking at the Male Librarian Stereotype," 104–5.

72. Wilson, *Stereotype and Status*, 16, as cited in Harris, *Librarianship*, 71.

73. Rosalee McReynolds, "A Heritage Dismissed," *Library Journal* 110 (1985): 26, as cited in Harris, *Librarianship*, 71–72.

74. Wilson, *Stereotype and Status*, 35.

75. Williams, "Glass Escalator," 261.

76. James V. Carmichael, "Gender Issues in the Workplace: Male Librarians Tell Their Side," *American Libraries* 25 (1994): 227-231, as cited in Dickinson, "Looking at the Male Librarian Stereotype," 106.

77. Ann O'Brien, and Martin Raish, "The Image of the Librarian in Commercial Motion Pictures: An Annotated Filmography," *Collection Management* 17 (1993): 61–84, as cited in Dickinson, "Looking at the Male Librarian Stereotype," 106–7.

78. Harris, *Librarianship*, 77.

79. Edna Foley, "Nursing as a Profession for College Women," in *American Decades Primary Sources 1910–1919*, vol. 2, ed. Cynthia Rose (Detroit, MI: Gale, 2004), 429–32.

80. "Nursing Statistics," MinorityNurse.com, 2013, www.minoritynurse.com/minority-nursing-

statistics.

81.   "Quick Facts on Registered Nurses," US Department of Labor, Women's Bureau, accessed May 7, 2014, www.dol.gov/wb/factsheets/Qf-nursing.htm.

82.   Harris, *Librarianship*, 83.

83.   Ibid., 89.

84.   Williams, "Glass Escalator," 261.

85.   Claire Rayner, "What Do the Public Think of Nurses?" *Nursing Times* 80 (1984): 31, as quoted in Harris, *Librarianship*, 78.

86.   Robert J. Meadus, "Men in Nursing: Barriers to Recruitment," *Nursing Forum* 35, no. 3 (2000), 10, doi:10.1111/j.1744-6198.2000.tb00998.x.

87.   Harris, *Librarianship*, 78–79.

88.   Janice Rider Ellis and Celia Love Hartley, *Nursing in Today's World: Trends, Issues, and Management*, 8th ed. (Philadelphia: Lippincott Williams and Wilkins, 2003), and Sarah Kearns, "Why the Public Image of Nursing Is Important," *The Leader's Lounge* (blog), September 9, http://blogs.hcpro.com/nursemanagers/2009/09/why-the-public-image-of-nursing-is-important, as cited in Morteza Rezaei-Adaryani, Mahvash Salsali, and Eesa Mohammadi, "Nursing Image: An Evolutionary Concept Analysis," *Contemporary Nurse: A Journal for the Australian Nursing Profession* 43 (December 2012): 85.

89.   John Rosales, "Checking Out: Budget Hawks See Library Programs as an Easy Cut, but What's the Cost to Student Achievement?" *NEA Today Magazine*, 2011, www.nea.org/home/43952.htm.

90.   Marie L. Radford, "Librarian Stereotypes, Alive and Well, Alas," *Library Garden* (blog), May 21, 2010, http://librarygarden.net/2010/05/21/librarian-stereotypes-alive-well-alas.

91.   James R. King, *Uncommon Caring: Learning from Men Who Teach Young Children* (New York: Teachers College Press 1998), 138–39, as quoted in Marcus Weaver-Hightower, "Male Preservice Teachers and Discouragement from Teaching," *Journal of Men's Studies* 19, no. 2 (2011): 98, doi:10.3149/jms.1902.97.

92.   Weaver-Hightower, "Male Preservice Teachers," 103.

93.   Ibid., 105.

94.   Sarah Jo Sandefur and Leeann Moore, "The 'Nuts and Dolts' of Teacher Images in Children's Picture Storybooks: A Content Analysis," *Education* 125 (2004): 41.

95.   Ibid., 43.

96.   Ibid., 47.

97.   Rick Breault, "The Celluloid Teacher," *Educational Forum* 73 (2009): 306–17, doi:10.1080/00131720903166820.

98.   Williams, "Glass Escalator," 254.

99.   United States Bureau of Labor Statistics, *Current Population Survey*, 2011, as cited in Sarah D. Sparks, "Despite a Downturn, Few Men Attracted to Teaching Field," *Education Week* 31 (May 9, 2012): 10.

100.   Williams, "Glass Escalator," 256.

101.   Ibid., 261.

102.   Ibid., 263–64.

103.   "Pink-Collar Opportunities," *New York Times*, May 20, 2012, www.nytimes.com/interactive/2012/05/20/business/pink-collar-opportunities.html.

104.   Carmichael, "The Male Librarian."

105.   Shaila Dewan and Robert Gebeloff, "More Men Enter Fields Dominated by Women," *New York Times*, May 21, 2012, www.nytimes.com/2012/05/21/business/increasingly-men-seek-success-in-jobs-dominated-by-women.html.

106. Sandra Bem, "The Making of Images, A Psychological Perspective," in *Image-Making in Nursing*, ed. Carolyn A. Williams (Kansas City, MO: American Academy of Nursing, 1983), 42, as quoted in Harris, *Librarianship*, 83.
107. Harris, *Librarianship*, 84.
108. Ibid., 83.
109. Ibid., 84.
110. Amy Tennery, "The Term 'Pink Collar' Is Silly and Outdated—Let's Retire It," *Time*, May 23, 2012, http://business.time.com/2012/5/23/the-term-pink-collar-is-silly-and-outdated-lets-retire-it.
111. Harris, *Librarianship*, 75.
112. Ibid., 94–96.
113. Rose Marie Hoffman, L. DiAnne Borders, and John A. Hattie, "Reconceptualizing Femininity and Masculinity: From Gender Roles to Gender Self-Confidence," *Journal of Social Behavior and Personality* 15 (2000): 483.
114. Dirk Johnson, "A $42 Million Gift Aims at Improving Bedside Manner," *New York Times*, September 22, 2011, www.nytimes.com/2011/09/22/us/university-of-chicago-gets-42-million-gift-for-bucksbaum-institute.html.

Bibliography

American Library Association. "Table A-1: Number of Credentialed Librarians by Characteristic, 2009–2010." "Diversity Counts," last modified 2013. www.ala.org/offices/sites/ala.org.offices/files/content/diversity/diversitycounts/diversitycountstables2012.pdf.

Attebury, Ramirose Ilene. "Perceptions of a Profession: Librarians and Stereotypes in Online Videos." *Library Philosophy and Practice*, paper 433 (October 19, 2010). http://digitalcommons.unl.edu/libphilprac/433.

Badovinac, Branka, and Primož Južnic. "Aspects of Representation of Library and Information Science." *New Library World* 112, no. 7/8 (2011), 293–312.

Bird, Amanda. "The Under Representation of Women in a 'Feminized Profession.'" *Dalhousie Journal of Interdisciplinary Management* 3, no. 1 (2007). http://ojs.library.dal.ca/djim/article/view/2007vol3Bird/41.

Breault, Rick. "The Celluloid Teacher." *Educational Forum* 73, no. 4 (2009): 306–17. doi:10.1080/00131720903166820.

Carmichael, James V., Jr. "The Male Librarian and the Feminine Image: A Survey of Stereotype, Status, and Gender Perceptions" *Library and Information Science Research* 14, no. 4 (1992), 411–46.

Department for Professional Employees, AFL-CIO. "Fact Sheet 2011: Library Workers: Facts and Figures." http://ala-apa.org/files/2012/03/Library-Workers-2011.pdf.

Dewan, Shaila, and Robert Gebeloff. "More Men Enter Fields Dominated by Women." *New York Times*, May 21, 2012. www.nytimes.com/2012/05/21/business/increasingly-men-seek-success-in-jobs-dominated-by-women.html

Dewey, Melvil. "The Profession." American Library Journal 1 (September 1876–August 1877): 5–6, Google Play, https://play.google.com/store/books/details/the_library_journal?id=0R0DAAAAYAAJ.

Dickinson, Thad E. "Looking at the Male Librarian Stereotype." In *The Image and Role of the Librarian*, edited by Wendi Arant and Candance R. Benefiel, 97–110. Binghamton, NY: Haworth, 2002. Originally published in *Reference Librarian* 37, no. 78 (2003): 97–110.

Dilevko, Juris and Lisa Gottleib. "The Portrayal of Librarians in Obituaries at the End of the Twentieth Century." *Library Quarterly* 74 (2004): 152–80.

England, Paula, Michelle Budig, and Nancy Folbre. "Wages of Virtue: The Relative Pay of Care Work." *Social Problems* 49 (2002): 455–73.

Engle, Michael. "Remythologizing Work: The Role of Archetypal Images in the Humanization of Librarianship." Last modified August 8, 2006. http://ecommons.library.cornell.edu/bitstream/1813/3902/1/archetype.html.

Etzioni, Amitai. Preface to *The Semi-Professions and Their Organization: Teachers, Nurses, Social Workers*, edited by Amitai Etzioni. New York: Free Press, 1969.

Foley, Edna. "Nursing as a Profession for College Women." In *American Decades Primary Sources 1910–1919*, vol. 2, edited by Cynthia Rose, 429–32. Detroit, MI: Gale, 2004. Originally published in *American Journal of Nursing* 10 (1910), 532–36.

Frankel, Valerie. "Who Do You Want to Be in Bed?" *Self* 31 (May 2009): 158–63.

Harris, Roma M. *Librarianship: The Erosion of a Woman's Profession*. Norwood, NJ: Ablex, 1992.

Hoffman, Rose Marie, L. DiAnne Borders, and John A. Hattie. "Reconceptualizing Femininity and Masculinity: From Gender Roles to Gender Self-Confidence." *Journal of Social Behavior and Personality* 15, no. 4 (2000): 475–503.

Johnson, Dirk. "A $42 Million Gift Aims at Improving Bedside Manner." *New York Times*, September 22, 2011. www.nytimes.com/2011/09/22/us/university-of-chicago-gets-42-million-gift-for-bucksbaum-institute.html.

Luthmann, Abigail. "Librarians, Professionalism and Image: Stereotype and Reality." *Library Review* 56, no. 9 (2007): 773–80. doi:10.1108/00242530710831211.

Majid, Shaheen, and Azim Haider. "Image Problem Even Haunts Hi-Tech Libraries: Stereotypes Associated with Library and Information Professionals in Singapore." *Aslib Proceedings: New Information Perspectives* 60, no. 3 (2008): 229–41. doi:10.1108/00012530810879105.

Meadus, Robert J. "Men in Nursing: Barriers to Recruitment." *Nursing Forum* 35, no. 3 (2000): 5–12. doi:10.1111/j.1744-6198.2000.tb00998.x.

MinorityNurse.com "Nursing Statistics." 2013. www.minoritynurse.com/minority-nursing-statistics.

Passet, Joanne E. "Men in a Feminized Profession: The Male Librarian, 1887–1921." *Libraries and Culture* 28, no. 4 (1993): 385–402.

"Pink-Collar Opportunities." *New York Times*, May 20, 2012. www.nytimes.com/interactive/2012/05/20/business/pink-collar-opportunities.html.

"Pink-Collar Workers." In *Ready Reference: Women's Issues*, vol. 2, edited by Margaret McFadden, 667–68. Pasadena, CA.: Salem Press, 1997.

Radford, Marie L. "Librarian Stereotypes, Alive and Well, Alas." *Library Garden* (blog), May 21, 2010. http://librarygarden.net/2010/05/21/librarian-stereotypes-alive-well-alas.

Radford, Marie L., and Gary P. Radford. "Librarians and Party Girls: Cultural Studies and the Meaning of the Librarian." *Library Quarterly* 73, no. 1 (2003): 54–69.

Rezaei-Adaryani, Morteza, Mahvash Salsali, and Eesa Mohammadi. "Nursing Image: An Evolutionary Concept Analysis." *Contemporary Nurse: A Journal for the Australian Nursing Profession* 43 (December 2012): 81–89.

Rosales, John. "Checking Out: Budget Hawks See Library Programs as an Easy Cut, But What's the Cost to Student Achievement?" *NEA Today Magazine*, 2011. www.nea.org/home/43952.htm.

Sandefur, Sarah Jo, and Leeann Moore. "The 'Nuts and Dolts' of Teacher Images in Children's Picture Storybooks: A Content Analysis." *Education* 125 (2004): 41–55.

Seale, Maura. "Old Maids, Policeman, and Social Rejects: Mass Media Representations and Public Perceptions of Librarians." *Electronic Journal of Academic and Special Librarianship* 9, no. 1 (2008): http://southernlibrarianship.icaap.org/content/v09n01/seale_m01.html.

Strecker, Candi. "Sex in the Stacks: Librarian Porn Novels Reviewed" ChipRowe.com, 2011. www.chiprowe.com/articles/library.html.

Tennery, Amy. "The Term 'Pink Collar' Is Silly and Outdated—Let's Retire It." *Time*, May 23, 2012. http://business.time.com/2012/5/23/the-term-pink-collar-is-silly-and-outdated-lets-retire-it.

US Bureau of Labor Statistics, *Current Population Survey*, 2011, as cited in Sparks, Sarah D. "Despite a Downturn, Few Men Attracted to Teaching Field." *Education Week* 31 (May 9, 2012): 10.

US Department of Labor, Women's Bureau. "Quick Facts on Registered Nurses." Accessed May 7, 2014. www.dol.gov/wb/factsheets/Qf-nursing.htm.

Weaver-Hightower, Marcus. "Male Preservice Teachers and Discouragement from Teaching." *Journal of Men's Studies* 19, no. 2 (2011): 97–115. doi:10.3149/jms.1902.97.

Williams, Christine L. "The Glass Escalator: Hidden Advantages for Men in the 'Female' Professions." *Social Problems* 39, no. 3 (1992): 253–67. www.jstor.org/stable/3096961.

Wilson, Pauline. *Stereotype and Status: Librarians in the United States*. Contributions in Librarianship and Information Science, no. 41. Westport, CT: Greenwood, 1982.

CHAPTER 5

From Sensuous to Sexy

The Librarian in Post-Censorship Print Pornography

David D. Squires

Among the many calls for progressive librarianship in the now classic compendium *Revolting Librarians* is a short chapter encouraging librarians to "practice a few sensuous exercises."[1] One exercise recommends that readers imagine themselves in the centerfold of the *Library Journal*. The sensuous librarian, thought Kathleen Glab, would act as an antidote to the common misperception "that all librarians had silver hair, wore half glasses, tailored suits, sensible shoes, and had their index fingers permanently frozen into a pointing position."[2] Published in 1972, Glab's chapter made her declaration for physically gratifying library work at the same juncture when a trend in popular fiction began to represent librarians in the process of shedding not only "the old maid-Marian-Librarian image" but also the conservative clothes and stodgy professionalism that Glab identifies as part of the stereotype.[3] Dansk Blue Books, a small imprint owned by the California-based smut mogul Milton Luros, published an early example of such fiction the year prior to *Revolting Librarians*.* Written pseudonymously by Rod Waleman, *The Young Librarian* marks the emergence of a pornographic subgenre that presents librarians less as old maids and more

---

Thanks to Lindsay Braddy and Caitlin Shanley, two librarians who defy all stereotypes, for providing me encouragement during the early drafting stages. I owe a very special thank you to Leah Benedict whose generous gift of several Greenleaf Classics made this essay possible.

* For more on Luros, see Earl Kemp's fanzine *eI* 7, no. 4 (August 2008), available at http://efanzines.com. Luros published his final adult magazine in 1972, the same year *Revolting Librarians* came out. Titled *Sensuous Living*, it promotes love for all the shapes, smells, and feelings of a physically gratified life.

often as attractive young women, inhibited by library decorum but congenitally oversexed.[4] This chapter argues that, like the sensuous librarian, representations of the sexy librarian in pulp pornography emerged from a historically specific bid to cultivate an erotic public sphere from liberal institutions of reading.

If the common stereotype of shushing librarians imagines library employees as unsensuous agents of social repression, librarian pornography refashions them as victims of repression—and invariably ripe for liberation. The protagonist of *The Young Librarian*, Linda Brumiglia, embodies the trope in the "demure knee-length" dress she wears to work, which the narrator explains as "in contrast to the attractive dresses in Linda's closets with their provocative miniskirts."[5] Even her demure dress, however, stands out against the backdrop of her boss's "ministerial garb" and "bland, colorless efficiency."[6] In this case, the library itself represents a stifling social institution that keeps Linda from realizing the potential pleasure of her "tall-bodied, superb figure."[7] Unlike the silver-haired authoritarian that Glab invokes to capture the popular image of librarians, Linda chafes against the employee hierarchy that keeps her secluded in a far corner of the library where she works in the cataloger's office, obediently following rules imposed by her superiors. The sight of her head librarian, a woman described in the same terms Glab uses to describe the old maid stereotype, makes Linda lament the "somewhat smothering embrace of library employment."[8] Miss Patten's "white-haired semi-senescence" provides the young librarian with motivation to wear her raven-black hair down and yearn for a sexual awakening.[9]

By the early 1970s, the image of librarians as prim old women had been cemented in the popular imagination as a cultural icon, providing the foundational trope that librarians and pornographers reimagined as something far sexier. While Glab's cheeky suggestions for increasing the sensuousness of library work undoubtedly have inspired generations of enterprising librarians, Waleman's more explicitly pornographic representation of cataloger Linda Brumiglia has set the tone for a proliferation of sexy librarian imagery that reaches far beyond pornography. The 2003 sequel to *Revolting Librarians*—*Revolting Librarians Redux*—includes a brief overview of the scope of the sexy librarian phenomenon. Cindy Indiana lists advertisements, cartoons, hardcore pulp novels, mainstream and pornographic movies, along with several librarian-run websites dedicated to cataloging even more examples.[10] Jessamyn West, Martin Raish, Dan Lester, and Candi Strecker have gone a long way toward documenting the widespread cultural interest in pornographic representations of librarians.[11] Yet interpretations of the cultural significance of these representations have not been elaborated. Indiana attributes the phenomenon to a misplaced sense of irony: "The media sees an opportunity for humor in suggesting that even a librarian might enjoy sex."[12] Strecker similarly chalks up the pornographic fascination with uniformed women to sexist assumptions about women in the professional world: "Part of the arousal factor seems to based [sic] on the paradox that a woman might be brainy and slutty."[13] While both theories pinpoint the contradictory Madonna-whore dynamic that most sexy librarians embody, neither explains what these images might mean to librarians or patrons.

The frumpy librarian stereotype, on the contrary, has received considerable attention from academic librarians concerned that it contributes to a pervasive professional devaluation. Several of the most theoretically nuanced elaborations of that stereotype come from Marie and Gary Radford, who together have worked to bring critical theory into conversation with investigations of librarian stereotypes. Using Michel Foucault's theory of discourse, for instance, they have usefully explicated the seeming paradox embodied by the stereotypically buttoned-down librarian: at once the gatekeeper of public propriety and the butt of endless cracks at outmoded conservatism. As the Radfords put it, "The female librarian is presented as fearsome, but, beneath the stern exterior, there is nothing to fear: there is only a woman."[14] The sexy stereotype takes the misogyny even further, moving from "only a woman" toward a sexual fantasy featuring foreboding librarians turned librarian sexpots.

If the sexist attitudes coloring much librarian-themed pornography were not already apparent, the Radfords' Foucauldian analysis would make them easy to recognize. Their analysis has usefully explicated the way that a professional discourse of library services easily bends toward cultural fantasies of librarians servicing patrons. Foucault's theory of discourse, however, does less to explain the coincidental emergence of a sexy librarian trope alongside a feminist-inspired vision of sensuous librarianship. I explain that historical coincidence by contextualizing the library, pulp publishing, and obscenity law within a shared field of cultural production. Historically specific interpretation of the sexy librarian stereotype uncovers its roots in a 20th-century free speech movement that culminated with a series of high profile Supreme Court cases. Those cases deregulated print pornography, left librarians to renegotiate acquisition policies, and, eventually, changed library collections across the country. The fundamental assumption that this chapter elucidates is that a change in collection policy welcomes a change in the public a library serves, opening avenues to revamp the cultural associations that underlie librarian stereotypes.

Libraries: Lusty or Musty?

One of the most significant aspects of the Radfords' discursive analysis is their insistence that we approach stereotypes of the librarian as continuous with stereotypes of the library. They see fear of complex library systems as the background from which a fearsome librarian emerges in the popular imagination. Similarly, the sexy librarian emerges from what Candi Strecker describes as "the erotic potential of the library setting" with its distinctive mix of public and private space organized by isolated stacks.[15] Cultural understanding of libraries, as much as librarians, contributes to the appeal of the particular fantasies that library porn constructs for readers. Most of the sexy librarians populating moving image pornography and mainstream advertising never set foot in a library. The hardcore pulps published during the 1970s and 1980s, however, invariably use the library as at least a backdrop, even when the main action—sexual and otherwise—happens elsewhere. As Avi Steinberg put it in an article for *The Paris Review Daily*, "Porn books still feel the compulsion to tell a story, to make the glasses and bun *mean* something."[16]

His reading of librarian pornography situates the golden age of librarian porn in relation to a much earlier libertine tradition, best known for its association with the notorious Marquis de Sade. Historians understand the libertines' rejection of aristocratic mores as contributing to the rise of liberal democracy.* Steinberg describes some of the most renowned titles from the period—including *Bang the Librarian Hard, Hot Pants Librarian, The Librarian Gets Hot,* and *The Librarian Loves to Lick*—as an "earnest libertine revival."[17] By his account, they portray mid-20th-century sexual liberation and public librarianship as belonging to the same progressive trajectory that leads toward liberalism flourishing in body and mind. More recent librarian porn, he argues, "reveals a zeitgeist of anxiety" that correlates the librarian's neglected sex life with the extinction of the library.[18] Access to information has indeed played an important role in developing the robust public spheres necessary for maintaining a democratic society, but Steinberg's characterization of librarian porn from the 1970s takes an overly sanguine attitude toward the various depictions of the library that those novels present. While his main example, *Bang the Librarian Hard,* features a protagonist who uses sex as a means of promoting the library, other titles of the era portray the library as a cultural institution that stifles individuality, including creative and sexual expression.

In fact, portrayals of the library as a repressive institution are common. For example, in *The Young Librarian,* when cataloging work stifles her individuality, Linda discovers that taboo sexual practices provide a cathartic outlet for otherwise frustrated emotions. Sex with other women and minors lets her cut across the grain of professional propriety enforced by her superiors at the library and convinces her that she will not end up a shriveled old maid like the head librarian, Miss Patten. If *The Young Librarian* presents a unique case for coming so early in the 1970s and for featuring so little of the library setting that helps define the genre, it nonetheless provides a sense of the library as a potentially contentious social institution.

A more typical example of the genre titled *The Naughty Librarian* came out in 1981 under the Greenleaf Classics colophon. Responsible for several smaller imprints, including Heatherpool Press and Patch Pockets, Greenleaf published an entire line of librarian-themed adult books that all looked nearly identical. The covers feature an ink drawing—in this case,

---

* For the best work on pornography's relationship to democracy, see Lynn Hunt, ed. *The Invention of Pornography* (New York: Zone Books, 1993). In response to a reader's comment, Steinberg indicates that he consulted her introduction to the volume during his research.

of a woman wearing large-framed glasses and her hair in a bun. Propped up on a pile of hardcover books, her right hand grasps the back of a man's head, pulling his face toward her bare breasts, while another man watches from behind a nearby bookshelf with his mouth agape. The drawing conforms to the depiction of the novel's protagonist, library employee Sandy Lewis, who the narrator describes according to strict generic conventions. "Her drab clothes, thick glasses and spinsterish hairdo," we learn at the outset, hide "the gorgeous wanton woman beneath."[19] Although one scene placed late in the story does involve Sandy naughtily assisting a patron in the stacks while her boss looks on, the novel opens with Sandy playing the voyeur. She masturbates while watching two teens in a storeroom of the library because, even as her 21st birthday approaches, the narrator laments, Sandy has yet to find a sex partner of her own.

It turns out the teens noticed her watching them, as Sandy learns by overhearing their postcoital conversation. The girl sees her as a tragic figure: "It's too bad the only fun she can have is watching someone else fuck."[20] The boy, however, takes a far less sympathetic view, insisting that such a "bow-wow" couldn't expect anything more. Their exchange represents an especially significant moment for the novel because, in addition to introducing the baseline librarian stereotype, it provides Sandy with the motivation to transform her look and transcend her station at the library. More immediately, even, it propels the narrative into the second sex scene as Sandy convinces the local beefcake gym owner to become her personal sex trainer. The description of her disrobing for the first time intends to reveal more about the main character than simply her "lush curves" and "uplifted fullness." The novel takes the opportunity to turn the spectacle of Sandy's nude body into a metaphysical epiphany about her sexual identity: "Layer by layer, Sandy's true beauty was revealed. Once the thick glasses were removed and the heavy bun loosened, she looked totally different— and totally feminine."[21] Shedding her shapeless clothes reveals the truth of her shapely body, which in turn stands in as a sign of the purity of her gender and the unbridled sexuality that she soon achieves.

Sandy's considerable achievement, however, necessitates a career change. Whereas Glab hoped that sensuous librarians would transform the way employees and patrons experienced the library, the sexy librarian of pulp pornography would just as soon transform her personal life by leaving the library behind. After vindicating herself by seducing the teenage boy who likened her to a dog, Sandy leaves her post at the circulation desk to become the secretary and sexual incentive at a small, all-male business firm. Her new boss, the hunky patron who ravished her on a pile of books in a secluded corner of the library, introduces the staff by offering her as a bonus to anyone who closes a big contract. The offer takes Sandy aback at first, but when her first "fringe benefit" lover asks her at the end of the novel if she regrets leaving the library, she assures him that she does not. "I'm glad I'm done with musty, dusty books and catering to musty, dusty people!"[22] Contrary to Steinberg's examples, the library and the librarian stereotype figure here as obstacles that the protagonist must overcome to liberate herself from the confining sexual conventions of an earlier age. In other words, *The Naughty Librarian* and many similar titles worked to entrench rather than challenge the old maid stereotype, while simultaneously offering a vision of sexual liberation fraught with sexist assumptions about women in the professions.

Librarians for Liberation

Liberation from cultural conservatism is a defining preoccupation of the classic librarian-themed titles. While the library plays various roles— sometimes a repressive social institution, sometimes a hub of promiscuous community engagement—the narrative arc always moves toward new kinds of freedom from the somewhat smothering embrace of old-fashioned values. Another librarian title from Greenleaf Classics, *Horny Licking Librarian*, makes the point abundantly clear as every single character who works with Polly Prentiss at Hardwick School masks their libidinal urges in caricatured forms of Victorian morality. The assistant librarian, "a very shy and puritanical young man," is engaged to a woman who won't kiss him until they marry, which her parents will not allow until he establishes his career.[23] With a little work, Polly manages to seduce him and finds out that he's a natural lover. He notices in turn that Polly demonstrates an entirely different attitude toward rules when at home in bed than she does at the library. "She sure wasn't like the woman he knew at work," the narrator explains. "That Miss Prentiss wore her hair in a prim bun, glared at any student who even breathed loudly, and was always cold and efficient. But the Miss Prentiss he saw now was a wild woman. . . . She wasn't at all uptight about revealing her pleasure."[24] The severity of her adherence to library rules eases and quickly turns into outward contempt for such regulations once she begins seducing other colleagues and students on campus.

The novel's most defiant moment occurs when the headmaster finds Polly enthusiastically engaged with three men, two employees and a student. He dismisses them all from the school at once, but Polly manages to charm him with kinky sex. Early in the novel we learn that the headmaster is a sort of censorship crusading Comstock figure,* "probably the biggest prude who ever lived. The rumor was that he pissed ice water. If he caught any student or faculty member having anything to do with sex, he kicked them out of Hardwick instantly. People had been expelled just for reading about sex."[25] Cracking the censorship nut represents a complete subversion of the "stern moral principles and strict standards of conduct" that define the educational institution's tradition.[26] When the headmaster finally joins the orgy at the end of the novel he completes the simple allegory of sexual liberation. But the gesture toward his ban on illicit reading material gives the narrative more than a symbolic resonance with the very real censorship laws regulating pornographic materials.

One reason these novels worry so much about their own status as antirepressive folktales for mature audiences is that, unlike today, print pornography held not only a culturally contentious place in American society but also a legally contentious place in the US judicial system. Explicit references to the regulation of reading materials create a self-reflexive narrative technique that aims at enlisting readers in the same pursuit of sexual expression that absorbs the lusty librarians in these novels. The articulation of a desire for freedom from sexual norms and censorship regulations goes even beyond the narrative to define the tone of the paratext framing Greenleaf Classics. Many of the librarian-themed titles include a brief

---

* For more on Anthony Comstock's life and legacy, see Anna L. Bates, *Weeder in the Garden of the Lord* (Lanham, MD: University Press of America, 1995).

foreword attributed to the publisher that offers a liberal justification for the novel's redeeming social value. *The Naughty Librarian,* for example, begins with a three-paragraph note that summarizes and interprets the narrative to follow:

> In this story, a female librarian has learned to be outward and honest with her sexual desires, and she becomes a woman whom many would brand as a slut and others would merely call liberated. She is a woman dedicated to becoming a sexually liberated soul—a person who not only feels sexually free, but who has been compelled to unshackle others from the bonds of puritanism and censorship.[27]

However vexed an image of sexual freedom the novel offers up, the book itself could exist only because of an unshackling of censorship laws.

The librarian-themed adult books published in the 1970s and 1980s, and the stereotypes they forwarded, followed in the wake of a decades-long legal battle over definitions of obscenity that effectively ended in 1967. Beginning with the 1933 decision that James Joyce's *Ulysses* did not "excite sexual impulses or lustful thoughts,"[28] the anti-censorship campaign came to a head in the 1960s with a series of cases provoked by titles from the Grove Press catalog. Grove's founder, the self-fashioned anti-censorship crusader Barney Rosset, knowingly published banned books with the intention of defending them in court. His legal strategy for defending novels such as *Lady Chatterley's Lover, Tropic of Cancer,* and *Naked Lunch* involved marshaling expert testimony from established authors, critics, and even the American Library Association to confirm their literary value, thus circumventing the definition of an obscene text as lacking any redeeming social value.[†] The strategy proved effective for Grove but also forced an uneasy distinction between illicit masterpieces with inherent artistic merit and smutty pulp that merely pandered to lascivious tastes. The US Supreme Court demonstrated the legal force of that distinction in 1966

---

† In the landmark First Amendment case Roth v. United States, Justice William Brennan explained the reach of obscenity law: "implicit in the history of the First Amendment is the rejection of obscenity as utterly without redeeming social importance." Roth v. United States. 354 US 476 (1957). Full-text available at www.law.cornell.edu.

when it took up a case against Putnam's edition of John Cleland's 18th-century novel *Memoirs of a Woman of Pleasure* along with two separate cases against popular pornographers Ralph Ginzburg and Edward Mishkin. Putnam received the Court's go-ahead while Ginzburg and Mishkin received jail time.[29]

Because Grove Press fought so many landmark obscenity cases, many accounts of what literary historian Loren Glass has recently called "the end of obscenity"* attribute the mid-20th-century liberalization of print regulations entirely to Rosset's efforts.[30] In fact, another case in 1967 has the distinction of extending the freedoms Rosset secured for legitimate presses to the underground world of pulp pornography. When an undercover cop arrested Robert Redrup for selling him Greenleaf titles *Lust Pool* and *Shame Agent*, Greenleaf's founder William Hamling offered to cover his legal fees if he pled not guilty. The case ended up in the US Supreme Court, where the majority opinion decided that written materials sold to willing adults were protected under the Constitution.[31] Paperback sex book publishers finally had a court sanction to operate lawful, full-scale business, and Greenleaf took full advantage by issuing increasingly frank descriptions of sex.† The carefully, if minimally, rendered plot lines and paratexts that insisted on the social significance of sexual liberation kept the novels within the bounds of the law. In the ever-evolving field of obscenity law, the paratext also provided a built-in argument for the redeeming social value of any given title.

Relaxed print regulations meant that a greater number of sexually explicit texts became available in the market place, including the novels that popularized sexy librarian stereotypes. The cultural reverberations of anticensorship campaigns were quick to reach institutions of reading in the public sphere. Libraries in particular became privileged sites of contention for debates about access to sexual materials. As long as pornographic

---

* Glass borrows his chapter title "The End of Obscenity" from Charles Rembar, *The End of Obscenity* (New York: Random House, 1968). Rembar provides a classic example of Grove-centric interpretations of print deregulation. His influence persists in popular accounts such as Fred Kaplan, "The Day Obscenity Became Art," *New York Times*, July 21, 2009, A21.

† According to Frederick Lane, the *Redrup* decision also allowed photographic pornography to move toward increasingly explicit imagery. Frederick S. Lane, *Obscene Profits* (New York: Routledge, 2000), 27–28.

works were illegal, of course, libraries had no reason to consider collecting them. However, with the newly legitimated status of sexually explicit classics such as *Memoirs of a Woman of Pleasure*, librarians had to reconsider their role in mediating between the public and material collections. Should they redouble censorial efforts to live up to their perceived role as custodians of community standards? Or should they champion liberal ideals of intellectual and informational freedom? In the wake of the obscenity trials, public debates about the redeeming social value of pornographic works permeated professional debates in the form of anxiety not only over book collections but also over librarians' commitments to liberty, democracy, and the future of state-sponsored libraries.‡

When the American Library Association entered a brief as amicus curiae in support of *Tropic of Cancer* in 1964, it set the tone for liberating the library from what Morris Ernst and William Seagle once dubbed "the subterranean censorship" of acquisition policies. Writing in 1928, Ernst and Seagle pointed to selection practices developed in London during the Victorian era that effectively banned so-called objectionable books: "If the libraries agreed among themselves not to stock a book the publisher might just as well decide to sell it for so much waste paper; it had been relegated to limbo."[32] With the emergence of more affordable books, libraries exercised considerably less control over the literary marketplace. Yet Ernst and Seagle's concern that public libraries in the United States had adopted a similar practice to supervise their readers' tastes resonated in the post-censorship era in which Greenleaf's librarian titles flourished. With the old maid stereotype of librarians fully formed by the mid-20th century, discussions about how libraries and librarians should handle sexually explicit materials invariably touched on popular perceptions of their work.

In 1971, for instance, Bill Katz wrote an article about magazine selection that echoes points Ernst and Seagle make about the importance of catering to patron demand. "Despite the wide interest in the subject," writes Katz, "the erotic is an area most librarians fail to appreciate—at least in

---

‡ For an excellent account of the contentious debates about pornography during this period see, Whitney Strub, *Perversion for Profit* (New York: Columbia University Press, 2010). Chapter 5, "The Permissive Society," is especially relevant.

terms of their public collections."[33] His nod to the popular idea of librarians as unerotic fogies relates to his conviction that librarians had "heavily damaged" their image by trying to keep smut out of the stacks.[34] Repairing that image, he argued, meant aligning library collections with popular culture. For Katz, incorporating pornography into public collections meant keeping up with the progress forged by a liberal democracy, making pornography in libraries "a sort of ultimate test of freedom."[35] Much as uninhibited sexual expression constitutes the ultimate liberation for librarians in pornography, pornography in the library constitutes the ultimate sign of freedom for at least one librarian. Reading the professional literature alongside the pornographic literature demonstrates, perhaps ironically, that the anti-censorship ethos encapsulating Greenleaf and progressive librarians in a common vocational spirit dovetailed with a shared yearning for a more provocative archetypal librarian.

Promiscuous Public Images

Not all librarians got caught up in the zeitgeist of sexual liberation, although debates about how to handle sex materials had a widespread impact on professional librarianship. According to Kathleen Molz, editor of the *Wilson Library Bulletin* during the 1960s, a rich mine of material interpreting the sexual revolution in literature "can be found in the lesser-known journals of special interest to one of the most overlooked participants in the erotica business: the public librarian."[36] For her own part, Molz believed that adults who wanted tawdry entertainment should have the freedom to obtain it. Professionally, however, she insisted, "it does not lie within the responsibility of a public library to indulge every vagary of human taste."[37] The problem for librarians was to decipher a cultural field turned topsy-turvy by the emergence of what Molz calls "the high pornography." While the lowbrow production of Greenleaf's pulp pornography—which included cheap paper and explicit covers—marked it as unsuitable for library collections, most of Grove Press's catalog and several of Greenleaf's nonfiction publications created a gray area. How should librarians handle the collection of Supreme Court obscenity decisions from 1973 that Greenleaf published with a scathing introduction on the dangers of state censorship? Or the nonfiction study *Sex, Censorship and Pornography* that boasted over 50 pages of explicit images for reference? Did they constitute legitimate research materials?[38] For Molz, the path toward answering those difficult questions did not consist in running away from the image of libraries as "conservative, square, or what you will," but rather in honing a more critical reception of "a literature squalid in style, poor in effect."[39] She worried more about librarians looking frivolous than repressive.

The identity crisis plaguing post-censorship librarians did not escape the people responsible for Greenleaf Classics. They targeted librarians as fodder for pornographic fantasy precisely because—in addition to the apparent obsession with women in uniform—they regarded the library as insufficiently responsive to the changing social climate of the late 20th century. Despite the American Library Association's strong statement in their brief for the *Tropic of Cancer* trial that "a patron of a library has a right to read in the library any book of his choice," the library continued to represent an area of cultural access off-limits to Greenleaf Classics.[40] As the publisher puts it in the foreword to Heather Brown's novel *The Librarian's Naughty Habit*, "One profession, that of librarian, reflects the uneven progress of social change."[41] Lucky for librarians, Greenleaf had a plan to help. By presenting the story of Samantha, an ambitious and adventurous young woman who "finds herself suddenly confronted by a sexual liberalism which challenges her curiosity," the publisher hopes to cast "a new light onto a profession long stereotyped."[42] The novel is, it promises, "a chronicle of our times. The story of a woman trapped in a tide of social change."[43]

The Librarian's Naughty Habit is somewhat unique among librarian pornography in that it relies on very few of the generic character types that usually signify *librarian*. Told entirely in the first person, the novel treats readers to more of the protagonist's internal character than her external physique. Samantha never describes herself wearing a bun, thick-rimmed glasses, or dowdy clothes. Nor does she fervently defend library decorum. The path to sexual liberation for Samantha involves fostering a public sex culture at her library. Beginning and ending with scenes that involve the dubious place of sex materials in the library, the narrative dramatizes contemporary professional anxieties over how the growing public acceptance of, and in some cases demand for, pornography will complicate standard best practices. Although she responds to the challenge in farcical ways, Samantha finds herself, much like librarians of the period, learning to mediate between patron desires for sexual content and library protocol. As it progresses, the narrative makes increasingly clear that at stake in Samantha's ongoing negotiation with sex materials is the same concern over image that catalyzed the divergent professional perspectives represented by Bill Katz and Kathleen Molz.

Samantha's story begins with the head of circulation asking her to determine whether a new acquisition could go out for standard shelving. A standard assignment, Samantha explains, except "this time there was an exceptional quality about her request because the book she wanted me to read was one of those sex manuals."[44] Like some of Greenleaf's nonfiction titles, sex manuals notoriously flouted censorship regulations by packaging sexually explicit images as reference material. When a patron researching a term paper for his physiology of reproduction class asks to look at the book, Samantha has to inform him that her boss has not yet approved it for circulation. In the next chapter she lies to the head of circulation about the graphic nature of the book so that it can go out to the stacks, where she finds the student masturbating. Their encounter culminates in a threesome with another member of the library staff. The novel suggests at the outset that what libraries allow on their shelves has direct bearing on how patrons relate to librarians.

Samantha's instinct to bend the rules toward providing patrons access to sex materials intensifies at the end of the novel when the head librarian, Mr. Smiley, tasks her with single-handedly running the library's meager public relations office. Facing budget cuts at the hands of the city council because of public indifference to the library, Mr. Smiley asks her to increase library traffic by two or three hundred patrons in just a few days. Samantha strikes upon the idea of showing a popular film, thinking that changing the library's offerings will also change the extent of its public reach. The novel gestures toward early 1970s porno chic, a period when several pornographic films had wide theatrical releases, as Samantha describes her research process for deciding what to screen.* "To my surprise, one type of movie seemed to be beating everything else cold. Nobody went to westerns anymore. Or war pictures. Spy pictures were dead. Nobody was interested in musicals these days. And certainly not family pictures. Sex was what everybody was interested in."⁴⁵ Here, as in the opening scene, research leads the novel's characters toward sexual discovery. Cooperative interaction between library materials, staff, and patrons creates a promiscuous public library that attracts people from far beyond "the small fraction of the public it ordinarily attracted."⁴⁶

After a brief moment of reflection to think about whether or not a skin flick has any place in the library, Samantha decides to order *Hitchhikin' Housewife*, accidentally agreeing to take the X-rated version normally available only for private viewings. Needless to say, the screening is a success— a crowd of noisy youngsters shows up to see a film that the local police had banned in theaters. By the end of the film "reality became a part of fantasy" as the audience erupts into a spontaneous orgy.⁴⁷ Rather than focusing on the transformation of Samantha's image and identity, *The Librarian's Naughty Habit* shifts attention to the transformation of the public that the public library serves. It not only grows, giving Mr. Smiley the numbers he needs for his budget presentation at the city council, it also changes character as Samantha's programming efforts tend toward the promotion of a public sex culture. Samantha's efforts eventually result in a radically changed perspective of the library: the city council recognizes it as a thriving cultural institution, far from the musty, dusty scene of cultural decay that many popular representations of librarians and the library imply.

Although outlandish in the extreme, the climax of *The Librarian's Naughty Habit* goes against the grain of popular renderings to offer an optimistic representation of the library. The layered image of promiscuous library patrons indiscriminately indulging in sex as they watch a promiscuous hitchhiker have sex on screen depicts the possibility of sex materials organizing, rather than fracturing, a public. The absurd, and admittedly crude, rendering speaks to the difficulty of imagining such a possibility.

---

* For more on the moment of "porno chic," see Loren Glass, "Bad Sex: Second-Wave Feminism and Pornography's Golden Age," in *Cultural Expressions of Evil and Wickedness*, ed. Terrie Waddell (New York: Rodopi, 2003), 97–112.

As Michael Warner points out in *The Trouble With Normal*, a seminal explication of sexual politics in the United States, "There is very little sense in this country that a public culture of sex might be something to value, something whose accessibility is to be protected."[48] With the deregulation of the printed word, however, both librarians and pornographers set about reimagining public libraries as institutions that actively cultivate public sex culture. Not exactly a model for sexual freedom but nonetheless moving beyond the mere tolerance posited by censorship debates, the librarian in 1970s and 1980s pulp pornography gave a farcical face to the cultural significance of anti-repressive institutions of reading.

Library professionals probably would not do well to enlist Samantha, Sandy, Linda, and Polly as poster children in the campaign to overturn librarian stereotypes. Yet closer attention to a historically particular form of cultural production that made the "sexy librarian" a conventional stereotype might provide an object lesson on the deep connections between the public library's social function and public perception of librarians. At the very least, several decades after its emergence, librarian pornography provides those of us invested in understanding the impact of popular representations of librarians with a unique occasion for collectively negotiating the benefits of access to a public sphere that promotes promiscuous imagination.

Notes

1. Kathleen Glab, "The Sensuous Librarian," in *Revolting Librarians*, ed. Celeste West and Elizabeth Katz (San Francisco: Booklegger, 1972), 20.
2. Ibid., 19.
3. Ibid., 20.
4. Rod Waleman, *The Young Librarian* (Copenhagen, Denmark: Dansk Blue Books; North Hollywood, CA: Brandon House, 1971). Page numbers correspond to reprint by Olympia Press, 2007.
5. Ibid., 5.
6. Ibid.
7. Ibid., 8.
8. Ibid., 7.
9. Ibid.
10. Cindy Indiana, "In the Stacks and in the Sack: An Undercover Look at Librarians and Erotica," in *Revolting Librarians Redux*, ed. K. R. Roberto and Jessamyn West (Jefferson, NC: McFarland, 2003), 100–103.
11. See Jessamyn West, "Naked Librarians," accessed <date of access>, www.jessamyn.com/

naked/index.html; Martin Raish, "Librarians in the Movies: An Annotated Filmography," last updated August 5, 2011, http://emp.byui.edu/raishm/films/introduction.html; Candi Strecker, "Sex in the Stacks: Librarian Porn Novels Reviewed," ChipRowe.com, accessed July 17, 2013, www.chiprowe.com/articles/library.html. "The Image of Librarians in Pornography," Dan Lester's extensive bibliography (formerly at www.riverofdata.com/librariana/porn), unfortunately no longer exists.

12. Indiana, "In the Stacks and in the Sack," 101.
13. Strecker, "Sex in the Stacks."
14. Marie L. Radford and Gary P. Radford, "Power Knowledge, and Fear: Feminism, Foucault, and the Stereotype of the Female Librarian," *Library Quarterly* 67, no. 3 (July 1997): 261.
15. Strecker, "Sex in the Stacks."
16. Avi Steinberg, "Checking Out," *Paris Review Daily* (blog), December 26, 2012, www.theparisreview.org/blog/2012/12/26/checking-out.
17. Steinberg, "Checking Out."
18. Ibid.
19. Laura Quincy, *The Naughty Librarian* (San Diego: Heatherpool, 1981), 6.
20. Ibid., 10.
21. Ibid., 13.
22. Ibid., 149.
23. Nick Eastwood, *Horny Licking Librarian* (San Diego: Patch Pockets, n.d.), chap. 2. Plain text e-book available at http://neatopotato.net/xnovel.
24. Ibid., chap. 3.
25. Ibid.
26. Ibid., chap. 8.
27. Quincy, *Naughty Librarian*, 1.
28. United States v. One Book Entitled Ulysses by James Joyce, 191 US 545 (1934). Full text of the decision is available online at www.law.cornell.edu.
29. Ralph Ginzburg et al., Petitioners, v. United States. Edward Mishkin, Appellant, v. State of New York. 383 US 463 (1966). Full text of the decision is available online at www.law.cornell.edu.
30. Loren Glass, *Counter Culture Colophon* (Stanford, CA: Stanford University Press, 2013).
31. Robert Redrup, Petitioner v. State of New York. 386 US 767 (1967).
32. Morris L. Ernst and William Seagle, "The Subterranean Censorship," *Bookman* 68, no. 1 (September 1928): 37.
33. Bill Katz, "The Pornography Collection," *Library Journal* 96 (December 1971): 4065.
34. Ibid., 4061.
35. Ibid., 4066.
36. Kathleen Molz, "The Public Custody of the High Pornography," *American Scholar* 36, no. 1 (Winter 1966–67): 93.
37. Ibid., 101–102.
38. Stanley Fleishman, *The Supreme Court Obscenity Decisions* (San Diego: Greenleaf Classics, 1973); Donald H. Gilmore, *Sex, Censorship and Pornography* (San Diego: Greenleaf Classics, 1969).
39. Molz, "High Pornography," 103.
40. Fleishman, *Supreme Court Obscenity Decisions,* 218.
41. Heather Brown, *The Librarian's Naughty Habit* (San Diego: Greenleaf Classics, 1976), 3. Page numbers correspond to reprint by Olympia Press, 2006.
42. Ibid.

43. Ibid.
44. Ibid., 5.
45. Ibid., 100.
45. Ibid.
47. Ibid., 112.
48. Michael Warner, *The Trouble with Normal* (Cambridge, MA: Harvard University Press, 2003), 171.

Bibliography

Bates, Anna L. *Weeder in the Garden of the Lord: Anthony Comstock's Life and Career.* Lanham, MD: University Press of America, 1995.

Brown, Heather. *The Librarian's Naughty Habit.* San Diego: Greenleaf Classics, 1976. Reprinted by Olympia Press, 2006.

Eastwood, Nick. *Horny Licking Librarian.* San Diego: Patch Pockets, n.d. Plain text e-book available at http://neatopotato.net/xnovel.

Ernst, Morris L., and William Seagle. "The Subterranean Censorship." *Bookman* 68, no. 1 (September 1928): 36–40.

Fleishman, Stanley. *The Supreme Court Obscenity Decisions.* San Diego: Greenleaf Classics, 1973.

Gilmore, Donald H. *Sex, Censorship and Pornography.* San Diego: Greenleaf Classics, 1969.

Glab, Kathleen. "The Sensuous Librarian." In *Revolting Librarians,* edited by Celeste West and Elizabeth Katz, 19–21. San Francisco: Booklegger, 1972.

Glass, Loren. "Bad Sex: Second-Wave Feminism and Pornography's Golden Age." In *Cultural Expressions of Evil and Wickedness: Wrath, Sex, Crime,* edited by Terrie Waddell, 97–112. New York: Rodopi, 2003.

———. *Counter Culture Colophon: Grove Press, The Evergreen Review, and the Incorporation of the Avant-Garde.* Stanford, CA: Stanford University Press, 2013.

Hunt, Lynn, ed. *The Invention of Pornography: Obscenity and the Origins of Modernity, 1500–1800.* New York: Zone Books, 1993.

Indiana, Cindy. "In the Stacks and in the Sack: An Undercover Look at Librarians and Erotic." In *Revolting Librarians Redux: Radical Librarians Speak Out,* edited by K. R. Roberto and Jessamyn West, 100–103. Jefferson, NC: McFarland, 2003.

Kaplan, Fred. "The Day Obscenity Became Art." *New York Times,* July 21, 2009, A21.

Katz, Bill. "The Pornography Collection." *Library Journal* 96 (December 1971): 4060–66.

Kemp, Earl. *eI* 7, no. 4 (August 2008). http://efanzines.com/EK/eI39.

Lane, Frederick S. *Obscene Profits: Entrepreneurs of Pornography in the Cyber Age.* New York: Routledge, 2000.

Lester, Dan. "The Image of Librarians in Pornography." River of Data. www.riverofdata.com/librariana/porn. Site discontinued but available through web.archive.org.

Molz, Kathleen. "The Public Custody of the High Pornography." *American Scholar* 36, no. 1 (Winter 1966–67): 93–103.

Quincy, Laura. *The Naughty Librarian.* San Diego: Heatherpool, 1981.

Radford, Marie L., and Gary P. Radford. "Power Knowledge, and Fear: Feminism, Foucault, and the Stereotype of the Female Librarian." *Library Quarterly* 67, no. 3 (July 1997): 250–66.

Raish, Martin. "Librarians in the Movies: An Annotated Filmography" Last updated August 5, 2011. http://emp.byui.edu/raishm/films/introduction.html.

Ralph Ginzburg et al., Petitioners, v. United States. Edward Mishkin, Appellant, v. State of New

York. 383 US 463 (1966).

Rembar, Charles. *The End of Obscenity: The Trials of Lady Chatterley, Tropic of Cancer, and Fanny Hill.* New York: Random House, 1968.

Robert Redrup, Petitioner v. State of New York. 386 US 767 (1967).

Roth v. United States. 354 US 476 (1957).

Steinberg, Avi, "Checking Out." *Paris Review Daily* (blog). December 26, 2012. www.theparisreview.org/blog/2012/12/26/checking-out.

Strecker, Candi. "Sex in the Stacks: Librarian Porn Novels Reviewed." ChipRowe.com. Accessed July 17, 2013. www.chiprowe.com/articles/library.html.

Strub, Whitney. *Perversion for Profit: The Politics of Pornography and the Rise of the New Right.* New York: Columbia University Press, 2010.

United States v. One Book Entitled Ulysses by James Joyce. 191 US 545 (1934).

Waleman, Rod. *The Young Librarian.* Copenhagen, Denmark: Dansk Blue Books; North Hollywood, CA: Brandon House, 1971. Reprinted by Olympia Press, 2007.

Warner, Michael. *The Trouble with Normal: Sex, Politics and the Ethics of Queer Life.* Cambridge, MA: Harvard University Press, 2003.

West, Jessamyn. "Naked Librarians." Jessamyn.com. Accessed November 8, 2013. www.jessamyn.com/naked/index.html.

CHAPTER 6

Rainbow Warriors

Stories of Archivist Activism and the Queer Record

Terry Baxter

> Laugh and cry and tell stories. Sad stories about bodies stolen, bodies no longer here. Enraging stories about the false images, devastating lies, untold violence. Bold, brash stories about reclaiming our bodies and changing the world.
>
> ~ Eli Clare, *Exile and Pride: Disability, Queerness, and Liberation*[1]

The banner on Dusty Archive Kitten Deaths states

> "Whenever you use 'musty' [or 'dusty'] in an article about Archives, the ghost of Schellenberg kills a kitten"
>
> ~Brad Houston
>
> Exposing reliance upon schema and stereotypes for archives and libraries in the press.[2]

This Tumblr site was set up in early 2014 to counter media articles that portray archives as dark, musty caves and archivists as antisocial Gollums hoarding their precious documents.* One such article was published recently in the *New York Times*, describing the work of archivist Bruce

---

* See http://dustyarchivekittendeaths.tumblr.com for a variety of examples of current media stereotypes of archives and archivists.

Abrams, recently retired from the state of New York. The descriptions were less than flattering:

> …this mazelike archive he treated as his own personal, cloistered garden… with the requisite reserve and slight social unease that one expects from a dedicated archivist… One problem with the job, he said, was that he was often interrupted in his archiving to retrieve files for the public.[3]

Archivists responded in dismay on social media about their portrayal as socially reserved guardians of secreted documents whose use by the public constitutes interference with the important duties of archiving. Archivist Amanda Hill's immediate tweet—"nyti.ms/1kmSMPO 'One problem with the job… was that he was often interrupted… to retrieve files for people.' THAT WAS HIS JOB."[4]—received 18 responses within the day, most of which decried the article's unchallenged stereotyping of archivists.*

These are not new conceptualizations of archives and archivists. A 1984 report to the Society of American Archivists titled *The Image of Archivists: Resource Allocators Perceptions*, found that archivists are viewed as introverted professionals who like to work on their "troves" of documents in solitude and have trouble relating their value or the value of their archives to resource allocators and the public.[†] This trope remained remarkably consistent into the 21st century. As I noted in 2011, "If a person was to rely on generalities, the average archivist would be a middle-aged white woman, similar to the cardigan-and-glasses-wearing librarian, or maybe even Jocasta Nu, head librarian of the Jedi archives."[5]

---

* For other examples, see *Meredith Halsey*, "The Popular Perception of Archivists," Meredith Halsey (blog), February 1, 2014, http://meridithhalsey.wordpress.com/2014/02/01/the-popular-perception-of-archivists, and "One day, non-specialists will write about info professionals in a non-cringeworthy way. Porcine fliers may also occur." (Brad Houston [@herodoctusjr], tweet, January 31, 2014, https://twitter.com/herodotusjr/status/429263577908641792).

† The Society of American Archivists published the Levy Report (December 1984) with analysis by its Task Force on Society and Archives in December 1985. Both are available at http://www2.archivists. org/sites/all/files/Image-of-Archivists-Levy1984.pdf.

But the fact of the matter is that archives and archivists are not (if they ever were) inwardly focused professionals concerned primarily about their boxes of stuff. Archivists are engaged with the people who use archives and consistently develop innovative and creative ways to promote their records and the ways in which they can be used.[‡]

There are a number of reasons for the changing views of archivists, but four stand out. First is the changing demographics of archivists. This subject warrants an entire essay of its own. The composition of the archives profession is much different in 2014 than it was in 1964 or 1984. The starkest changes are age, gender, and education. Fifty years ago, the majority of archivists were middle-aged men with bachelor's degrees in the humanities. Archivists coming into the profession today are overwhelmingly millennial women with master's degrees in library and information science.[§] While there is no definitive correlation between these demographics and views of archivists, it seems reasonable to infer that higher levels of education and professionalization at a younger age could relate to archivists' increasing desire to define themselves and not just accept outsider stereotypes.[6]

The second reason is the changing technology landscape within which archivists work. While the current social networking tools employed by archivists generate a lot of flash, in many ways it is the more mundane work of online descriptive tools and digitized collections that have democratized access to archives and brought more archivists into contact with more people. As seen above, archivists are also getting relatively younger and are adept at using technology, especially social networking tools. While the media focuses many of its current image stories on either dusty archives or hipster archivist narratives, it is the facility with technology, especially socially connective technology, that has brought real

---

‡ For a detailed review of the modern archivist and archives, see Kate Theimer, "What Is the Meaning of Archives 2.0?" *American Archivist* 74 (Spring/Summer 2011): 58–68.

§ The most definitive work on archives demographics is the A*Census, which was conducted in 2004 and reported on and analyzed in the 2006 Fall/Winter issue of *American Archivist*. For more recent data, see Terry Baxter, "Gender Balance in the Heritage Professions," presentation to the Pacific Northwest Historians Conference, Spokane, WA, November 2009.

change to the way archivists are viewed.[*]

The third reason emerges from the nature of archival work. Much of the work in the first half century of formal archives programs centered around processing and preservation activities. Access, while not exclusively aimed at "serious researchers," aimed to meet the needs of the academic community. These activities allowed archivists to perform their jobs for years with minimal need for public interaction. The last 30 years in the profession have seen that balance flip—processing has taken a backseat to enhanced access and outreach. This has forced archivists to interact with a much broader public spectrum in more creative ways.[7]

The fourth reason, and the subject of the remainder of this chapter, is the rise of the activist archivist. Archival activism has changed the face of archivists from passive catalogers of "sacred relics" to active users and promoters of powerful agents of social change. In some ways, there is a relationship between the rise in archival activism and the rise in community archives. Archival activism relies strongly on the connection built through direct and personal work with a specific community. It creates a trusting relationship with community members that sees the community's vision as important and the archives as a means of furthering that vision. Activist archivists have changed the way communities view them by reinventing themselves—from external experts who can be easily stereotyped, into internal comrades whose passion and skills must be engaged with individually.

This chapter discusses activist archivists in Portland, Oregon's, queer community. But similar stories are unfolding across the United States. From Occupy Wall Street archives in New York[8] to distillery archives in Kentucky to Southeast Asian expat archives in Irvine,[†] archivists are changing the way they connect with and consequently are seen by the communities they serve.

---

[*] For recent articles on the image of librarians and archivists, see Alison Leigh Cowan, "Leaving Cloister of Dusty Offices, Young Archivists Meet Like Minds," www.nytimes.com/2013/04/29/ nyregion/archivists-bringing-past-into-future-are-now-less-cloistered.html, and Jordan G. Teicher, "This Is What a Librarian Looks Like," www.slate.com/blogs/behold/2014/02/11/kyle_ cassidy_photographs_librarians_at_the_american_library_association.html.

[†] The University of Kentucky has been collecting oral histories and archives related to the Buffalo Trace Distillery. For more information see Buffalo Trace Oral History Project, www.nunncenter. org/buffalotrace/about. The Southeast Asian Archive was established at the University of California Irvine in 1987. For more information, see http://seaa.lib.uci.edu.

Rand Jimerson, in *Archives Power*, discusses the fragility and ephemeral nature of individual and collective memory. He quotes historian Richard White: "Only careless historians confuse memory and history. History is the enemy of memory. The two stalk each other across the fields of the past, claiming the same terrain."[9] In contrast with memory, archives, while not the neutral fact buckets they have seemed in the past, provide tangible evidence of things that have happened. This evidence can be interrogated and interpreted by anyone. Archives allow stories to be told that have a basis in reality and that can be investigated and analyzed.

History contains traces and sources. Traces are things that remain of the past that were not created with the intention of transmitting information about the past. Sources are purposefully constructed to serve as an account of past events. Both are useful, but the former have less of a chance for manipulation. By collecting archives containing both trace and source, community archivists move their claims for equality and justice from a realm of personal rhetoric, collective memory, or community myth to one of substantiated and reviewable narratives. The establishment of an archive immediately provides legitimacy to the stories told. It roots them in evidence and establishes that however this evidence may be interpreted by their or others' histories, it documents real things done by real people.

In the spring of 1970, less than a year after the Stonewall Riots, two reporters from the Portland independent newspaper *Willamette Bridge* and a young gay man who had tried to place a classified ad looking for love joined forces to form the Portland Gay Liberation Front.[10] This organization was the first openly political civil rights organization in Oregon centered on queer rights.[‡] Queer history in Portland was in evidence from (and even before) the founding of the city in 1845. There are repeated references in sources to the existence of a variety of sexual and gender minorities and, more prominently, laws devised to criminalize both their existence and

‡ The author is using *queer* as a term for sexual and gender minorities that are not heterosexual or gender-binary. As a cis, heterosexual archivist I work hard to insure that the historical record is diverse and includes the stories of all humans. Mistakes in terminology in this text are unintended and regretted.

their activities. While there are certainly instances of protest in the record,* most of the documented activity included the enactment of sodomy laws, laws to sterilize "perverts," and nearly uniform public hostility to queer people of any sort.†

Portland's gay rights movement was an early offshoot of national gay rights organizations. Its emergence in 1970 also coincided with an explosion of movements designed to obtain, expand, and protect civil rights for a number of marginalized groups. Civil rights, the Equal Rights Amendment, the American Indian Movement, Brown Power, and other movements battled for an equal place in a diverse America challenging mainstream culture. To many bewildered Americans, the calls for equality and justice seemed to appear out of thin air and represented a threat to their normative lives. In this same year, historian Howard Zinn confronted an audience of archivists about their attempts to approach archives with a neutral stance. "The archivist, even more than the historian and the political scientist, tends to be scrupulous about his neutrality, and to see his job as a technical job, free from the nasty world of political interest: a job of collecting, sorting, preserving, making available, the records of the society," Zinn declared.[11] However, he continued, "The existence, preservation, and availability of archives, documents, records in our society are very much determined by the distribution of wealth and power."[12] Zinn added that archival collections were "biased towards the important and powerful people of the society, tending to ignore the impotent and obscure."[13] Many archivists trace the birth of archival activism to this presentation.

The history and nuance of archivist activism could fill its own volume, and in fact has. Rand Jimerson's 2005 Society of American Archivists address, "Embracing the Power of Archives," and subsequent 2009 book,

---

* For example, Dr. Marie Equi lived openly as a lesbian in Portland nearly 100 years ago and was publicly advocating for a variety of women's rights and adopted a child with her then partner Harriet Speckart; see www.oregonencyclopedia.org/entry/view/equi_marie_1872_1952_.

† While this subject is too broad to discuss fully here, some basic survey sources include a timeline of queer history in Portland compiled by GLAPN at http://pdxqueerhistory.wikispaces.com/Timeline+of+PDX+Queer+History; Ariel Gore's *Portland Queer* (Portland, OR: Lit Star, 2009), which provides both memoir and fiction narratives of the Portland queer experience; and Peter Boag's "Does Portland Need a Homophile Society?" (*Oregon Historical Quarterly* 105, no. 1 (2004): 6–39.), which discusses Portland's queer scene post–WWII.

Archives Power, provide the most wide-ranging articulation of archivist activism.[14] In general, it has been a call from some archivists to the profession to recognize that archives are not neutral; that they can be selected, preserved, and used to promote social justice.

While many historians were familiar with Zinn's bias for decades, mainstream archivists had not spent much time emphasizing the documentary heritage of marginalized groups—neither through appraisal and collection efforts, through description and other access mechanisms, nor through outreach and advocacy efforts. In fact many archivists in this era consciously avoided any sense that they were "politicizing" their collections and believed (and tried to project an image of) strict neutrality. This stance resembled, to nonarchivists, the same stereotypically meek aspect of their sister professionals, librarians. But for archivists, this attitude was the result of professional theory that did not see significant revisions in professional practice until the 1980s.[15]

That left much of the early queer archival work in the hands of community archivists. Community archives can be seen as "the grassroots activities of documenting, recording and exploring community heritage in which community participation, control and ownership of the project is essential."[16] Early queer activists recognized that their community heritage and community perspectives on its interpretation needed to be preserved. In the absence of recognizable efforts from mainstream historians and archivists, communities took on this responsibility themselves. Take this description of the creation of the Lesbian Herstory Archives:

> At one meeting in 1974, Julia Stanley and Joan Nestle, who had come out before the Gay Liberation Movement, talked about the precariousness of lesbian culture and how so much of our past culture was seen only through patriarchal eyes. Deborah Edel, Sahli Cavallo and Pamela Oline, with histories ranging from lesbian-feminism to political lesbianism, joined in and, thus, a new concept was born—a grassroots Lesbian archives.[17]

Many of these early archival activists did not equate themselves with "professional" archivists or archivist organizations. They saw these as tools of the dominant cultural narrative and distrusted them to either collect and care for their records or to interpret them as authentically as they could do themselves.

The Lesbian Herstory Archives was not the earliest queer community archives.* Between 1942 and 1971, pioneering queer community archivist Jim Kepner collected material related to queer topics, issues, and individuals. Kepner was one of the founders of One Inc., which founded the educational One Institute and began publishing *One Magazine* in 1953. This magazine would become the first widely distributed publication for gay and lesbian people in the United States. The magazine featured articles, editorials, short stories, book reviews, and letters to the editor. In 1971, Kepner named his collection, then housed in his rented Hollywood apartment, the Western Gay Archives. His archives would later move to a storefront space in Hollywood, becoming the National Gay Archives, and later, the International Gay and Lesbian Archives, to reflect the growing scope of the collections. The archives would later be renamed ONE National Gay and Lesbian Archives. In October 2010, the collections at ONE Archives became a part of the USC Libraries system. Today, ONE Archives is the oldest continuing LGBTQ organization in the United States and the largest repository of LGBTQ materials in the world.†

The period between 1971 and 1992 emphasized action over documentation. Portland Pride was established in 1971 both to commemorate Stonewall and to provide a celebration for the queer community. A series of laws were enacted, most of which either decriminalized homosexual activity or provided increasingly broad workplace protections for queer Portlanders. And of course there was AIDS. The first AIDS death in Portland occurred in 1982. Within a year the Cascade AIDS Project was formed to advocate for AIDS research and treatment.

---

* For a general review of major archives, see Aimee Brown, "How Queer 'Pack Rats' and Activist Archivists Saved Our History: An Overview of Lesbian, Gay, Bisexual, Transgender, and Queer (LGBTQ) Archives, 1970–2008," in *Serving LGBTIQ Library and Archives Users*, ed. Ellen Greenblatt, 121–35, (Jefferson, NC: McFarland, 2010).

† For more information, see "History," ONE Archives at the USC Libraries, 2013, http://one.usc. edu/about/history.

Fears about AIDS and hostility to "special rights" for gays and lesbians led to a conservative Christian backlash. The Oregon Citizens Alliance (OCA) began a six-year campaign to repeal gay rights and demonize queer citizens. The OCA had early success. In 1988, it proposed Measure 8, a referendum that both repealed the existing executive order barring state government workplace discrimination against gay people and created a statute that prohibited workplace protections from being enacted. The measure passed by a 53–47 percent margin.[18]

Emboldened by their success, the OCA proposed Measure 9 in 1992.[19] This measure gained international notoriety for its proposal to amend Oregon's Constitution to prevent "special rights" for queer people by "recogniz[ing] homosexuality, pedophilia, sadism and masochism as abnormal, wrong, unnatural, and perverse." The ballot measure was defeated, 56 percent to 44 percent.[‡] That same year, the Oregon Court of Appeals declared the [1988] Measure 8 unconstitutional.[20] As a result, the OCA's only statewide victory was nullified.

The defeat of Measure 9 happened for a number of reasons. Opponents outspent the OCA 6 to 1 on lobbying. Major newspapers and politicians of both parties opposed it.[21] Attitudes about queer people were becoming more accepting. But a major reason for the change was the coalescence of a revived gay rights movement. This movement came together to fight continued attempts of the OCA to introduce local antigay discriminatory laws. Basic Rights Oregon was formed in 1996 in direct response to OCA attacks and has continued to the present as a force in queer rights advocacy.

Just as importantly, and two years earlier in 1994, a key institution in the fight for basic human rights for queer people was created. The Gay and Lesbian Archives of the Pacific Northwest (GLAPN) was established. GLAPN credits community historian Allan Berube with convincing gay and lesbian organizations to begin collecting material that documented the queer experience, especially rights activism.[22] While Berube's influence is clear, it is also reasonable to see the role of resurgent activism in the collection of the community's documentation.

---

‡ Taylor Clark, "Straight and Narrow," *Willamette Week*, March 9, 2005, www.wweek.com/portland/article-4191-1992.html. Although this was a resounding defeat, opponents of Measure 9 were dismayed that over 638,000 Oregonians had voted for it.

There is no clear evidence that opponents to Measure 9 saw GLAPN as a source of activism. It had only recently been established and had not had much time to share its mission and holdings. What is clear is that queer activists saw themselves as a community that was open about itself and up-front about its demands to be accorded the same place in the broader culture as any other community. I would argue that the documented stories now publicly available in an archives, dedicated not just to queer people in general but to queer people in the northwest, provided fuel for activists of Basic Rights Oregon and allowed them to craft personal and powerful messages based on local narratives.

This sense of archivists "using" archives to effect social change was not even really nascent at this time. Most professional archivists, steeped in archival literature and education that emphasized selection of, preservation of, and equitable and open access to archival collections, saw the politicization of archives as imprudent at best, and at worst unethical. The OCA continued to promote a series of local and statewide initiatives trying to limit or roll back the rights of queer people. These initiatives were thwarted by a combination of legislative action, case law, and changes in voting that reflected changing public attitudes. By 2000, the OCA was effectively dismantled.

Within four years, one of the most controversial actions related to queer rights in Portland occurred. In March 2004, a group of the Multnomah County Commissioners, based on advice from the County Attorney, instructed the county marriage licensing office to issue marriage licenses to any two people who met the requirements in county code, effectively including queer couples. Over an eight-week period, Multnomah County issued 3,022 marriage licenses to same-sex couples.[23] On April 20, the county was instructed by the Multnomah County Court to cease issuing marriage licenses, and the state was instructed to register those licenses already issued.[24]

In November 2004, Oregon voters enacted Measure 36, which constitutionally defined marriage as between one man and one woman.[25] The measure passed by a 57 to 43 percent margin, failing only in Multnomah and Benton counties.[26] In April 2005, the Oregon Supreme Court ruled in *Li and Kennedy v. State of Oregon* that Multnomah County did not have authority to issue marriage licenses to same sex couples and that they were void when issued.[27]

In response, the 2004 Wedding Album Project was initiated by the Multnomah County Board of Commissioners in 2005 to commemorate the one-year anniversary of 3,022 same-sex couples receiving marriage licenses in the city of Portland, Oregon.[28] The county sent a letter to all of the couples to whom they issued marriage licenses between those five weeks explaining the purpose of the project. The invitation requested that couples contribute photographs, written memories, or other materials relating to their marriages. The county arranged for volunteers to collect the records and display them in the lobby of the Multnomah Building for the month of March 2005. The letter also stated that, following the exhibit, the materials would be donated to the Oregon Historical Society and made available for research. The county collected materials from 260 of the more than 3,000 same-sex couples who received marriage certificates from Multnomah County.

By the time the materials for the Wedding Album Project were collected in 2005, the marriage certificates had been voided by the state of Oregon. Yet despite the disappointment of the album contributors, many of them praised the marriages and the county's controversial decision as having had a positive impact on their lives. The decision to allow same-sex marriages—if even for a brief five-week period—represented to them the county's recognition and acceptance of the lives they had established for themselves. Many of the couples, traveling from as far away as New York, had been together for decades, while others for only a few years. The materials in the albums document not only these marriages, but also the stories of relationships and the personal struggles survived in the face of opposition.[29]

The Wedding Album Project is interesting for several reasons. First and foremost, it is important documentation of the queer community's response to the brief, historic time when gay marriage was legal in Multnomah County. At this time, only Massachusetts authorized gay marriage, and the documentation of the emotional response of couples in Multnomah County to the expression of their civil rights provided one brick in the path to the realization of marriage equality for all Americans.

Second, the Wedding Album Project was a purposefully constructed collection. The Board of County Commissioners decision was controversial in many ways. Commissioners Linn, Cruz, Naito, and Rojo de Steffey had purposefully excluded Commissioner Roberts, a likely opponent, from their discussions of same-sex marriage. They also skirted the spirit of Oregon's Public Meetings Law to insure that they could act without public review of their deliberations.[30] But the commissioners also viewed themselves as activists, using whatever means necessary to pursue a just cause. The Wedding Album Project allowed them to document what they saw as the positive outcome of their work without having to include a record of the way in which they accomplished it.

Finally, the Wedding Album Project Archives was deposited with the Oregon Historical Society archives and not with the Multnomah County Archives. Either could have been an appropriate choice, but by choosing the one that emphasizes the cultural record instead of the official archives of county government action, I would contend that the commissioners were purposefully emphasizing their role as community activists instead of as politicians.

This episode highlights the need to understand that archives have power. That is why they are so popular with activists. But power is not the same as truth. Archives are used by people with their own agendas and biases. Tom Hyry and Michelle Light recognized early on that archivists should not shy away from these in their selection and description of archives.[31] Rand Jimerson urged archivists to reject neutrality and to apply objectivity as best as possible in their work with archives.[32] This notion, not fully accepted in the professional archives community even now, implies that archivists bring a variety of backgrounds, beliefs, filters, and biases to their work.* Consequently, it is in their best interests to openly state what those issues are, strive to be as objective as possible in their work, and recognize that their professional decisions have direct and real impact on the communities in which they work.

---

* The most recent issue of the *American Archivist* includes a set of point-counterpoint articles debating whether it is in the profession's best interest to embrace archival activism. See Mark A. Greene, "A Critique of Social Justice as an Archival Imperative: What Is It We're Doing That's All That Important?" and Randall Jimerson, "Archivists and Social Responsibility: A Response to Mark Greene," *American Archivist* 76 (Fall/Winter 2013).

The nature of archivist activism was debated in practice in 2008 by the Society of American Archivists (SAA). In the wake of Proposition 8 in California,[33] SAA's Diversity Committee and the Lesbian and Gay Archivists Roundtable (LAGAR) petitioned the SAA Council to publicly advocate for equal civil rights, including marriage, among its membership. This request stirred up a wide-ranging and sometimes contentious discussion of the role of advocacy, especially regarding social issues that are not directly records-related.[†] In the end, the SAA Council decided to add sexual orientation to its nondiscrimination policy.

In 2011, the Cascade AIDS Project (CAP) began gathering material to celebrate its 25th anniversary.[34] Incorporated in 1986, the Portland nonprofit has been at the center of local efforts to reduce and eventually eliminate HIV/AIDS in the local community. It provides both educational outreach and direct services to clients with AIDS. CAP began to gather the organization's history—documents, photos, and the stories of staff, clients, and volunteers. In doing so, it assembled a record of the far-reaching effects of HIV and AIDS in Portland and the strength, love, and community that have rallied to fight the virus.

While its archives has been used for traditional research, they have also played a valuable role in CAP's outreach efforts. In addition to the more familiar documents, the collection has a wide variety of ephemera, oral histories, and a memory plaque with the names of every person who has died of AIDS in Oregon. The CAP archives are used regularly to augment presentations and educational sessions. In contrast to how archives are often seen—pristine, reserved, academic—these archives are intended to build emotional connection.

At a recent presentation celebrating World AIDS Day, the volunteer archivist for CAP, Allan Giles, brushed aside concerns about thumbtacking early posters and t-shirts to the display board. "These archives display their marks with pride," stated Giles. "They are meant to be used and touched. They are how we connect with people" (conversation with author, December 4, 2013).

---

† For example, see Terry Baxter, "I <3 Equality," *Beaver Archivist*, blog post and comments, February 2, 2009, http://terryx.wordpress.com/2009/02/11/i-3-equality.

This sense of purposeful connection also marked the Radical Library Crawl in 2011.[35] Based on the popular Oregon Archives Crawl,* it offered people the opportunity to visit specialized feminist and queer libraries, view their collections, meet their librarians, and even get library cards. People crawled from Bitch Media to In Other Words Bookstore to Q Center. In each location, it was clear that these organizations were presenting their collections—archives and books—in a unique way to engage new audiences and to connect them to their missions.

For approximately 40 years, queer archives have been collected in Portland. These archives have both documented and contributed to the slow march to full civil rights for queer people. Archives like GLAPN or CAP provide evidence of things that have happened, letting people review and analyze them. But activism often proceeds more from the heart than from the head.

Archivists have been advocating for decades for a more diverse historical record.[†] But in many ways, it has only been in the last 10 years or so that the archives profession has come to see community archives and the people who manage them as partners in the maintenance of the historic record. I would argue that the willingness to partner with community archivists is necessary in diversifying the archival record. It is also a consequence of archivists beginning to see themselves as active participants in the world around them and not merely observers documenting it. The act of connecting, of contextualizing, is at the heart of the archival endeavor, and it works best from the inside, not the outside.

These queer archives, often community archives preserved and maintained by the groups that created them, provide a voice to people who have too often been excluded from the broader narrative, allowing the stories of queer people and their struggle for equality and acceptance to be told. They matter for two broad reasons. The first is that the story of hu-

---

* The Oregon Archives Crawl is a popular event held in Portland during Archives Month. It is a creative way for Oregon archivists to engage with people who would not normally use archives. For a good review by the creators of the event, see Diana Banning and Anne Prahl, "Public Crawls to Oregon's Archives," *Archival Outlook*, November/December 2010: 18.

† For a broad survey of diversity initiatives in the archives profession, see Elizabeth W. Adkins, "Our Journey towards Diversity—And a Call to (More) Action," *American Archivist* 71 (Spring/ Summer 2008): 21–49.

man history is much more diverse now than it has ever been. Individuals and groups are preserving their own history and demanding that it be included in the broader narrative. The diversification of the American (and human) record matters. It is not only a more equitable approach to history, but a truer story. We have long moved beyond a belief that history is built on the stories of the powerful and privileged. But we are still learning the stunning diversity of stories being told. These stories are made possible by archivists who are actively promoting a diverse record by their selection and promotion of all records.

This leads to the second reason. We all have the responsibility to work for a better world. The stories we tell each other are powerful, with the ability to move hearts and change minds. Archivists have the ability to make those stories vibrant, more truthful, and more diverse. To do so they must reject and dispel the stereotypes that they are unwilling to share their resources and themselves. They need to take their collections, their skills, and their hearts out into the world and engage with communities who want to have their stories told and heard.

But archivists also need to beware of building a new stereotype. Archivists are not superheroes, jumping into communities and using their expertise to "save" them. Archives power, activist archivists, community archivists—all of these terms are frames that describe the increasing engagement of archivists with communities. If that engagement is not collaborative, however, seeing the mission and values of the community as important as the archives, archivists risk losing the trust necessary to use archives in the service of positive social change.

Archives have been central to the ability of queer people in Portland to assert the same rights as any other people and to feel welcome as valued and desired members of the community. But this worked only because archivists were willing to shrug off their stereotypes as dusty awkward loners, roll up their sleeves, and get into the community mix.

In *Camino Real*, Gutman discusses The Survivor and The Dreamer with The Generalissimo: "You said, 'They're harmless dreamers and they're loved by the people.' 'What,' I asked you, 'is harmless about a dreamer, and what,' I asked you, 'is harmless about the love of the people? Revolution only needs good dreamers who remember their dreams."[36] Old views of archivists would never see them as dreamers. But times change. Archivists and communities continue to dream, survive, and work together, using the records of deeds and words, to build a better world for all.

Notes

1. Eli Clare, *Exile and Pride* (Cambridge, MA: South End Press, 1999): 136.
2. Dusty Archive Kitten Deaths, Tumblr site, accessed January 16, 2014, http://dustyarchive-kittendeaths.tumblr.com.
3. Corey Kilgannon, "New York Court Archivist Isn't Letting Retirement Stop Him," *New York Times*, January 31, 2014, www.nytimes.com/2014/02/02/nyregion/new-york-court-archivist-isnt-letting-retirement-stop-him.html.
4. Amanda Hill (@mandahill), tweet, January 31, 2014, https://twitter.com/mandahill/status/429590915993575424.
5. Terry Baxter, "Going to See the Elephant: Archives, Diversity and the Social Web," in *A Different Kind of Web*, ed. Kate Theimer (Chicago: Society of American Archivists, 2011), 295.
6. Kate Theimer, "What is the Meaning of Archives 2.0?" *American Archivist* 74 (Spring/Summer 2011): 67.
7. Mark A. Greene and Dennis Meissner, "More Product, Less Process: Revamping Traditional Archival Processing," *American Archivist* 68 (Fall/Winter 2005): 208–263.
8. Hiten Samtani, "The Anarchists: Who Owns the Occupy Wall Street Narrative?" *Brooklyn Ink*, December 26, 2011 http://thebrooklynink.com/2011/12/26/39230-the-anarchists-who-owns-the-occupy-wall-street-narrative.
9. Richard White, quoted in Randall C. Jimerson, *Archives Power* (Chicago: Society of American Archivists, 2009), 193.
10. George T. Nikola, "How the Oregon LGBT Movement Was Born," Gay and Lesbian Archives of the Pacific Northwest, last revised July 30, 2013, www.glapn.org/6130nicolagaymovement.html.
11. Howard Zinn, "Secrecy, Archives, and the Public Interest," *Midwestern Archivist* 2, no. 2 (1977): 20.
12. Ibid.
13. Ibid., 21.
14. Jimerson, *Archives Power*. The full text of Jimerson's 2005 address can be found at www.archivists.org/governance/presidential/jimerson.asp.
15. Reto Tschan, "A Comparison of Jenkinson and Schellenberg on Appraisal," *American Archivist* 65 (Fall/Winter 2002): 176–95.
16. "Community Archives Approach," Prairienet, 2011, www.prairienet.org/op/digarch/approaches-for-smaller-community-institutions/community-archiving.
17. "History and Mission," Lesbian Herstory Archives, accessed December 20, 2013, www.lesbianherstoryarchives.org/history.html.
18. Lauren Cowen, "Vote for Measure 8 Shocks Opponents," *Oregonian*, November 10, 1988, F16.
19. "Government Cannot Facilitate, Must Discourage Homosexuality, Other 'Behaviors,'" in "Initiative, Referendum and Recall: 1988–1995," Oregon Blue Book, http://bluebook.state.or.us/state/elections/elections21.htm.

20.   Charles E. Beggs, "Oregon's Anti-Gay Law Unconstitutional, Appeals Court Rules," *AP News Archive*, November 12, 1992, www.apnewsarchive.com/1992/Oregon-s-Anti-Gay-Law-Un-constitutional-Appeals-Court-Rules/id-fab7a94f6b00f866b06e820c09b60ea2.

21.   Phil Keisling, *Voters Pamphlet* (Salem: State of Oregon, 1992), 99–127, http://library.state.or.us/repository/2010/201003011350161/ORVPGenMari1992.pdf.

22.   "A History of GLAPN," Gay and Lesbian Archives of the Pacific Northwest, accessed December 20, 2013, www.glapn.org/1007glapnhistory.html.

23.   Associated Press, "Oregon to Register Same-Sex Marriages," *Washington Post*, July 10, 2004, A12, www.washingtonpost.com/wp-dyn/articles/A39903-2004Jul9.html.

24.   Li v. State of Or., No. 0403-03057 (4th J.D. Or., Apr. 20, 2004), https://www.aclu.org/files/FilesPDFs/bearden%20opinion.pdf.

25.   "Amends Constitution: Only Marriage Between One Man and One Woman Is Valid or Legally Recognized as Marriage," in "Initiative, Referendum and Recall: 2000–2004," Oregon Blue Book, http://bluebook.state.or.us/state/elections/elections22a.htm.

26.   Oregon Secretary of State, "November 2, 2004, General Election Abstract of Votes, State Measure 36," accessed May 6, 2014, www.oregonvotes.gov/doc/history/nov22004/abstract/m36.pdf.

27.   Li v. State of Or., 110 P.3d 91 (Or. 2005).

28.   Amanda Binder, "Guide to the Multnomah County (Or.) Wedding Album Project Records, 2004–2005," Northwest Digital Archives (NWDA), 2007, http://nwda.orbiscascade.org/ark:/80444/xv84834.

29.   Ibid.

30.   Les Zaitz, "Multnomah County's Same-Sex Marriage Controversy Puts Open Meetings Law in Limelight," *Oregonian*, March 12, 2004, accessed via Oregonlive.com on April 2, 2014, www.oregonlive.com/portland/index.ssf/2013/12/multnomah_countys_same-sex_mar.html.

31.   Tom Hyry and Michelle Light, "Colophons an Annotations: New Directions for the Finding Aid," *American Archivist* 65 (Fall/Winter 2002): 216–30.

32.   Jimerson, *Archives Power*, 290–95.

33.   "Proposition 8: Eliminates Right of Same-Sex Couples to Marry," California Online Voter Guide, November 2008 General Election, 17th Edition," California Foundation, www.calvoter.org/voter/elections/2008/general/props/prop8.html.

34.   Cascade AIDS Project Archives, home page, 2011, www.caparchives.org/home.

35.   Katie Lockwood, "Radical Library Crawl," message to Pdxrr mailing list, October 13, 2011, http://lists.radicalreference.info/pipermail/pdxrr/2011-October/000004.html.

36.   Tennessee Williams, *Camino Real* (New York: Dramatists Play Service, 1953), 24.

Bibliography

Adkins, Elizabeth W. "Our Journey towards Diversity—And a Call to (More) Action." *American Archivist* 71 (Spring/Summer 2008): 21–49.

Associated Press. "Oregon to Register Same-Sex Marriages." *Washington Post,* July 10, 2004, A12. www.washingtonpost.com/wp-dyn/articles/A39903-2004Jul9.html.

Baxter, Terry. "Going to See the Elephant: Archives, Diversity and the Social Web." *A Different Kind of Web: New Connections between Archives and Our Users,* edited by Kate Theimer, 74–303. Chicago: Society of American Archivists, 2011.

———. "I <3 Equality." *Beaver Archivist* (blog). February 2, 2009. http://terryx.wordpress.

com/2009/02/11/i-3-equality.

Binder, Amanda. "Guide to the Multnomah County (Or.) Wedding Album Project records, 2004-2005." Northwest Digital Archives (NWDA), 2007. http://nwda.orbiscascade.org/ark:/80444/xv84834.

Brown, Aimee. "How Queer 'Pack Rats' and Activist Archivists Saved Our History: An Overview of Lesbian, Gay, Bisexual, Transgender, and Queer (LGBTQ) Archives, 1970-2008." In *Serving LGBTIQ Library and Archives Users: Essays on Outreach, Service, Collections and Access*, edited by Ellen Greenblatt, 121–35. McFarland, 2010.

Clare, Eli. *Exile and Pride: Disability, Queerness, and Liberation*. Cambridge, MA: South End Press, 1999.

Dusty Archive Kitten Deaths. Tumblr site, accessed January 16, 2014, http://dustyarchivekitten-deaths.tumblr.com.

Gay and Lesbian Archives of the Pacific Northwest. "A History of GLAPN." Accessed December 20, 2013. www.glapn.org/1007glapnhistory.html.

Greene, Mark A. "A Critique of Social Justice as an Archival Imperative: What Is It We're Doing That's All That Important?" *American Archivist* 76 (Fall/Winter 2013): 302–34.

Halsey, Meredith. "The Popular Perception of Archivists." *Meredith Halsey* (blog), February 1, 2014. http://meridithhalsey.wordpress.com/2014/02/01/the-popular-perception-of-archivists.

Hyry, Tom, and Michelle Light. "Colophons and Annotations: New Directions for the Finding Aid." *American Archivist* 65 (Fall/Winter 2002): 216–30.

Jimerson, Randall C. *Archives Power*. Chicago: Society of American Archivists, 2009.

———. "Archivists and Social Responsibility: A Response to Mark Greene." *American Archivist* 76 (Fall/Winter 2013): 335–45.

Keisling, Phil. *Voters Pamphlet: State of Oregon General Election November 3, 1992*. Salem: State of Oregon, 1992. http://library.state.or.us/repository/2010/201003011350161/ORVPGen-Mari1992.pdf.

Kilgannon, Corey. "New York Court Archivist Isn't Letting Retirement Stop Him." *New York Times*, January 31, 2014. www.nytimes.com/2014/02/02/nyregion/new-york-court-archi-vist-isnt-letting-retirement-stop-him.html.

Li v. State of Or., 110 P.3d 91 (Or. 2005).

Li v. State of Or., No. 0403-03057 (4th J.D. Or., Apr. 20, 2004). https://www.aclu.org/files/FilesPDFs/bearden%20opinion.pdf.

Nikola, George T. "How the Oregon LGBT Movement Was Born." Gay and Lesbian Archives of the Pacific Northwest, last revised July 30, 2013. www.glapn.org/6130nicolagaymovement.html.

Oregon Secretary of State. "November 2, 2004, General Election Abstract of Votes, State Measure 36." Accessed May 6, 2014. www.oregonvotes.gov/doc/history/nov22004/abstract/m36.pdf.

Prairienet. "Community Archives Approach." 2011. www.prairienet.org/op/digarch/approaches-for-smaller-community-institutions/community-archiving.

Samtani, Hiten. "The Anarchists: Who Owns the Occupy Wall Street Narrative?" *Brooklyn Ink*, December 26, 2011. http://thebrooklynink.com/2011/12/26/39230-the-anarchists-who-owns-the-occupy-wall-street-narrative.

Theimer, Kate. "What Is the Meaning of Archives 2.0?" *American Archivist* 74 (Spring/Summer 2011): 58–68.

Zinn, Howard, "Secrecy, Archives, and the Public Interest." *Midwestern Archivist*. 2, no. 2 (1977): 20–21.

CHAPTER 7

Unpacking Identity

Racial, Ethnic, and Professional Identity and Academic Librarians of Color

Isabel Gonzalez-Smith, Juleah Swanson, and Azusa Tanaka

In 2007, an Association of College and Research Libraries white paper on racial and ethnic diversity in academic librarianship noted, "Although the current environment for recruitment, retention, and advancement of people of color in academic librarianship remains virtually unchanged since the appearance of the 2002 ACRL White Paper,[1] methods and strategies for addressing the issue seem to be evolving."[2] Unfortunately, the same can be said in 2013, which raises the question of why, in spite of evolving efforts, does racial and ethnic diversity among academic librarians remain virtually unchanged?

Despite an abundance of existing literature on diversity in libraries, we lack a multidimensional view on the experiences of academic librarians of color, thus calling for a different lens in research. To get to the root of diversity issues, we must first begin to understand the vocabulary, theory, and context that shape the discussions of diversity, race, and ethnicity in our profession. By applying identity theory, academic librarianship stands to increase its understanding of the success of diversity initiatives and the impact diversity has on its professionals. This exploratory chapter serves as an introduction to racial, ethnic, and professional identity theory to allow us to dig into the deeper, more imperative questions about the experiences of academic librarians of color.

In 2012, the American Library Association released the results of a 2009–2010 "comprehensive study of gender, race, age, and disability in the library profession"[3] entitled *Diversity Counts*, which found that only 13.9 percent of academic librarians are nonwhite.[4] Disappointingly, the number of nonwhite academic librarians in 2010 decreased by 0.5 percent from the *Diversity Counts* figures in 2000* while the percentage of nonwhites in the United States population increased 20.5% from 2000 to 2010.[5]

Meanwhile, the number of students of color enrolled in college grew 56 percent, whereas the percentage of white students within the total college student population dropped from 67 percent to 58 percent.† For academic librarians, these changing demographics suggest that the student bodies they support are increasingly diversifying. However, as Lorna Peterson critiques, analysis of changing demographics does not tell the full story of what is occurring on campuses and in libraries across the country: "History shows that it is not numbers that dictate the distribution of power and resources."[6] The demographics in higher education of students, faculty, and librarians are not a sufficient indicator of whether or not academic libraries provide effective services to all students and faculty. How can we even begin to understand our students and faculty if we do not yet acknowledge the complexities of race and ethnicity within our profession?

To illustrate the sometimes invisible or overlooked dynamics of race within libraries, in 2004, John Berry compiled a formative list of examples modeled after the classic article by Peggy McIntosh entitled, "White Privilege: Unpacking the Invisible Knapsack."[7] In his list, Barry exposed commonplace examples of white privilege in libraries such as, "I am never asked in my profession to speak for all the people of my racial group."[8] In an article on the invisibility of race in library and information science,

---

* Table B-5 in the *Diversity Counts* update indicates that 14.4 percent of librarians in higher education were nonwhite in 2000. The total of nonwhite librarians in higher education in 2009–2010 was 13.9 percent according to Table A-5 American Library Association, "Table A-5: Number of Higher Education Credentialed Librarians by Characteristic, 2009–2010" and "Table B-5: Number of Higher Education Credentialed Librarians by Characteristic, 2000," in *Diversity Counts* 2012 update (Chicago: American Library Association, 2012), www.ala.org/offices/sites/ala.org.offices/files/content/diversity/diversitycounts/diversitycountstables2012.pdf.

† Enrollment growth data for students of color is from 2001 to 2011. White student percentage of total student population data is from 1998 to 2008. Young M. Kim, *Minorities in Higher Education* (Washington, DC: American Council on Education, 2011), 2-3, http://diversity.ucsc.edu/resources/images/ace_report.pdf.

Todd Honma asks, "Why is it that scholars and students do not talk openly and honestly about issues of race and LIS? Why does the field have a tendency to tiptoe around discussing race and racism, and instead limit the discourse by using words such as 'multiculturalism' and 'diversity'? Why is the field so glaringly white, yet no one wants to talk about whiteness and white privilege?"[9]

The questions Honma raises are a call for greater understanding and more meaningful conversations about diversity among librarians. Yet when we begin to consider this call to action, we are faced with more questions.

How does diversity impact the academic librarian's sense of self? More specifically, how do academic librarians of color perceive themselves in a predominantly white profession, and how can we interpret these perceptions to better understand their experiences? The library profession actively encourages diversity through initiatives such as recruitment, residency programs, scholarships, and mentorship to attract and retain librarians of color. As the statistics previously indicated, in spite of ongoing recruitment and retention efforts, the percentage of academic librarians of color in the profession has decreased. Why is this occurring? Perhaps by looking through the lens of identity theory, we will be able to shed light on the experiences of academic librarians of color and how these experiences shape the profession.

Though we want to be able to answer these questions, we cannot begin to conduct meaningful research in this area until we first explore the theoretical foundations of such questions. We must first understand what identity theory is and how professional, racial, and ethnic identities shape our sense of self. By developing a foundational understanding of identity theory, we, as academic librarians, gain a greater context for previous studies and can move forward with future research on diversity within the library profession.

This chapter presents exploratory work on professional, racial, and ethnic identity theory and its application in our understanding of diversity and academic librarianship. To supplement research on identity theory, academic librarians of color were asked to share their experiences in the profession in their own words. Alongside the discussions of identity theory, quotes and anecdotes are found throughout this chapter, in italics, from academic librarians of color. Although these anecdotes may better explain the material, each is a unique story rather than a generalizable statement. The thoughts and experiences of one academic librarian of color cannot speak for all academic librarians of color. The combination of theory and personal narratives serves as a starting point for facilitating future conversations about race, diversity, and academic librarianship.

Words Matter: Race, Ethnicity, and People of Color

Throughout this chapter, we intentionally use the term *librarian of color,* derived from the idiomatic phrase *people of color.* To better understand the history and meaning of the term *people of color,* we begin by looking at the evolution and implications of race and ethnicity.

These two words, *race* and *ethnicity,* have been manipulated, altered, and redefined multiple times over the course of American history as snapshots of society's categorization of its own people. One example is the origin of the term *Hispanic,* coined by the Richard Nixon administration for the 1970 census.[10] In 2003, the *New York Times* reported that the US Census Bureau declared Hispanics the largest minority group, clarifying this population as an ethnicity, not a race.[11] In another elaboration of racial and ethnic classification, Paul Leung describes the "artificial categorization" of Asian Pacific Islanders that "lumps" various groups under one label.[12] Leung also draws parallels to people labeled black, stating, "Blacks, too, are not homogenous, with cultural variations of origin in Africa, the West Indies, or the Caribbean as well as geographical differences in the United States."[13]

In 1994, the *New Yorker* published a powerful piece by Lawrence Wright that expanded on the fierce history of racial and ethnic classifications controlled by the United States government.[14] Wright supports claims that racial and ethnic classifications essentially represent politics. Data and statistics are created and utilized in a way that end up shaping American identities and result in "political entities" with representation, lobbying interests, and social/political/economic needs. These examples illustrate the argument that race and ethnicity are synthetic and amorphous by nature. In other words, just as Dewey is a classification system for books, we use and manipulate race as a classification system for people.

Not only are race and ethnicity fabricated categories, they lack consistent and replicable meaning over time. Across professions, the inconsistent construction and use of race and ethnicity is problematic. Anthropologists have critiqued race as "not a biological fact but a social fact, a social construction."[15] Some psychologists have called *race* and *ethnicity* sociopolitical and sociocultural terms with inconsistent definitions and multiple influences.[16] Other psychologists have expressed concern with the treatment of *race* and *ethnicity* as interchangeable terms because their definitions have morphed and evolved multiple times over social history.[17] Finally, doctors and health professionals have also critiqued the lack of a scientific basis for racial and ethnic classification, which has resulted in varying definitions, lack of consensus on terminology, data collection inconsistencies, problems of misclassification, inaccurate counting, and much more.[18]

Some may interpret *people of color* to denote African Americans, while others assume it implies the actual color of your skin. Although its origins stem from the abolition era in the United States and later the African American community, the term *people of color* has evolved into a sociopolitical idiom of unity and solidarity among marginalized racial and ethnic communities.[19] The term goes beyond, and replaces, the meaning of *minority* or *nonwhite*.[20]

In 1988, William Safire's "On Language: People of Color" in *The New York Times* emphasized that "people of color … should not be used as a synonym for black."[21] The contemporary meaning of *people of color* took shape after the development of the term *women of color*. Loretta Ross, a reproductive justice activist and scholar, asserts that the origin of the phrase *women of color* took place during discussions at the National Women's Conference in 1977, where coalition building among racial and ethnic delegate groups began to take shape.[22] The term *people of color* draws upon the intentions of the phrase *women of color* as a means of coalition building and invoking solidarity.

The library profession has adopted similar terminology. The phrase *librarians of color* has been used increasingly to include underrepresented racial and ethnic groups in the profession. In 1972, E. J. Josey, a black librarian and activist, published "What Black Librarians Are Saying," in which Vivian D. Hewitt used the phrase *librarians of color* in reference to "minority" people.[23] Since 2006, the Joint Conference of Librarians of Color (JCLC) has convened twice with the sponsorship of five American Library Association ethnic caucuses.* These affiliate groups originate from the 1970s as a response "to a perceived lack of support inside the ALA in dealing with the many issues affecting underrepresented librarians and users."[24] In 1998, the American Library Association established the Spectrum Initiative with aims to address "the underrepresentation of librarians of color within the current workforce."[25] These are only a few examples of how the library profession has addressed diversity initiatives using *librarians of color* to identify librarians from underrepresented groups. The vocabulary used in the profession to describe diversity issues, initiatives, and stakeholders reflects the climate of not only the library sphere but also parent institutions and American society.

In researching this chapter, the authors discovered that a concise, accessible definition of *person of color* was difficult to find. The definition given in the *Sage Encyclopedia of Race, Ethnicity, and Society* most closely resembled our understanding of *person of color* as referring to racial and ethnic minority groups.[26] Thus, to best express our understanding of the term *person of color*, we, the authors, define the term beyond the literal color of one's skin. We are defining the term as referring to individuals who reside in the United States and who belong to minoritized racial and ethnic groups, including but not limited to African, African American, Alaskan Native, Arab, Asian, Latino, Native American, Pacific Islander, and multiracial.

Some argue that the phrase *people of color* is limited. One argument is that the term lumps diverse identities into one mass, overlooking the unique experiences among the various racial and ethnic identities, as well as the racism that can exist within and among these communities.[27] The term cannot be used carelessly, ignoring the fact that our ethnic and racial differences are what create our sense of identity and individual or communal narratives. It does not touch upon intricacies and issues like colonization, diaspora, indigeneity, immigration, nationality, and so much more. Still, the term is useful because it invites conversation regarding our groups' histories, struggles, politics, and status.

Since 1997, the US Census has abided by the standards for race and ethnicity as provided by the US Office of Management and Budget that categorizes America's diverse population into five main categories individuals can self-identify from: *White, Black* or *African American, American Indian or Alaskan Native, Asian,* and *Native Hawaiian or Other Pacific Islander.*[28] Race and ethnicity are social constructs, and the terms we use to describe ourselves racially and ethnically bear more psychological meaning than scientific merit.[29] They lack significance without human influence. When we asked academic librarians of color to use their own words to claim their racial or ethnic identity, the responses demonstrated the dynamic and dramatically multidimensional ways we self-identify given an open forum sans check boxes:

> *Puerto Rican from New York City*

> * * *

> *African-American, West Indies heritage, first generation American*

> * * *

> *Ipai/Kumeyaay westerners call us Native American*

Words do matter. They matter in the construction of our identities, how others define us, and how we choose to self-identify in a greater context. Like the words we choose to identify, define, and categorize ourselves, identity is complex, varied, and dynamic.

Identity Theory
What Is Identity?

Identity is the complex understanding of the fundamental question "Who are you?"[30] "Identities are inescapably *both* personal *and* social not only in their content, but also in the processes by which they are formed, maintained, and changed over time."[31] Each person has multiple forms of an identity existing individually, relationally, or socially, like gender, race, religion, ethnicity, sexuality, place of residence, profession, etc.

For the purposes of this chapter, the most prominent elements of identity theory to understand are these:

1. Identity is always in flux, with different meanings in various contexts and times.

2. Individuals develop a sense of self within a social context as intimate as family or school and as grand as government or history.[32]

We shape our understandings of who we are, or our sense of self, based on our social surroundings at every level. Though multiple forms of identity shape our sense of self, in this chapter we focus on two categories—professional identity and racial and ethnic identity—to build an understanding of how these identities can shape the sense of self among academic librarians of color.

Professional Identity

Unlike a job that an individual simply performs to fulfill a necessity like paying the bills, what distinguishes a profession from an occupation is that participants are expected to develop an identity based on the work, position, and values of that profession.[33] Values constructed by a profession may guide its professionals. For example, doctors are guided by professional values outlined in the Hippocratic Oath and library professionals find guidance through values outlined in the American Library Association Code of Ethics. A few academic librarians of color shared how the library profession is incorporated into their sense of self:

> *Being a librarian is more than a job to me; it is part of my identity.*

* * *

> *[Librarianship has] definitely impacted my professional sense of self, as I have found great personal fulfillment working in this profession.*

Becoming a professional involves more than education or the attainment of specialized knowledge. One study on professional identity among female lawyers found that "successful participation in the field involves more than the simple acquisition of legal skills; it also requires the assimilation of a range of corporeal and psycho-social characteristics."[34] These findings are key. To be socialized into a profession, one "must master a particular substantive body of knowledge, and [one] must internalize an appropriate professional identity."[35] Therefore, to be successful as an academic librarian, as with any profession, one must not only acquire the necessary skills and knowledge for the job, but also assimilate the characteristics, values, and norms of the profession. As an example, one academic librarian of color shared how values have shifted since joining the profession:

> *I think being an academic librarian makes me think about some*
> *issues that I had not really pay [sic] too much attention to before,*
> *such as censorship, or academic freedom.*

As academic librarians, we can be at different levels of professional identity formation and development. "Professional identity forms over time with varied experiences and meaningful feedback."[36] Some may feel a strong identity as an academic librarian while others may feel this professional identity is less salient.

The library itself is a site for professional identity formation. "All professions and individual workplaces are systems of power relations and, hence, important sites of identity formation."[37] Yet, as Honma suggests, a critical look into the sociopolitical history of libraries reminds us of the library's past as a place of exclusion rather than inclusion—as we want it to be today.[38] In 1972, James R. Wright, a black librarian, recounted an adolescent memory of being turned away from the public library "because I was born black in America," a reminder that libraries have participated in systems of racial power and oppression.[39] For one academic librarian of color, this history still resonates:

> *I feel librarianship has made my sense of identity stronger. As a*
> *graduate student I learned that libraries contributed a lot to the*

> *fight for intellectual freedom … and that libraries are an example*
> *of the constitution at work (information access, privacy, etc.). At the*
> *same time, I learned that these great public institutions, which now*
> *do so much for the freedom and equality for their users, were not*
> *above limiting information access for minorities during and before*
> *the civil rights era. Now, as a librarian of color, I feel I have a little*
> *bit more of an obligation to provide a consistent and equal level of*
> *service in each interaction with a member of the community.*

What happens when an individual's values come into conflict with the profession or place of work or library in which one is employed? When comparing the values of an individual to the values or culture of an organization, "Organizational culture is probably the more powerful force, which means that if persons for various reasons can *not* move to another organization, they will probably be subjected to strong pressures to conform to that culture and to change their own value system."[40]

Academic libraries, as workplaces situated within larger institutions, have their own value systems and structures of power and reward, such as the tenure system, that contribute to the professional identity of the librarians employed there. Power and reward structures in an organization contribute to a type of "psychological contract" between an employee and employer. Edgar Schein outlines the psychological contract in his classic text on employee-employer relationships:

> Through various kinds of symbolic and actual events, a "psy-
> chological contract" is formed which defines what the employ-
> ee will give in the way of effort and contributions in exchange
> for … organizational rewards in the form of pay and benefits
> and an organizational future in the form of a promise of pro-
> motion or other forms of career advancement. This contract is
> "psychological" in that the actual terms remain implicit; they
> are not written down anywhere.[41]

This means that an implicit system of contributions and rewards exists and functions between an employer and an employee. For example, though there may be explicit terms on conducting research and publishing for promotion or tenure of an academic librarian, there may also be implicit expectations that these contributions focus on specific topics within the field or be published in certain prestigious journals.

Research on the tenure system in higher education suggests that the value placed on the contributions of faculty of color may carry unequal weight in comparison to contributions from white counterparts. "White faculty who have historically dominated the power brokers of higher education institutions are more likely to fit into and perpetuate previously defined research agendas and values."[42] In academic librarianship, a study by Damasco and Hodges found that many academic librarians of color perceive race as a reoccurring factor that influences their ability to achieve tenure and promotion. Examples include selection of service and committee work, barriers to research and publication, and access to mentorship.[43] These findings suggest that people of color find remnants of exclusion and discrimination embedded within the reward structure and organizational values of academia and academic libraries.

Damasco and Hodges recommend a mutual understanding between libraries and academic librarians on the definition of value in the tenure and promotion process: "Library faculty of color must find ways to demonstrate the value … and library administrators must actively appraise and promote diversity research, service, and programming within the larger organizational culture."[44] The library profession should question how academic librarians of color are impacted by a possible disconnect between their values and the values of the institution. How does a librarian of color navigate the development of a professional identity when one's values may not align with those of the institution?

Racial and Ethnic Identity

A common misconception lies in the belief that *race* and *ethnicity* are interchangeable terms. The distinction between racial and ethnic identities of people of color are similarly misunderstood. It is important to recognize the distinction between the two concepts in order to begin to understand how they may impact the experiences of academic librarians of color.

Racial identity theory "emphasizes the manner in which individuals respond to and internalize their actions to sociopolitical conditions of oppression."[45] In the context of librarianship, one academic librarian of color shared,

> When you are an African American librarian, you stand out. For good or bad, you stand out.

For this particular librarian, identity is influenced by what it means to be African American as well as what it means to be a professional in the library world. Racial identity refers to how individuals psychologically develop responses to socially constructed messages of race dominance and nondominance. Furthermore, racial identity models developed by psychologists elaborate that racial identity is "the process of development by which individual members of the various socioracial groups overcome the version of internalized racism that typifies their group in order to achieve a self-affirming and realistic racial-group or collective identity."[46] In short, people can experience their sense of racial identity on a spectrum, from self-loathing due to racism projected onto them to pride in identifying with one's racial group.

An individual can experience racism in many forms that can be explicit or not. Racial microaggressions are implicit, daily slights and negativities toward people of color, done by individuals who communicate, intentionally or unintentionally, messages of racism either verbally or behaviorally.[47] A few academic librarians of color recounted experiences of microaggressions at the workplace:

> When patrons or guests ask to speak to an administrator or manager (I am a library director) and they seem surprised when I introduce myself as such.

* * *

> [A student] asked to speak to a "real librarian'" [...] not sure if it is because I looked young, or wasn't an old white lady, but he had a

hard time believing I was a librarian. My coworker also felt that it
was because I was a person of color.

As psychologists Helms and Cook state:

> The racial identity models are intended to describe the process
> of development by which individual members of the various
> socioracial groups overcome the version of internalized racism
> that typifies their group in order to achieve a self-affirming and
> realistic racial-group of collective identity. The need for suck
> development exists because society differentially rewards or
> punishes members of societally ascribed racial groups accord-
> ing to their racial classifications.[48]

In short, members of socioracial groups who experience racism, directly or indirectly, develop mechanisms and responses to such experiences that to one degree or another impact their racial identity.

An example of a response individuals feel in relation to their racial
identity is the feeling of isolation when functioning in a larger, dominant
society. This is illustrated when some academic librarians of color expressed that they felt isolated working in a dominantly white profession:

> *I feel more like a foreigner in a very strange land in [the] library*
> *world.*

* * *

> *I feel more disconnected from my cultural heritage because of the*
> *homogenous community and lack of diversity in my institution and*
> *profession.*

Yet our individual experiences are multidimensional and dynamic.
Therefore, racial identity is not a static concept but has stages or levels of
development varying among individuals. This means that some academic
librarians of color may have a strong racial identity, that is, a strong sense
of racial self, while others do not.

Racial identity theory focuses on the large-scale, societal impact race has on an individual; ethnic identity theory focuses closer to home. Ethnic identity touches on the degree to which individuals identify with the values, norms, languages, and beliefs of their particular ethnic group.[49] Notions of belonging, membership, group affiliation, and emotional connection and commitment to one's ethnic group all fall under ethnic identity.[50] Examples of this in the library profession are the ALA ethnic caucuses, which function as products of ethnic group affiliation and provide librarians with a sense of support and community. Some academic librarians of color shared their feelings of belonging and association:

> *[I] have met some wonderful people through ALA, JCLC, and RE-FORMA that have probably "boosted" my "ethnic" identity.*

* * *

> *The Spectrum community has helped to foster my positive ethnic identity.*

* * *

> *Meeting other people of mixed racial backgrounds who do not look "ethnic." It's made me feel less alone and more empowered.*

Furthermore, another study on ethnic identity measured and compared the ethnic identity scores—measures of the ability to relate oneself to one's own ethnic background—of African American, Asian American, Hispanic, and white high school students. This research found that ethnic minority groups had significantly higher ethnic identity scores than their white counterparts.[51] It is possible, then, that ethnic identity could resonate strongly within the sense of self of an academic librarian of color.

Ethnic identity theory can be used in practice to better understand and develop recruitment and mentoring opportunities for academic librarians of color. In *Pathways to Progress: Issues and Advances in Latino Librarianship,* Ortega and Ramos describe a need for Latino librarians to proactively recruit and mentor Latino library science students in a "disproportionately white" profession.[52] They argue that recruiting individuals with the language skills and cultural understanding of this particular ethnic group helps to better serve the growing Latino population in the United States. What this proposed recruiting and mentoring strategy taps into is an understanding of ethnic identity theory and the sense of belonging it can invoke. Ortega and Ramos also note that not every Latino speaks Spanish, illustrating the point that not only does the profession need more diversity, it requires diversity within all of its possible ranges.

Ortega and Ramos also encourage increasing the visibility of librarianship by promoting awareness of the profession to Latinos as early as high school. If we apply ethnic identity theory, we can understand the importance of students and future librarians seeing people of their same ethnic group as librarians already in the profession. Therefore, increasing the visibility of such role models will increase the chances that students of color in higher education will find the profession a welcoming, supportive, and viable career choice. Sergio Chaparro notes, "I strongly believe that recruitment for the LIS profession has its base in the visibility factor. The more we see Latinos in the profession, the more compelled we feel to emulate their efforts."[53]

Ethnic identity theory can also be applied in our understanding of librarian-student interactions. In 2012, a study on academic librarian approachability tested variables such as race/ethnicity, age, and gender and revealed that race does indeed play a role in the patron's perception of the librarian.[54] Subjects identified with librarians who most resembled their own racial/ethnic characteristics and rated those librarians as the most approachable. The researchers further connected librarian approachability to student retention and academic success, especially for students of color, who use the library more often than their white peers.[55] Again, Ortega and Ramos suggest a model for mentoring students where "a minority faculty member is matched with a similar minority student" and state that such models "create a nurturing relationship where a faculty member will support and advise the student."[56] The experience of one academic librarian of color illustrates a supportive relationship that is fostered with students of the same background:

> When I conduct instruct [sic] sessions where first-generation students are present, I am more conscious and able to relate to their personal experiences and particular information literacy challenges. Because of our similar backgrounds I tend to better understand and relate to their college experience....

Using the ethnic identity lens, we can understand how a relationship between mentor and mentee or instructor and students of shared ethnic backgrounds can be nurturing, providing both parties with a strong sense of community, belonging, support, and contribution. It is important to note, however, that racial and ethnic identity frameworks address the emotional and mental impact of an individual's experience of being part of racial and ethnic groups; they do not measure behaviors or actions.

Finally, Stephen Quintana, a counseling psychologist, summarized racial and ethnic identity theories and models into five major points:

1. Individuals explore racial/ethnic identity and develop an ethnic group consciousness during adolescence.

2. Encounters with racism trigger racial identity exploration and movement through development levels.

3. Racial identity development ranges from self-loathing to positive identification or pride in one's racial group.

4. Adolescents are prepared by others to develop an awareness of racial discrimination they will or may experience.

5. Racial and ethnic identity development occurs in various levels or stages.[57]

For academic libraries, it is important not only to understand racial and ethnic identity theory, but also to distinguish between the two in order to more accurately address the specific needs of both academic librarians of color and students of color. To consider both racial and ethnic identity is to recognize a more holistic approach to diversity in academic libraries.

Identity Is Multidimensional

These theories alone may be digestible and relatively comprehensible, but when we begin to look at each identity theory in relation to others, the notion of identity becomes much more complex. As illustrated throughout this chapter, many elements can impact how individuals self-identify, such as time, history, generation, size of community, and geography or region.[58] The freedom to claim one's identity, particularly racially and ethnically, can be empowering for people of color. We saw examples of this earlier when librarians of color provided rich responses to a question on self-identification of one's race or ethnicity. A recent piece on National Public Radio featured a young Dominican Republic woman who "came out" as racially black and culturally Latina.[59] Her story and others illustrate that our identities as individuals are claimed, dynamic, and subject to change as well as coexisting with other aspects of identity.

Because identities come in a multitude of forms coexisting with one another, a person can have a gendered, religious, racial, ethnic, political, and professional identity all at the same time. Sociologist Cary Costello describes three different concepts on how multidimensional identities may coexist. The first concept is the idea that identities seamlessly blend "like ingredients mixed together in just the right proportions to create a unique cake of selfhood."[60] In other words, our identity is singular, an amalgamation of all our identities, mixed into one self.

The second concept states that identities are contextual, existing only within the space and time of a given context.[61] For example, one academic librarian of color revealed,

> I am multiracial & multiethnic, and how I identify changes depending on who I am with and where in the world I am.

The idea of identity as contextual and the librarian's acknowledgement of mediating a contextual identity suggest that what we look like and who we are physically may not influence our identity at every moment. Instead, "context shapes and influences the salience of a racial or ethnic identity."[62]

The third, and perhaps more complex and nuanced, concept of identity is one where identities are independent of one another and possibly change over time, creating the potential for either harmony or conflict with other independent identities:

> The self is like a room full of furniture. Each piece of furniture is an identity.... Some identities are always found in the room, like grandma's rocking chair, but others are more like a trendy zebra-striped footstool: unlikely to be there in ten years.... Just as grandma's rocking chair and the trendy footstool coexist awkwardly, so can one's religious identity and one's sexual identity, or one's racial identity and one's professional identity.[63]

As stated earlier, identity is always in flux, like a room with trendy furniture and old furniture, rearranged and changing over time.

This chapter touches upon only a small fraction of identity for academic librarians of color: race, ethnicity, and professionalism. However, we must remember and acknowledge that the salience of any particular aspect of an individual's sense of self will vary. For some librarians, their sexual, political, or gender identity deeply enriches and impacts their experience in the workplace more than their race. We must understand that identity is never static but ever dynamic.

Conclusion

The number of academic librarians of color in the profession is disproportionately small compared to the diverse student bodies we are charged with serving. A new approach to diversity literature is the application of professional, racial, and ethnic identity theory. Much like the term *people of color*, identity theories carry a practicality. Identity theories get to the psychological root of how an individual forms their sense of self and continues to function in society. As individuals, we form our identities from many avenues and messages, including the vocabulary used by others to identify who you are in society. Terminology, history, statistics, and institutional structures all play a role in a complex system that impacts individuals in one shape or another.

As people of color enter and work in the predominantly white profession, the library field should question what impact the disproportionate representation has on its existing professionals and on potential librarians. The lenses of professional, racial, and ethnic identity allow us to, first, recognize and, second, begin to understand the experiences librarians of color may have and carry. To strengthen diversity initiatives of the library profession, we must understand what shapes people's sense of self, what strengthens it, what challenges it, and what supports it. Although these models do not explain social injustices, discrimination, racism, and prejudice, they do provide us with tools for understanding the experiences carried by people of color who are affected in one way or another by these factors.

Identity theories allow us to look further into how these experiences impact librarians of color and their perceptions of working within the library profession. This chapter has been intended to clarify why words matter, what identity theories are, and how they can be applied. Future qualitative research can apply the identity theories outlined in this chapter and begin to discern whether a pattern of common experiences exists among academic librarians of color. We hope to continue this conversation on race and diversity within the profession through further research, and we hope you, too, will join us in exploring these complex issues in our profession.

Notes

1. Ad Hoc Task Force on Recruitment and Retention Issues, *Recruitment, Retention and Restructuring* (Chicago: Association of College and Research Libraries, 2002), www.ala.org/acrl/proftools/recruiting/recruitment.
2. Teresa Y. Neely and Lorna Peterson, *Achieving Racial and Ethnic Diversity among Academic and Research Librarians,* white paper (Chicago: Association of College and Research Libraries, 2007), 8, www.ala.org/acrl/sites/ala.org.acrl/files/content/publications/whitepapers/ACRL_AchievingRacial.pdf.
3. "Diversity Counts," American Library Association, accessed April 25, 2014, www.ala.org/offices/diversity/diversitycounts/divcounts.
4. American Library Association, "Table A-5: Number of Higher Education Credentialed Librarians by Characteristic, 2009–2010," in *Diversity Counts* 2012 update, (Chicago: American Library Association, 2012), www.ala.org/offices/sites/ala.org.offices/files/content/diversity/diversitycounts/diversitycountstables2012.pdf.

5. United States Census Bureau, "The White Population: 2010," *United States Census Bureau*, September 2011, http://www.census.gov/prod/cen2010/briefs/c2010br-05.pdf, 3, table 1.

6. Lorna Peterson, "Alternative Perspectives in Library and Information Science: Issues of Race," *Journal of Education for Library and Information Science* 37, no. 2 (1996): 172.

7. Peggy McIntosh, "White Privilege: Unpacking the Invisible Knapsack," *Peace and Freedom*, July/August 1989, 9–10, reprinted in *Independent School* 49, no. 2 (1990): 31–35.

8. John Berry, "White Privilege in Library Land," *Library Journal* 129, no. 11 (2004): 50.

9. Todd Honma, "Trippin' over the Color Line: The Invisibility of Race in Library and Information Studies," *InterActions: UCLA Journal of Education and Information Studies* 1, no. 2 (2005): 1, http://escholarship.org/uc/item/4nj0w1mp.

10. Francesca A. Jenkins, "Latinos, Hispanics, or What?" *Hispanic Outlook in Higher Education* 19, no. 14 (2009): 17.

11. Lynette Clemetson, "Hispanics Now Largest Minority, Census Shows," *New York Times*, January 22, 2003, www.nytimes.com/2003/01/22/us/hispanics-now-largest-minority-census-shows.html.

12. Paul Leung, "Multicultural Competencies and Rehabilitation Counseling/Psychology," in *Handbook of Multicultural Competencies in Counseling and Psychology 2003*, ed. Donald B. Pope-Davis et al. (Thousand Oaks, CA: Sage Publications, 2003), 449.

13. Ibid.

14. Lawrence Wright, "One Drop of Blood," *New Yorker*, July 1994, 46–55.

15. Isabel Espinal, "A New Vocabulary for Inclusive Librarianship: Applying Whiteness Theory to Our Profession," in *The Power of Language/Poder de la Palabra*, ed. Lillian Castillo-Speed (Englewood, CO: Libraries Unlimited, 2001), 134.

16. Janet E. Helms, "Some Better Practices for Measuring Racial and Ethnic Identity Constructs," *Journal of Counseling Psychology* 54, no. 3 (2007): 236, doi:10.1037/0022-0167.54.3.235; Janet E. Helms and Regine M. Talleyrand, "Race Is Not Ethnicity," *American Psychologist* 52, no. 11 (1997): 1247, doi:10.1037/0003-066X.52.11.1246; Stephen M. Quintana, "Racial and Ethnic Identity: Developmental Perspectives and Research," *Journal of Counseling Psychology* 54, no. 3 (2007): 259.

17. Helms and Talleyrand, "Race Is Not Ethnicity," 1246.

18. Robert A. Hahn and Donna F. Stroup, "Race and Ethnicity in Public Health Surveillance: Criteria for the Scientific Use of Social Categories," *Public Health Reports* 109, no. 1 (1994): 7.

19. Salvador Vidal-Ortiz, "People of Color," in *Encyclopedia of Race, Ethnicity, and Society*, ed. Richard T. Schaefer, (Thousand Oaks, CA: Sage Publications, 2008), 1037–38.

20. Ibid., 1038.

21. William Safire, "People of Color," On Language, *New York Times Magazine*, November 20, 1988, www.nytimes.com/1988/11/20/magazine/on-language-people-of-color.html?src=pm.

22. Andrea Plaid, "For Your Women's History Month: Loretta Ross on the Origin of 'Women of Color,'" *Racialicious* (blog), March 3, 2011, www.racialicious.com/2011/03/03/for-your-womens-history-month-loretta-ross-on-the-origin-of-women-of-color; "Document 25: The Minority Caucus: It's Our Movement Now," in *How Did the National Women's Conference in Houston in 1977 Shape a Feminist Agenda for the Future?* ed. Thomas Dublin, Stephanie Gilmore, and Kathryn Kish Sklar (Binghamton: State University of New York at Binghamton, 2004), 156–57.

23. Vivian D. Hewitt, "Special Libraries, Librarians and the Continuing Education of Black People," in *What Black Librarians Are Saying*, ed. E. J. Josey (Metuchen, NJ: Scarecrow, 1972),

273.

24. Alma C. Ortega and Marisol Ramos, "Recruiting and Mentoring: Proactive Mentoring: Attracting Hispanic American Students into Information Studies," in *Pathways to Progress*, ed. John L. Ayala and Salvador Güereña (Santa Barbara, CA: Libraries Unlimited, 2012), 104.

25. "Spectrum—Scholarship Overview," American Library Association, accessed May 7, 2014, www.ala.org/offices/diversity/spectrum/scholarshipinformation.

26. Vidal-Ortiz, "People of Color," 1037–38.

27. Janani, "What's Wrong with the Term 'Person of Color'?" *Black Girl Dangerous* (blog), March 20, 2013, www.blackgirldangerous.org/2013/03/20/2013321whats-wrong-with-the-term-person-of-color.

28. United States Census Bureau, "About Race," *Census.gov*, accessed May 10, 2014, http://www.census.gov/population/race/about.

29. Jean S. Phinney, "When We Talk about American Ethnic Groups, What Do We Mean?" *American Psychologist* 51, no. 9 (1996): 918.

30. Vivian L. Vignoles, Seth J. Schwartz, and Koen Luycks, "Introduction: Toward an Integrative View of Identity," in *Handbook of Identity Theory and Research*, ed. Vivian L. Vignoles, Seth J. Schwartz, and Koen Luycks (New York: Springer, 2011), 2, doi:10.1007/978-1-4419-7988-9_1.

31. Ibid., 5.

32. Hardin L. K. Coleman et al., "An Ecological Perspective on Cultural Identity Development," in Pope-Davis et al., *Handbook of Multicultural Competencies*, 40.

33. Cary Gabriel Costello, *Professional Identity Crisis* (Nashville, TN: Vanderbilt University Press, 2005), 17.

34. Hilary Sommerlad, "'Becoming' a Lawyer: Gender and the Processes of Professional Identity Formation," in *Calling for Change*, ed. Shelia McIntyre and Elizabeth Sheehy (Ottawa, ON: University of Ottawa Press), 165, http://muse.jhu.edu/books/9780776615530.

35. Carrie Yang Costello, "Changing Clothes: Gender Inequality and Professional Socialization," *NWSA Journal* 16, no. 2 (2004): 153.

36. Herminia Ibarra, "Provisional Selves: Experimenting with Image and Identity in Professional Adaptation," *Administrative Science Quarterly* 44, no. 4 (1999): 765.

37. Sommerlad, "'Becoming' a Lawyer," 159.

38. Honma, "Trippin' over the Color Line."

39. James R. Wright, "The Public Library and the Black Experience," in *What Black Librarians Are Saying*, ed. E. J. Josey (Metuchen, NJ: Scarecrow, 1972), 224.

40. Edgar H. Schein, *Career Dynamics* (Reading, MA: Addison-Wesley, 1978), 83.

41. Ibid., 112.

42. Uma M. Jayakumar et.al., "Racial Privilege in the Professoriate: An Exploration of Campus Climate, Retention, and Satisfaction," *Journal of Higher Education* 80, no. 5 (2009): 556, doi:10.1353/jhe.0.0063.

43. Ione T. Damasco and Dracine Hodges, "Tenure and Promotion Experiences of Academic Librarians of Color," *College and Research Libraries* 73, no. 3 (2012): 294.

44. Ibid.

45. Alvin N. Alvarez and Erin F. Kimura, "Asian Americans and Racial Identity: Dealing with Racism and Snowballs," *Journal of Mental Health Counseling* 23, no. 3 (2001): 194.

46. Janet E. Helms and Donelda A. Cook, *Using Race and Culture in Counseling and Psychotherapy* (Boston: Allyn and Bacon, 1999), 84.

47. Derald Wing Sue et al., "Racial Microaggressions in Every Life: Implications for Clinical Practice," *American Psychologist* 62, no. 4, (2007): 271.

48. Ibid.
49. Alvarez and Kimura, "Asian Americans and Racial Identity," 194.
50. Glenn Gamst, Christopher T. H. Liang, and Aghop Der-Karabetian, *Handbook of Multicultural Measures* (Thousand Oaks, CA: Sage Publications, 2011), 89.
51. Frank C. Worrell, "Ethnic Identity, Academic Achievement, and Global Self-Concept in Four Groups of Academically Talented Adolescents," *Gifted Child Quarterly* 51, no.1 (2007): 24, doi:10.1177/0016986206296655.
52. Ortega and Ramos, "Recruiting and Mentoring," 104–5.
53. Sergio Chaparro, "Common Denominators in the Development of Latino Library Leadership," in *Pathways to Progress: Issues and Advances in Latino Librarianship*, ed. John L. Ayala and Salvador Güereña (Santa Barbara, CA: Libraries Unlimited, 2012), 2.
54. Jennifer L. Bonnet and Benjamin McAlexander, "Structural Diversity in Academic Libraries: A Study on Librarian Approachability," *Journal of Academic Librarianship* 38, no. 5 (2012): 282.
55. Ibid., 284.
56. Ortega and Ramos, "Recruiting and Mentoring," 113.
57. Quintana, "Racial and Ethnic Identity," 259.
58. Joseph E. Trimble, Janet E. Helms, and Maria P. P. Root, "Social and Psychological Perspectives on Ethnic and Racial Identity," in *Handbook of Racial and Ethnic Minority Psychology*, ed. Guillermo Bernal et al., (Thousand Oaks, CA: Sage Publications, 2003), 240.
59. NPR Staff, "A Latina Teen 'Comes Out' as Black," *Code Switch: Frontiers on Race, Culture, and Ethnicity* (blog), June 6, 2013 (6:56 p.m.), National Public Radio, www.npr.org/blogs/code switch/2013/06/06/189305074/a-latina-teen-comes-out-as-black.
60. Costello, *Professional Identity Crisis*, 24.
61. Ibid.
62. Gamst et al., *Handbook of Multicultural Measures*, 91.
63. Costello, *Professional Identity Crisis*, 24.

Bibliography

Ad Hoc Task Force on Recruitment and Retention Issues. *Recruitment, Retention and Restructuring: Human Resources in Academic Libraries*. Chicago: Association of College and Research Libraries, 2002. www.ala.org/acrl/proftools/recruiting/recruitment.

Alvarez, Alvin N., and Erin F. Kimura. "Asian Americans and Racial Identity: Dealing with Racism and Snowballs." *Journal of Mental Health Counseling* 23, no. 3 (2001): 192–206.

American Library Association. "Diversity Counts." Accessed April 25, 2014. www.ala.org/offices/diversity/diversitycounts/divcounts.

———. *Diversity Counts* 2012 update. Chicago: American Library Association, 2012. www.ala.org/offices/sites/ala.org.offices/files/content/diversity/diversitycounts/diversitycountstables2012.pdf.

———. "Spectrum—Scholarship Overview." Accessed May 7, 2014. www.ala.org/offices/diversity/spectrum/scholarshipinformation.

Berry, John D. "White Privilege in Library Land." *Library Journal* 129, no. 11 (2004): 50.

Bonnet, Jennifer L., and Benjamin McAlexander. "Structural Diversity in Academic Libraries: A Study on Librarian Approachability." *Journal of Academic Librarianship* 38, no. 5 (2012): 277–286.

Chaparro, Sergio. "Common Denominators in the Development of Latino Library Leadership." In *Pathways to Progress: Issues and Advances in Latino Librarianship*, edited by John L. Ayala and Salvador Güereña, 1–6. Santa Barbara, CA: Libraries Unlimited, 2012.

Clemetson, Lynette. "Hispanics Now Largest Minority, Census Shows." *New York Times*. January 22, 2003. www.nytimes.com/2003/01/22/us/hispanics-now-largest-minority-census-shows.html.

Coleman, Hardin L. K., Romana A. Norton, Gina E. Miranda, and Laurie McCubbin. "An Ecological Perspective on Cultural Identity Development." In *Handbook of Multicultural Competencies in Counseling and Psychology*, edited by Donald B. Pope-Davis, Hardin L. K. Coleman, William Ming Liu, and Rebecca L. Toporek, 38–58. Thousand Oaks, CA: Sage Publications, 2003.

Costello, Carrie Yang. "Changing Clothes: Gender Inequality and Professional Socialization." *NWSA Journal* 16, no. 2 (2004): 138–55.

Costello, Cary Gabriel. *Professional Identity Crisis: Race, Class, Gender, and Success at Professional Schools*. Nashville, TN: Vanderbilt University Press, 2005.

Damasco, Ione T., and Dracine Hodges. "Tenure and Promotion Experiences of Academic Librarians of Color." *College and Research Libraries* 73, no. 3 (2012): 279–301.

"Document 25: The Minority Caucus: It's Our Movement Now." In *How Did the National Women's Conference in Houston in 1977 Shape a Feminist Agenda for the Future?* edited by Thomas Dublin, Stephanie Gilmore, and Kathryn Kish Sklar, 156–57. Binghamton: State University of New York at Binghamton, 2004.

Espinal, Isabel. "A New Vocabulary for Inclusive Librarianship: Applying Whiteness Theory to Our Profession." In *The Power of Language/Poder de la Palabra: Selected Papers from the Second REFORMA National Conference*, edited by Lillian Castillo-Speed, 131–49. Englewood, CO: Libraries Unlimited, 2001.

Gamst, Glenn, Christopher T. H. Liang, and Aghop Der-Karabetian. *Handbook of Multicultural Measures*. Thousand Oaks, CA: Sage Publications, 2011.

Hahn, Robert A., and Donna F. Stroup. "Race and Ethnicity in Public Health Surveillance: Criteria for the Scientific Use of Social Categories." *Public Health Reports* 109, no. 1 (1994): 7–15.

Helms, Janet E. "Some Better Practices for Measuring Racial and Ethnic Identity Constructs." *Journal of Counseling Psychology* 54, no. 3 (2007): 235–46. doi:10.1037/0022-0167.54.3.235.

Helms, Janet E., and Donelda A. Cook. *Using Race and Culture in Counseling and Psychotherapy: Theory and Process*. Boston: Allyn and Bacon, 1999.

Helms, Janet E., and Regine M. Talleyrand. "Race Is Not Ethnicity." *American Psychologist* 52, no. 11 (1997): 1246–47. doi:10.1037/0003-066X.52.11.1246.

Hewitt, Vivian D. "Special Libraries, Librarians and the Continuing Education of Black People." In *What Black Librarians Are Saying*, edited by E. J. Josey, 268–74. Metuchen, NJ: Scarecrow, 1972.

Honma, Todd. "Trippin' over the Color Line: The Invisibility of Race in Library and Information Studies." *InterActions: UCLA Journal of Education and Information Studies* 1, no. 2 (2005): 1–26. http://escholarship.org/uc/item/4nj0w1mp.

Ibarra, Herminia. "Provisional Selves: Experimenting with Image and Identity in Professional Adaptation." *Administrative Science Quarterly* 44, no. 4 (1999): 764–91.

Janani. "What's Wrong with the Term 'Person of Color'?" *Black Girl Dangerous* (blog), March 20, 2013. www.blackgirldangerous.org/2013/03/20/2013321whats-wrong-with-the-term-person-of-color.

Jayakumar, Uma M., Tyrone C. Howard, Walter R. Allen, and June C. Han. "Racial Privilege in the Professoriate: An Exploration of Campus Climate, Retention, and Satisfaction." *Journal of Higher Education* 80, no. 5 (2009): 538–63. doi:10.1353/jhe.0.0063.

Jenkins, A. Francesca. "Latinos, Hispanics, or What?" *Hispanic Outlook in Higher Education* 19, no. 14 (Apr 20, 2009): 16–18.

Kim, Young M. *Minorities in Higher Education, Twenty-Fourth Status Report, 2011 Supplement.* Washington, DC: American Council on Education, 2011. http://diversity.ucsc.edu/resources/images/ace_report.pdf.

Leung, Paul. "Multicultural Competencies and Rehabilitation Counseling/Psychology." In *Handbook of Multicultural Competencies in Counseling and Psychology*, edited by Donald B. Pope-Davis, Hardin L. K. Coleman, William Ming Liu, and Rebecca L. Toporek, 439–55. Thousand Oaks, CA: Sage Publications, 2003.

McIntosh, Peggy. "White Privilege: Unpacking the Invisible Knapsack." *Peace and Freedom*, July/August 1989, 9–10, reprinted in *Independent School* 49, no. 2 (1990): 31–35.

National Public Radio. "A Latina Teen 'Comes Out' as Black," *Code Switch: Frontiers on Race, Culture, and Ethnicity* (blog), June 6, 2013 (6:56 p.m.). www.npr.org/blogs/codeswitch/2013/06/06/189305074/a-latina-teen-comes-out-as-black.

Neely, Teresa Y., and Lorna Peterson. *Achieving Racial and Ethnic Diversity among Academic and Research Librarians: The Recruitment, Retention, and Advancement of Librarians of Color,* white paper. Chicago: Association of College and Research Libraries, 2007. www.ala.org/acrl/sites/ala.org.acrl/files/content/publications/whitepapers/ACRL_AchievingRacial.pdf.

Ortega, Alma C., and Marisol Ramos. "Recruiting and Mentoring: Proactive Mentoring: Attracting Hispanic American Students into Information Studies." In *Pathways to Progress: Issues and Advances in Latino Librarianship*, edited by John L. Ayala and Salvador Güereña, 103–24. Santa Barbara, CA: Libraries Unlimited, 2012.

Peterson, Lorna. "Alternative Perspectives in Library and Information Science: Issues of Race." *Journal of Education for Library and Information Science* 37, no. 2 (1996): 163–74.

Phinney, Jean S. "When We Talk about American Ethnic Groups, What Do We Mean?" *American Psychologist* 51, no. 9 (1996): 918–27.

Plaid, Andrea. "For Your Women's History Month: Loretta Ross on the Origin of 'Women of Color.'" *Racialicious* (blog), March 3, 2011. www.racialicious.com/2011/03/03/for-your-womens-history-month-loretta-ross-on-the-origin-of-women-of-color.

Quintana, Stephen M. "Racial and Ethnic Identity: Developmental Perspectives and Research. "*Journal of Counseling Psychology* 54, no. 3 (2007): 259–70.

Safire, William. "People of Color." On Language, *New York Times Magazine*, November 20, 1988. www.nytimes.com/1988/11/20/magazine/on-language-people-of-color.html?src=pm.

Schein, Edgar H. *Career Dynamics: Matching Individual and Organizational Needs.* Reading, MA: Addison-Wesley, 1978.

Sommerlad, Hilary. "'Becoming' a Lawyer: Gender and the Processes of Professional Identity Formation." In *Calling for Change: Women, Law, and the Legal Profession*, edited by Shelia McIntyre and Elizabeth Sheehy, 159–77. Ottawa, ON: University of Ottawa Press, 2006. http://muse.jhu.edu/books/9780776615530.

Sue, Derald Wing, Christina M. Capodilupo, Gina C. Torino, Jennifer M. Bucceri, Aisha M. B. Holder, Kevin L. Nadal, and Marta Esquilin. "Racial Microaggressions in Every Life: Implications for Clinical Practice." *American Psychologist* 62, no. 4, (2007): 271–86.

Trimble, Joseph E., Janet E. Helms, and Maria P. P. Root. "Social and Psychological Perspectives on Ethnic and Racial Identity." In *Handbook of Racial and Ethnic Minority Psychology*, edited by Guillermo Bernal, Joseph E. Trimble, Ann Kathleen Burlew, and Frederick T. Leong, 239–75. Thousand Oaks, CA: Sage Publications, 2003.

United States Census Bureau. "About Race." *Census.gov*, Accessed May 10th, 2014. http://www. census.gov/population/race/about/.

United States Census Bureau, "The White Population: 2010," *United States Census Bureau*, September 2011, http://www.census.gov/prod/cen2010/briefs/c2010br-05.pdf.

Vidal-Ortiz, Salvador. "People of Color." In *Encyclopedia of Race, Ethnicity, and Society*, edited by Richard T. Schaefer, 1037–38. Thousand Oaks, CA: Sage Publications, 2008.

Vignoles, Vivian L., Seth J. Schwartz, and Koen Luycks. "Introduction: Toward an Integrative View of Identity." In *Handbook of Identity Theory and Research*, edited by Vivian L. Vignoles, Seth J. Schwartz, and Koen Luycks, 1–30. New York: Springer, 2011. doi:10.1007/978-1-4419-7988-9_1.

Worrell, Frank C. "Ethnic Identity, Academic Achievement, and Global Self-Concept in Four Groups of Academically Talented Adolescents." *Gifted Child Quarterly*, 51, no.1 (2007): 23–38. doi:10.1177/0016986206296655.

Wright, James R. "The Public Library and the Black Experience." In *What Black Librarians Are Saying*, edited by E. J. Josey, 220–26. Metuchen, NJ: Scarecrow, 1972.

Wright, Lawrence. "One Drop of Blood." *New Yorker*, July 25, 1994, 46–55.

CHAPTER 8

Librarians and Felines

A History of Defying the "Cat Lady" Stereotype

Dorothy Gambrell and Amanda Brennan

T'S EASY TO SEE HOW THEY COLLIDED. LIBRARIES HAVE BEEN HOME TO CATS SINCE THE MIDDLE AGES WHEN MONKS KEPT THEM AROUND THE MONASTERY AS HUNTERS, PROTECTING THEIR PRECIOUS MANUSCRIPTS FROM BEING EATEN BY MICE.[2]

THIS PRACTICE CONTINUED THROUGH THE 1800S IN GREAT BRITAIN, WHERE LOCAL GOVERNMENTS WOULD PAY LIBRARIES TO HOUSE THESE TINY, FURRY PREDATORS. [3]

FELINES PROTECTING LITERATURE BECAME A PERMANENT FIXTURE WITH THE OPENING OF THE NEW YORK PUBLIC LIBRARY'S MAIN BRANCH ON MAY 23, 1911.[4] THOUGH MODELED AFTER MUCH LARGER CATS, THE MARBLE STATUES SERVE AS GUARDIANS OF THE KNOWLEDGE HOUSED INSIDE THE LIBRARY.

IN 1908, WHILE THE NYPL WAS IN THE LATE STAGES OF ITS CONSTRUCTION, TWO BACTERIOLOGISTS AT THE PASTEUR INSTITUTE IN TUNISIA CAME ACROSS A NEW ORGANISM THEY NAMED TOXOPLASMA GONDII. [5]

IN 1970, GROUPS OF INDEPENDENT SCIENTISTS DISCOVERED THE ORGANISM COULD BE PASSED TO HUMANS VIA CAT FAECES.[6]

IN JANUARY 2013, THE CENTER FOR DISEASE CONTROL CONCLUDED MORE THAN 60 MILLION AMERICANS CARRIED TOXOPLASMA GONDII. [7] RECENT RESEARCH HAS LINKED T. GONDII WITH A NUMBER OF DISEASES INCLUDING SCHIZOPHRENIA, OCD AND ADHD.[8]

BUT JULIA CHILD [9] AND FLORENCE NIGHTINGALE [10] WERE BOTH KNOWN FOR THEIR DEEP FONDNESS OF CATS. KATY PERRY NAMED HER CAT KITTY PURRY AFTER HER STAGE NAME.[11]

CATS ARE KNOWN FOR THEIR SASSY PERSONALITIES, CURIOUS DEMEANORS, AND PASSION FOR KNOCKING EVERYTHING OFF A TABLE.

WHILE WE MAY NOT BE MUMMIFYING OUR CATS LIKE THE ANCIENT EGYPTIANS (LIKE ONE THAT IS CATALOGED IN NEW YORK'S CAZENOVIA LIBRARY [12]),

CLAP CLAP CLAP

and LIKE THE INTERNET

CAT PHOTOS LURK IN EVERY CORNER OF THE INTERNET.

LIBRARIES HAVE BEEN HOMES TO MANY CATS.

SQUEAKERS CALLED WILLET MEMORIAL LIBRARY AT WESLEYAN COLLEGE HIS HOME FROM 1985-2008. [13]

IN 1987, BRYANT PUBLIC LIBRARY'S CAT REGGIE [14] CAUSED LIBRARIAN PHYLLIS LAHTI TO LAUNCH THE LIBRARY CAT SOCIETY, BUILDING CONNECTIONS BETWEEN LIBRARIES WHO HAD CATS RESIDING IN THEIR STACKS.

THE MOST FAMOUS OF THESE CATS IS DEWEY READMORE BOOKS [15], WHO WAS FOUND FROSTBITTEN AND HUNGRY IN IOWA'S SPENCER PUBLIC LIBRARY IN 1988.

LIBRARIAN VICKI MYRON TOOK HIM IN, GIVING HOPE TO A TOWN HIT HARD BY AN ECONOMIC CRISIS. DURING HIS RESIDENCY, DEWEY BECAME A COMPANION FOR MANY LOCALS, INCLUDING THE RETIRED PATRONS WHO BEGAN STAYING AT THE LIBRARY LONGER AND THE HOMELESS MAN WHO WOULD PLACE DEWEY ON HIS SHOULDER AND TAKE HIM FOR WALKS AROUND THE STACKS. [16]

ONE FRIEND IN PARTICULAR WAS A MIDDLE SCHOOL STUDENT NAMED CRYSTAL. SHE WAS SEVERELY PHYSICALLY DISABLED AND WOULD OFTEN DO NOTHING BUT STARE AT THE FLOOR DURING HER LIBRARY VISITS.

DEWEY BEGAN TO JUMP ON HER WHEELCHAIR AS SHE CAME IN, GREETING HER WITH A SOFT PURR.

AS HER FRIENDSHIP WITH DEWEY GREW, SHE BEGAN TO SMILE MORE AND TAKE IN THE WORLD AROUND HER. LATER, SHE WOULD MAKE NOISES WHEN SHE ENTERED, CALLING TO DEWEY WHO WOULD RUN OVER AND JUMP IN HER LAP. [17]

AS STORIES LIKE THESE ABOUT DEWEY'S COMPANIONSHIP SPREAD, FANMAIL FROM AROUND THE GLOBE CAME POURING IN FOR THE CAT, FOLLOWED BY TOURISTS TRAVELING TO THE AREA TO GET A GLIMPSE OF DEWEY.

A COUPLE FROM NEW YORK SENT HIM MONEY EVERY YEAR ON CHRISTMAS AND HIS BIRTHDAY.

AFTER HIS DEATH IN 2006 AT AGE 19, MYRON RETIRED FROM THE LIBRARY. AT THE TIME OF HER RETIREMENT, SPENCER PUBLIC LIBRARY HAD 18,000 CARD-CARRYING MEMBERS [18], NEARLY TWICE THE TOWN'S POPULATION. SHE WENT ON TO WRITE FIVE BOOKS ABOUT DEWEY, ONE OF WHICH REACHED THE NEW YORK TIMES BEST-SELLER LIST.

THE MAGIC OF THIS LIBRARY CAT HAD SPREAD MUCH FARTHER THAN ANYONE COULD HAVE IMAGINED.

IF LIBRARIES AND THE INTERNET LOVE CATS SO MUCH, WHY HAS IT BECOME A NEGATIVE STEREOTYPE FOR LIBRARIANS, GUARDIANS OF THE WORLD'S INFORMATION, TO LOVE CATS TOO?

AS EARLY AS 2009 PEOPLE HAVE BEEN TRYING TO RECLAIM THE "CAT LADY" STEREOTYPE [19], INCLUDING CHICAGO LIBRARIAN ANNIE PHO.

SHE CHOSE THE HANDLE "CAT LADY LIBRARIAN" ON SOCIAL MEDIA AS A WAY OF OWNING BOTH STEREOTYPES. [20]

DESPITE THE FACT LIBRARIANS AND CAT LOVERS ALIKE ARE SEEN AS "UNDESIRABLE" [21], PHO DEFIES THESE NOTIONS BY NOT CONFORMING TO THE CLICHE IDEAS OF UNAPPROACHABLE SPINSTERS.

BY BUILDING STRONG CONNECTIONS WITH OTHER CAT-LOVING LIBRARIANS AND MAKING ADVANCES IN HER CAREER, PHO IS JUST ONE OF MANY LIBRARIANS WHO ARE DEDICATED TO CHANGING NEGATIVE IMPRESSIONS OF THE PROFESSION, ONE CAT AT A TIME.

Notes

1. Wikia, "Superman's Pal, Jimmy Olsen Vol 1 3," DC Comics Database, last modified June 6, 2013, http://dc.wikia.com/wiki/Superman%27s_Pal,_Jimmy_Olsen_Vol_1_3.
2. Allie B. Kagamaster, "History of Library Cats," Cat Channel, November 11, 2009, www.catchannel.com/magazines/catfancy/january-2010/history-of-library-cats.aspx.
3. Ibid.
4. "The Library Lions," New York Public Library, accessed September 14, 2013, www.nypl.org/help/about-nypl/library-lions.
5. J. P. Dubey, "History of the Discovery of the Life Cycle of *Toxoplasma gondii*," *International Journal for Parasitology* 39, no. 8 (2009): 877.
6. Ibid., 878.
7. "Parasites—Toxoplasmosis (*Toxoplasma* Infection)," Centers for Disease Control and Prevention, January 10, 2013, www.cdc.gov/parasites/toxoplasmosis.
8. Kathleen McAuliffe, "How Your Cat Is Making You Crazy," *Atlantic*, February 6, 2012, www.theatlantic.com/magazine/archive/2012/03/how-your-cat-is-making-you-crazy/308873.
9. Patricia Barey and Therese Burson, *Julia's Cats* (New York: Abrams Image, 2012).
10. Shana Lear, "Florence Nightingale's Felines," *Cat Fancy*, December 2011, www.catchannel.com/magazines/catfancy/december-2011/florence-nightingales-felines.aspx.
11. Stephanie Modkins, "Meet Kitty Purry, Singer Katy Perry's Cat," Examiner.com, February 27, 2010, www.examiner.com/article/meet-kitty-purry-singer-katy-perry-s-cat.
12. Mrs. Mecomber, "Egyptian Mummy at Cazenovia Library," New York Traveler, August 5, 2008, http://newyorktraveler.net/egyptian-mummy-at-cazenovia-library.
13. "Wesleyan's Library Cats," Wesleyan College, accessed September 14, 2013, www.wesleyancollege.edu/academics/library/cats.cfm.
14. Gary Roma, "Reggie," Iron Frog Productions, accessed September 14, 2013, www.ironfrog.com/librarycatsmap/mns-regg.html.
15. Dewey: The Small-Town Library Cat Who Touched the World, accessed September 14, 2013, www.deweyreadmorebooks.com.
16. Vicki Myron and Bret Witter, *Dewey's Nine Lives* (New York: New American Library, 2011), 4.
17. Ibid., 4.
18. Ibid., 19.
19. Nichole, "Cat Lady," *Feministe* (blog), July 17, 2009, www.feministe.us/blog/archives/2009/07/17/cat-lady.
20. Annie Pho, e-mail message to the author, February 3, 2013.
21. Annie Pho, e-mail message to the author, February 8, 2013.

Bibliography

Barey, Patricia, and Therese Burson. *Julia's Cats: Julia Child's Life in the Company of Cats*. New York: Abrams Image, 2012.

Centers for Disease Control and Prevention. "Parasites—Toxoplasmosis (*Toxoplasma* infection)." January 10, 2013. www.cdc.gov/parasites/toxoplasmosis/.

Dewey: The Small-Town Library Cat Who Touched the World. Accessed September 14, 2013. www.deweyreadmorebooks.com.

Dubey, J. P. "History of the Discovery of the Life Cycle of *Toxoplasma gondii*." *International Journal for Parasitology* 39, no. 8 (2009): 877–82.

Kagamaster, Allie B. "History of Library Cats." Cat Channel, November 11, 2009. www.catchannel.com/magazines/catfancy/january-2010/history-of-library-cats.aspx.

Lear, Shana. "Florence Nightingale's Felines." *Cat Fancy*, December 2011. www.catchannel.com/magazines/catfancy/december-2011/florence-nightingales-felines.aspx.

McAuliffe, Kathleen. "How Your Cat Is Making You Crazy." *Atlantic*, February 6, 2012. www.theatlantic.com/magazine/archive/2012/03/how-your-cat-is-making-you-crazy/308873.

Mecomber, Mrs. "Egyptian Mummy at Cazenovia Library." New York Traveler, August 5, 2008. http://newyorktraveler.net/egyptian-mummy-at-cazenovia-library.

Modkins, Stephanie. "Meet Kitty Purry, Singer Katy Perry's Cat." Examiner.com, February 27, 2010. www.examiner.com/article/meet-kitty-purry-singer-katy-perry-s-cat.

Myron, Vicki, and Bret Witter. *Dewey's Nine Lives: The Legacy of the Small-Town Library Cat Who Inspired Millions*. New York: New American Library, 2011.

New York Public Library. "The Library Lions." Accessed September 14, 2013. www.nypl.org/help/about-nypl/library-lions.

Nichole. "Cat Lady." *Feministe* (blog), July 17, 2009. www.feministe.us/blog/archives/2009/07/17/cat-lady.

Roma, Gary. "Reggie." Iron Frog Productions, accessed September 14, 2013. www.ironfrog.com/librarycatsmap/mns-regg.html.

Wesleyan College. "Wesleyan's Library Cats." Accessed September 14, 2013. www.wesleyancollege.edu/academics/library/cats.cfm.

Wikia. "Superman's Pal, Jimmy Olsen Vol 1 3." DC Comics Database. Last modified June 6, 2013. http:// dc.wikia.com/wiki/Superman%27s_Pal,_Jimmy_Olsen_Vol_1_3.

CHAPTER 9

Between Barbarism and Civilization

Librarians, Tattoos, and Social Imaginaries

Erin Pappas

The surface of the body, as the common frontier of society, the social self, and the psycho-biological individual; becomes the stage upon which the drama of socialization is enacted, and bodily adornment (in all its culturally multifarious forms, from body painting to clothing and from feather head-dresses to cosmetics) becomes the language through which it is expressed.

—Terry Turner, "The Social Skin."[1]

Body modifications, then, are always symbolic. That is to say, they stand for something beyond themselves.... The tattoo is not strictly itself, the ink under the skin.... [It is] a door that opens to a wonderland of ideas and memories, regrets and successes, and all the fear, hate, guilt, sin, love, sensitivity contained within.

—John A. Rush, *Spiritual Tattoo*[2]

Introduction: Whither Lydia?

Over the last few decades, tattoos have become ubiquitous. Once the exclusive provenance of sailors, bikers, convicts, strippers, and sideshow performers, they now adorn our athletes, pop stars, celebrity chefs, and artists. Despite the social prevalence of tattoos—a recent Harris Interactive survey places the number of Americans over age 18 with tattoos at 1 in 5, or roughly 20 percent of the adult population—they are still generally read as indicators of deviance.[3] The same survey reports that the non-tattooed are more likely than those with tattoos to have negative perceptions of those with ink, considering them more unstable and irresponsible.[4] Glossy magazines devoted to the art have been in circulation since the 1970s, now supplemented by dedicated blogs and Tumblr accounts; these, along with television programs such as *LA Ink* and *Miami Ink*, showcase designs of varying quality, origins, and style.[*] Online, user-submitted content is increasingly the norm; individuals are defined by the act of framing, in choosing what to reveal and what to conceal and how much personal information to disclose. Yet they cannot control the ways these images may spread and multiply. A picture posted on a niche Tumblr account may end up on BuzzFeed, a platform known for disseminating viral content. Such is the mimetic and meme-driven nature of the Internet. Pictures of tattoos adorning the bodies of regular people, not only celebrities, in this way circulate throughout the modern cultural landscape.

Though tattoos have been addressed in scholarship, especially in historical and anthropological literature, it is only in the last few decades that they have been seriously studied as part of an emergent Western tradition.[5] The genealogy of tattooing, in various eras and many cultures, points up the association with pathology: tattoos have been markers of

---

[*]   Magazines currently in circulation include *Skin Art, Inked, Tattoo Revue, Tattoo Flash, Skin & Ink, TATTOO, Inked, Urban!nk,* and a slew of trade publications. Tattoo conventions are also critical in the formation of the tattoo community. Online, the discourse and images proliferate still further. A search for "tattoo Tumblr" will turn up hundreds of unique blogs: those dedicated to tattoos worn by types of people—women, parents, hipsters, or people of color; to defining characteristics: "bad" ink, "quality" ink, traditional styles; and even to profession, such as the "Tattooed Librarians and Archivists" Tumblr (http://tattooedlibrariansandarchivists.tumblr. com), with an About banner that reads: "Hidden by white gloves, camouflaged by cardigans, or somewhere above sensible shoes is the tattooed librarian, archivist, or curator. Submit your ink today!"

deviance (as in subcultural or gang affiliation) or stigma (forms of mark-ing *qua* social control, where the body bears witness to a criminal past or prison stint) or signs of class (indicating abjection or certain labor practices).[†] Whenever the body can be "read" as a text of culture, nonnor-mative body projects like tattoos take on heightened import. From where we now stand, tattoos are paradoxically more mainstream while still car-rying a great deal of negative weight and semiotic baggage.[‡] The relative acceptability of tattoos is the result of a long discursive process whereby formerly deviant working-class practices have been appropriated and re-classified as "fine art."[§]

Scope Note: Method and Madness

In undertaking this project, I designed a survey with the specific intent of capturing narratively rich material coupled with basic demographic data. The survey instrument consisted of multiple-choice and open-ended questions and was an attempt to capture a snapshot of a population that is often speculated about (i.e., "tattooed librarians") but has not been in-terrogated directly. Obviously, the scope was limited from the outset, as I solicited the participation only of individuals who fit both the criteria of having tattoos and considering themselves librarians. The aims here were threefold: first, demographic, so as to gather concrete information about this population, rather than simply using available online images and commentary; second, semiotic, to elicit talk about particular signi-fiers that might or might not have bearing on professional personae; and

---

† For historical treatments of tattooing practices in Europe and America, see the essays in Jane Caplan, ed., *Written on the Body* (Princeton, NJ: Princeton University Press, 2000). Further read-ings can be gleaned from the bibliographies in Michael Atkinson, *Tattooed* (Toronto, ON: Uni-versity of Toronto Press, 2003), and Enid Schlidkrout, "Inscribing the Body," *Annual Review of Anthropology* 33 (2004): 319–44, both of which are less Eurocentric in their focus.

‡ In the project at hand, respondents posed similar questions. Why, they asked, should tattoos warrant such interest within the library profession when they are quite widespread in the popu-lace as a whole?

§ Consider, for instance, the way many elite tattoo artists look down on "flash" (standardized de-signs that adorn walls of tattoo parlors, from which customers can choose) and prefer to work with a client to design a custom piece. Custom work is as much a badge of uniqueness for the working artist as it is for the person whose body it will come to decorate.

third, discursive, in order to capture a particular sociohistoric moment in all its messy complexity. This analysis draws on my own theoretical background in linguistic anthropology and thus takes into account the self-perceptions of tattooed librarians, the discursive figurations they use to talk about themselves as subjects, and the ways in which they position others as social imaginaries.* More broadly, the project aims to situate the ways that seemingly frivolous conversations about tattooed librarians are actually part of a larger discourse about labor, gender, and subjectivity under late capitalism.†

The techniques here are those of the qualitative social scientist and humanities scholar, involving close reading of a small corpus of materials. Data for this project was gathered through a short survey designed with SurveyMonkey, which was then disseminated through the ALA Think Tank Facebook page (https://www.facebook.com/groups/ALAthink-TANK) and the Librarian Wardrobe Tumblr account (http://librari-anwardrobe.com). These two avenues of distribution proved more than adequate for the purposes of this project, given that its aim was (prelimi-nary) qualitative rather than (definitive) quantitative analysis.‡ In total, 184 responses were received. In no manner does this study purport to be

---

* Erving Goffman, *Frame Analysis* (Cambridge, MA: Harvard University Press, 1974). Drawing on Goffman, Michael Silverstein, and Mikhail Bakhtin, Paul Manning argues for a blurring of the distinction between "real" and "imagined" conversations, as the latter can provide ample insights into the implicit metapragmatic categories of the former (Paul Manning, "Barista Rants about Stupid Customers at Starbucks: What Imaginary Conversations Can Teach Us about Real Ones," Language and Communication 28 [2008]: 101–126).

† There is much to be said about the ways librarianship, as a heavily gendered vocational "calling," is complicit in the double bind of neoliberal personhood. For a more thorough analytic frame-work than I can provide here, see Maura Seale, "The Neoliberal Library," in *Information Literacy and Social Justice*, ed. Lua Gregory and Shana Higgins, 39-61 (Duluth, MN: Library Juice, 2013). It is worth noting many analyses rely on ontologies that treat gender as a given rather than taking it to be a socially constructed, ongoing, and performative facet that does not exhaust or define the subject. When I talk about "doing gender," it should be clear that the former belief is the commonly held cultural one, and the latter the one to which I hew. In the same vein, the concept of the social imaginary, in its historical specificity and broad application within social science, is teased out in the essays in Dilip Parameshwar Gaonkar and Benjamin Lee, eds., "New Imaginar-ies," special issue. Public Culture 14, no. 1 (2002).

‡ The bulk of the responses came within the first hour of posting. This was incredibly surprising, as I expected fewer than 50 people to respond in total, and also serves as a partial explanation as to why no other avenues (such as e-mail lists) were explored.

exhaustive in either scope or findings. Certainly the very social media vehicles used for distribution circumscribe the kind of respondents reached. By the same token, it would be methodologically naïve to assume that the experiences of 184 discrete respondents can stand in for a profession a thousand times larger than the sample size. Future work should and will interrogate intersections of class, sexuality, geography, and especially race in a more robust manner.

Ten questions comprised the survey material that undergirds this analysis, the first six of which gathered basic demographic information about age, gender, level of education, type of workplace, number of tattoos, and the age at which the respondent acquired their first tattoo. The final four questions were open-ended, asking respondents to describe their tattoos in terms of placement and design, what their tattoos meant to them, the reactions to their tattoos by others, and whether they considered "tattooed librarians" to be special.

Survey for Librarian Wardrobe

1. What is your gender?
    - Female
    - Male
    - Other (please specify)

2. What is your age?
    - 18 to 24
    - 25 to 34
    - 35 to 44
    - 45 to 54
    - 55 to 64
    - 65 to 74
    - 75 or older

3. What is the highest level of school you have completed or the highest degree you have received?
    - Less than high school degree
    - High school degree or equivalent (e.g., GED)
    - Some college but no degree

- Associate degree
- Bachelor degree
- Graduate degree
- PhD
- Other (please specify)

4. What type of library do you work in?
   - K-12
   - Public
   - Academic
   - Other (please specify)

5. How many tattoos do you have?
   - 1
   - 2
   - 3
   - 4
   - 5
   - More than 5

6. At what age did you get your first tattoo?

7. Describe your tattoos physically. (Placement, design, etc.)

8. Describe what your tattoos mean to you. (Meaning, significance, etc.)

9. How do others respond to your tattoos?

10. Is there something special about being a tattooed librarian?

The category of "librarian" was left purposefully underdetermined and kept separate from the degree obtained. In other words, librarian status was meant to be interpreted by the respondent rather than imposed by the categories of the survey. In other words, librarian status was meant to be interpreted by the respondent rather than imposed by the categories of the survey because the distinction between professional and paraprofessional staff, while important behind the scenes, does not typically enter into public perception. This divide also speaks to a larger debate about expert knowledge and the ways expertise is imagined, enacted, and performed.[6] Regardless of this lack of distinction, an overwhelming majority of the self-defined "librarian" respondents were also holders of master's and professional degrees: 87 percent of those surveyed held a master's. With regard to demographics, the respondents to this survey were also majority female, tended to work in academic or public libraries, and were predominantly between the ages of 25 and 44. The demographic information obtained correlates with information disseminated by ALA about the profession, though here a slightly higher percentage of respondents were female than in the profession overall (5 percent greater), and respondents tended to be younger than the identified mean age of 48.[*]

Of 184 respondents, 162 identified as female (88 percent), 21 as male (11.4 percent), and 1 as other (.6 percent, response given: "genderqueer"). The bulk of the respondents were between the ages of 25 and 34 (53 percent), with a slightly smaller grouping of 35-to-44-year-olds (32 percent). Those under the age of 25 (5.4 percent) and over the age of 45 (10 percent) made up the rest. The next question, answered by 182 of the respondents, concerned the number of tattoos that each individual had. By far, the highest concentration was for having a single tattoo: 56 respondents (31 percent) had only one; 46 respondents (25 percent) had two; 27 respondents (15 percent) had three; 11 respondents (6 percent), four; 6 respondents, (3 percent) five.

Interestingly, the numbers also clustered at the other end, given that 36 respondents (20 percent of the total) had more than five tattoos. Even this seemingly simple quantitative question invited commentary. Speaking through the comments and the expanded response sections, some people were unsure how to precisely quantify their tattoos—such as the 16 respondents with full or partial sleeves on their arms. Sleeves are intricate designs that can be expanded outward, covering ever-larger expanses of skin. Should this count as one big tattoo or many small ones? When visible, such designs clearly carry more communicative weight and visual impact than small black-ink tattoos that can be readily concealed.

---

[*] Note that the last large-scale survey conducted by ALA was in 1999. The profession reflected in my numbers is younger overall, though the profession at large may also be less gray than it was 15 years ago (Mary Jo Lynch "Age of Librarians," American Library Association, accessed October 15, 2013, www.ala.org/research/librarystaffstats/librarystaffstudies/ageoflibrarians).

In terms of age, the bulk of the respondents acquired their first tattoo prior to or during their early 20s. Breaking down the 180 responses received to that question by age bracket: 10 (5 percent) got their first tattoo before turning 18; 108 (60 percent) when they were between the ages of 18 and 23; 38 (21 percent) between the ages of 24 and 29; 13 (7 percent) between ages 30 and 35, 7 (3.8 percent) between ages 36 and 41; 3 (2 percent) between ages 42 and 47, and 3 (2 percent) after the age of 48. Looking at an even more granular level, the most prevalent age to get tattooed was 18, with 33 respondents (18 percent) reporting getting their first tattoo upon reaching the age when one may do so legally in the United States.* A few tentative conclusions can be drawn from this information. First, as this data set makes clear, the age when people got their first tattoo clearly falls at the younger end of the spectrum. Taken together, 65 percent of respondents were inked prior to the age of 24, which is prior to the onset of postgraduate study and subsequent professionalization. Taken as individuals, the librarians in this survey do not vastly differ from the broader demographic trend of North America, where approximately 20 percent of the adult population is tattooed. But as noted above, many respondents did not stop at just one tattoo, so at least some of these designs were undertaken as the respondent developed a professional role.

Bodies at Work

Communicative practice lies at the heart of tattooing, even if the tattoo is intended only as a message to oneself. Tattoos, however, carry different meanings for wearers and audiences. What role, if any, can tattoos play in the construction or dissemination of a professional persona? Given that the precepts of professionalism redirect focus away from the body as a source of labor, tattoos draw constant attention to the embodied self by being literally written on the skin. In the professional workplace, tattoos can impact relationships, perceptions, and paths to advancement. While generally outside the scope of this paper, a sizeable literature exists in the

---

* Geographic location was not part of the survey material. Despite using social media as the primary avenue of distribution, it seems reasonable to assume that most respondents are from the United States or, possibly, Canada.

field of human resources management about the practical implications of hiring individuals with tattoos.[7] For the employee, especially in the library field, guidebooks and manuals for the young professional can include tattoos in their purview: whether to have them, whether to hide them, and how they can impact working conditions and social relationships.[8] Even though tattoos are a by-now-prevalent middle-class practice, their relationship to particular forms of labor—gendered, embodied, and professional—is altogether less transparent, and, likewise, undertheorized.[†]

This subject may be familiar to those who follow professional e-mail lists, Facebook groups, opinion pieces, and blogs. In these places, discussions of what it means to be a librarian with tattoos, or the impacts and effects of tattooing on one's career, have been ongoing, with varying degrees of investment and interest.[‡] Still others express bafflement: why have tattoos, among all possible forms of body modification, become such a hot-button topic? The survey that forms the basis for this paper elicited similar responses. As one respondent put it, "No; I think it's ridiculous that it's become such a topic of interest. Is it a frenzied issue for those in other professions?" While forums do exist for talking about the acceptability of tattoos in other female-dominated professions, such as nursing, education, and social work, they appear less concerned with stereotypes per se and more caught up with the practical implications of visible ink on their job prospects.

As body modification, tattoos are unique because they are multivalent signs in ways that blue hair, a lip ring, or breast implants cannot be. While any of these may have personal import or provoke a response, tattoos invite complex semiotic readings that draw on pre-existing forms of iconography, narrative, and design. Tattoos can have multiple—simultaneously contradictory—meanings, depending on who is doing the interpreting. Thus while tattoos are "worn to be timeless and stable," they are still "sub-

---

† For more on the (gendered) body as a site of inscription, see Pippa Brush, "Metaphors of Inscription: Discipline, Plasticity, and the Rhetoric of Choice," *Feminist Review* 58 (Spring 1998): 22–43.

‡ For the purposes of this paper, I use the terms *tattooed librarian* and *librarian with tattoos* interchangeably. This heuristic helps simplify the analysis rather than the reality: not all who have tattoos have more than one, for instance, not all identify as librarians, and some may be engaged in different forms of labor but self-identify as librarians.

ject to extensive social, cultural, and individual polysemic and deconstructive readings that circumnavigate the wearer's intent with the choice of a design."[9] Tattoos are part of a broader class of signs with the potential for shifting signification: signs "which mean one thing to one group" can very easily "mean something else to another group, the same category being designated but differently characterized."[10] Owing to this semiotic richness, tattoos contain the fullest set of possibilities for (mis)interpretation. As with any form of adornment or decoration, tattoos have import beyond what a reductionist view implies.

Theorists have argued that in middle-class, postindustrial North America, tattoos are one of the ways in which individuals demarcate significant moments in their lives. Atkinson, for example, suggests that tattoos can harness the transformative power of rituals, that they "symbolically mark the passage from one self to another." Thus the tattoo is a "lasting reminder of the transition, and the manner in which the transition may be publicly communicated to others through bodily display."[11] Given the absence of socially pervasive rites of passage signifying the end of adolescence, individuals thus find their own way of marking their symbolic entry into adult society. Tattoos, being an increasingly common type of demarcation, can thus function as modern rites of passage. As the open-ended responses to this survey indicate, many respondents linked their tattoos to significant moments in their lives. The data about age strongly indicates that tattoos acquired in early adulthood might fulfill this role. More broadly, and as I explore more fully below, marking time and self in this manner crystallizes a type of highly individuated subject, one divorced from history, circumstance, and consequences, that both depends on and reinforces a neoliberal form of personhood.* Whether this can be classed as articulable desire on the part of the individual at the time, however, matters less than the way significant moments are taken up and incorporated into narrative trajectories that outline the self, foreground agency, and treat choices as purely a matter of individual will and desire.

---

* For purposes of this analysis, *neoliberalism* does not refer to the political economy of late capitalism per se, but rather denotes a kind of highly individuated subjectivity, one which exists apart from (and indeed, in spite of) the macro-level constraints of history, context, or society, albeit one that is made possible only under the conditions of late capitalism.

When asked how people responded to their tattoos, the answers were varied. Some took this as an opportunity to reinforce the distinction between the "work self" and the "real self." As Goffman points out in *Frame Analysis*, the ideas of self, stage, and role are themselves context-dependent:

> There is a relation between persons and role. But the relationship answers to the interactive system—to the frame—in which the role is performed and the self of the performer is glimpsed. Self, then, is not an entity half-concealed behind events, but a changeable formula for managing oneself during them. Just as the current situation prescribes the official guise behind which we will conceal ourselves, so it provides where and how we will show through, the culture itself prescribing what sort of entity we must believe ourselves to be in order to have something to show through in this manner.[12]

In these cases, the responses of patrons or coworkers were emphasized more strongly if those people saw the tattoos at all. A common practice was keeping the tattoo covered when in a professional setting or when the respondent did not want to engage in conversations about it. Indifference or disinterest were also common reactions, contrasting strongly with the narrative expectations of others. Other respondents mentioned the reaction of people in their lives to their ink. Parents and in-laws, especially, figured highly in these stories. Still others spoke explicitly about the ways patrons regarded their tattoos. In several cases, these interactions involved uninvited and unwanted commentary from (older, often male) patrons about the body of the (generally younger, female) librarian. A second trend, however, saw younger patrons responding positively to the body art of librarians, perhaps accompanied by verbal commentary signaling that individual's uniqueness compared to a (perceived) contrast set, i.e. "those other people who work here":

> Others respond pretty well. Sometimes people are very interested and complimentary, but of course, there are always people who do not like them. Sometimes at work I wear cardigans that cover my sleeve if I'm in a mood where I don't want to talk to someone about them. Yesterday I had a library patron ask to

see my arm and then he grabbed my wrist and flipped my arm around to see the other side. I don't really like it when people just take the initiative to grab me (it's art, but it's still attached to my body)! I just started library school at University of Wisconsin-Madison and the Director seemed very intrigued by all the tattoos in my incoming class. She seemed generally interested in tattoos and intrigued by them.

* * *

Living in a pretty conservative part of the country (southwest Missouri), people feel that they have the right to comment on my body and tattoos fairly often. Usually it's something like, "What's THAT supposed to be?", "Did that hurt?", or "Do you regret getting those?" Once while working with long sleeves (so my tattoos weren't visible) an older woman came up, gestured to a heavily tattooed teenager at the public computer, and loudly said, "Ugh, what would you do if that was your daughter?".

* * *

It varies. Mostly I get compliments. One coworker asked me (rather pointedly) if I regret my tattoos. Sometimes older male patrons make rude comments, but they also make rude comments about my age and hair, so they would probably be rude even if I didn't have tattoos.

* * *

Mostly people are curious, they ask if they hurt, why did I get them, what they mean. I've not had any negative responses. During my interview for my current library job, the assistant director said she thought my reader tattoo was awesome.

Responses to tattoos vary widely and depend on multiple contextual frames for their significance. In many cases, the person wearing the ink possesses the means to cover or conceal it, whether to discourage commentary, discussion, or debate, or simply express a preference for keeping the intimate self tucked away. These practices suggest that reactions and responses are dependent on multiple kinds of contexts: home and work; public and private; proximal and distal.

Making Narratives, Enacting Agency

For this project, a short survey seemed like a reasonable way of gathering information from far-flung individuals. It bears a superficial resemblance to ethnographies of virtual communities insofar as the informants are not co-located in space. The method, however, creates the appearance of community where none actually exists. Whereas blog commenters or e-mail list subscribers actively create communities of practice by way of regular, ongoing, and sustained interactions, that is not the case here. Ethnographies of tattooing have addressed this issue much more elegantly, in no small part by looking at the ways tattoo and community continually intersect and are re-created anew in physical and virtual spaces. In contrast, there is no "librarian tattoo community" to interrogate here. Its creation is merely an artifactual byproduct of the method, just as the "tattooed librarian" is much more a product of circulating discourses than it is a social reality.

Taking advantage of the open-ended questions, some respondents spelled out this distinction in more detail. When asked if there was anything special about being a tattooed librarian (Q10), the 171 responses were divided: 48 (28 percent) said "yes" agreed, 119 (79 percent) said "no," and 4 (2 percent) of the answers were ambiguous.[*] Approximately a third of the respondents saw a linkage between their profession and their tattoos, while the rest denied such an association. In the group that thought tattooed librarians were special, stereotypes were mentioned twice as often as in the second group. Those who didn't regard tattooed librarians as

---

[*] Looking at the data in retrospect, a forced choice between "yes" and "no" combined with space for an open-ended answer would have made the categorization much more straightforward. Were I to repeat this survey, I would also replace the word *special* with *interesting*, as the word invited antagonistic responses and made classification of the answers more difficult. The ambiguous answers were "Intrigue"; "researching for your next one is easier"; "never really thought about it"; and "lol."

special were also more likely to talk about their tattoos as having personal value—being "for the self"—rather than something to be shared with colleagues, coworkers, and patrons.

Several such respondents specifically mentioned that the decision to become a librarian was totally separate from their drive to get tattooed. Yet in the retelling, both of these decisions are framed by the rhetoric of individuation and personal choice:

> I don't know if it has so much to do with being a librarian. Although, I am a librarian and I love what I do, and most of them have root in literature of one form or another and history (not the dragon though, I just really wanted a big bad-ass dragon when I was 18). But my tattoos have been my shepherd through difficult times. So in a way, they helped to show me the way to myself. And somewhere in the middle of them I went to get my MLS and found what I was meant to do with my life. I've been trying to think of another tattoo that I might want for some time, but nothing has come to mind. Maybe I've found some peace through them, or maybe I'll wait until whatever comes next.

* * *

> Not really, maybe that's because I got my sleeve before I ever worked for the library. I knew it was something I always wanted and was intrigued by. I think if there's anything special about being a tattooed librarian it would be that we are breaking the old stereotypes of what a librarian should look like. In a broader sense, from a feminist perspective, I think being a tattooed woman is special and breaks stereotypes of traditional beauty, or what is beautiful in the eyes of the media. Last, I think libraries are so forward moving, and it works great to have a younger generation of librarians (tattoos or not) to be the advocates of what is to come.

* * *

Being tattooed is not related to my job as a librarian. I became a librarian to help people. When I am working with patrons I try to make sure I am always focused on the needs of the individual. I almost need to let my individuality fade away and just put myself in the patron's shoes. It's not about me, it's about them. That being said if a member has a question about tattoos I'll be glad to help them with any information I may have in the same way I would with music, gardening, raising ducks or any of my other interests.

* * *

I like to think that a tattoo is a long-term personal choice like getting married, having a child or adoption of a set of religious beliefs. All of these choices are special to the one choosing them, but I don't believe that a librarian with tattoos (or wearing a Star of David or a wedding ring) is any more or less special than one without.

* * *

Was tattooed long before being a librarian.—The tattoos are for myself, and not the general public. Mostly no-one sees them (and I don't have to explain)—I guess it's cool—but then it's cooler riding up to the library on my Ducati.

These responses create narratives that hinge on ideas of skin-bound personhood: tattoos are part of the individual's biography and body, but are not necessarily linked to their career. More than that, the tattoos have no other intended audience than the self; others who see them are merely incidental. A more subtle argument could be made for the highly individuated body as a site of inscription as a way of differentiating the "true self" from the "mass subject" prescribed by neoliberalism; yet, paradoxically, one can inhabit this position of subjectivity only within the precepts of neoliberalism.[13]

For the respondents who did find something special in being a tattooed librarian, the negation of stereotypes was a more common and explicit theme. Specifically, gendered stereotypes came under particular scrutiny. Some individuals inflected the gender distinction still further through the lenses of age, morality, or attitude. Though stereotypes were mentioned by both those who thought tattooed librarians were special and those who did not, those who found something special about the co-presence of tattoos and librarians were about twice as likely to mention them:

> I think it's unexpected, although three of my co-workers (all female librarians) also have tattoos, some of which are very elaborate and visible. It makes me laugh when I think about what a dichotomy there is between the more stereotypical image of [what] a librarian is and the one of a tattooed librarian. I think tattoos are becoming more culturally acceptable, but my colleagues and I all have ones that can easily be covered up if we are in a situation where they would be perceived as inappropriate or where we wouldn't want to be judged solely on the basis of our ink.

* * *

> There is, in the sense that it shows that not all librarians are stuffy old ladies who aren't up [to] date in the world. It gives us a different way to interact with patrons, and lets them know that we too have lives and interests and are progressive

* * *

> I like to think it makes me seem a little less like the stereotypical conservative, boring, no-fun librarian (I've been told I'm "too cool"/"too fun" to be a librarian, so that stereotype is definitely still alive and well).

* * *

> Tattooed librarians are a rebellion against the stereotypes of our profession. The epitomical image of a librarian is a sour-faced woman donning a severe bun and a cardigan. When people meet a tattooed librarian, it forces them to not only reconsider

their assumptions about the person, but about the library as an institution as well.

* * *

Being a tattooed librarian is awesome. I think it shows people that librarians can be more than just frumpy old ladies that remind you of your grandmother. It shows that librarians are a diverse and really interesting group of people!

* * *

I think there is something special about being a tattooed librarian, because they help break the mold or stereotypes people have about librarians, libraries, and even reading in general. I think it helps new generation relate to me in a different way than they may more conservative or traditional librarians.

* * *

Yes. It lends a sense of personal style & sense of individuality. It breaks with stereotypes of the "old fashioned" librarian.

Note that here the contrast set is between the speaking individual and the imagined figure of the "other," who is almost always described an older, uptight, sexless spinster. Once more, gender plays a paramount role in both the sides of this contrast set. The qualities of youthfulness, newness, and (presumably) self-determined sexuality are ascribed to the wearer of tattoos, who is a creature completely unlike the old-fashioned stereotype of the profession.

The language of these responses creates a narrative opposition between two kinds of librarians: "traditional" and "tattooed," which may simply be an echo of the current library discourse.* Origins aside, two different conceptual alignments emerge from these narrative responses. The first—around which clusters stronger language of selfhood, memory, and

---

* This argument is about narratives rather than practices; I am not imputing motives for tattooing.

identity— takes society at large as its frame of reference. Thus, librarians are not the contrast set: *everyone* is. And in the adult population at large, it would seem like "everyone has tattoos":

> No—a lot of people have tattoos. Also, I think people get overly excited about subverting the sexy-librarian stereotype. You have a tattoo—so does my grandfather—get over it.

* * *

> no more so than being a tattooed anything else! i don't really see how they intersect at all, except that "i have a tattoo" and "i am a librarian" are both true statements.

* * *

> Not particularly. I think it's special only because there are so many stereotypes about librarians and they tend to be rather feminine, and (traditionally) tattoos aren't feminine, at least in Western culture. However, I've never been particularly feminine, so I don't feel like there is a "stigma" to being tattooed. I dress rather conservatively, it's just who I am, not because I'm a librarian, so I think it's funny when people are shocked when I reveal my tattoos. But I feel like tats are becoming more and more common—or at least, more and more visibly common—and as we're part of the population, it's only natural that we would represent as much as any other profession.

* * *

> Not particularly! I think that it's probably quite common in the profession (and it's getting increasingly common in general anyway so I'm not sure that it's representative of anything more than that).

* * *

We are just like any other tattooed people, so no, I don't think so. Unless it shatters librarian stereotypes for someone, I don't find it to be a big deal. We are surrounded by tattooed people these days.

* * *

Lots of people have tattoos. Librarians still are seen in some areas of our culture as boring, staid, and not very interesting. Being tattooed makes me happy and being a librarian makes me happy and both make sense in my life.

* * *

I've never actually thought of myself as a tattooed librarian. I kind of always just thought that I'm [a] librarian who happens to have a few tattoos. I feel like it's more rare nowadays to not have tattoos so I don't see this as anything that special.

* * *

I think that we have to answer even more questions than non-tattooed librarians. But honestly, there are so many people with tattoos that it's hard to tie them all together by any one attribute.

The emergent subset in this case is not one of profession, but one of "regular people" who happen to have tattoos, which are themselves increasingly regular. This particular reading of body modification accomplishes two things. On the one hand, it points up individuality, where the skin-bound self makes choices for the self alone. And as socially acceptable, racially unmarked, middle-class practices, these choices are not understood as being constrained in any way.* At the same time, it implicitly acknowledges the capacity of other persons—other *selves*—to engage in the same kind

---

* The category of race was not addressed by the survey questions but would most likely prove fertile ground for future investigation.

of self-expression through ink. The person and the professional persona overlap only marginally.

Signs, Everywhere

Yet in practice, a few respondents noticed that the seemingly subversive image of the tattooed librarian was, in and of itself, becoming increasingly common. A few explicitly cautioned against what they saw as a prescriptive drive to dictate the appearances of others, as well as awareness that body policing goes both ways.

> No. I think it's dangerous to build a conception of what a librarian should look like, as if "real" librarians have certain characteristics, or "hip" librarians should look a certain way. I don't like to tie my own personal identity with my professional career.

* * *

> I really want a lit tattoo—I think I will "fit in" more with the scene with that ;)

* * *

> I don't think we are any different from non-tattooed librarians. I think what is really special is that tattoos almost make us not special—we're regular people just like tattooed doctors and gas station attendants and the ladies who sell things on QVC are regular people. Librarians have historically been perceived as shushing uptight bun heads, and tattoos may help distance ourselves from that image. Uptight people can't have tattoos, right? Also, I think a tattooed librarian may start to become the new stereotype, but at least that one sounds a little more fun.

* * *

> The one tattoo I have, and the others that I plan to get, are literary references. They obviously represent a love of and respect for

books and the written word. That is a big part of what made me want to be a public librarian in the first place.

Given that the types of tattoos were incredibly varied, only a small percentage of them could be immediately classified as being about librarianship, literature, or, more broadly, information. Some common themes do emerge, which align rather neatly with tattooing trends over the last few decades, among them: tribal designs; Celtic knotwork; Chinese or Japanese characters; nature imagery in the forms of stars, plants, flowers, and animals; names of people with significance to the wearer; calendar dates; and punctuation marks.

Singling out tattoos that could broadly be considered under the semantic cluster of *literature-library-information-knowledge*, a few of which are reproduced below, provides a small but interesting corpus. Among these, common themes were Dewey, Library of Congress, and Cutter numbers, books, and quotations:

> Inside right index finger S-h-h-h Right ankle beaded ankle bracelet with dropped zodiac signs of children and grandchildren.

* * *

> Script tattoo (book quote) that stretches between shoulder blades. Entirely black ink. Visible in shirts or dresses that have gently scooped necklines.

* * *

> Logo of favorite band on lower back. Video game character on lower stomach. Eagle on back of neck. Library symbol and dewey decimal numbers on inner wrist.

* * *

> Tiny Dewey decimal number at top center of back. Large piece covering entire upper left arm - black and white architectural.

Flurry of snowflakes: based on the photographs by Kenneth Libbrecht, start at shoulder cap and go down back/side, ending at upper thigh Scandinavian-inspired knotwork puffin: outline of puffin body in knotwork, realistic puffin head, Iron Age shears and skeleton keys incorporated into design, located on upper back in the "between tank top straps" area Library of Congress call number: lower abdomen.

* * *

1. First tattoo: binary code tattoo of my first girlfriend's birthday. upper right arm. Black ink 2. Logo of hometown newspaper, eagle upper left chest. Black ink. 3. Skull with tally marks on its forehead, in front of a star, upper left arm. Black ink. 4. The word "like," as per the instruction of feminist author Shelly Jackson's skin project to tattoo words on random people for a short story. Serif font, lower right ankle 5. The phrase "Nous tous somme savages," in a block format, serif font. Savages was mistakenly misspelled, right rib cage. Black ink. 6. An eagle on top of a stack of books with the words "Books are weapons in the war of ideas." WWII propaganda image. Signifies earning MLS from Indiana University. Back of left calf. Black ink 7. The word "vegan" tattoo'ed inside of lower lip. 8. Silhouette of an eagle, logo of the punk band Tragedy, upper right chest. Black ink. 9. Two zombie koi fish, tails tied together with a red ribbon. Placed on left rib cage/back and extends past the hip. Full color. 10. Full color symbolic heart on fire with wings. Lower right ankle 11. Kentucky cardinal right wrist. Red and black 12. Black Flag bars, lower left ankle. Full black 13. Beer bottle with a heart on a label, inner right ankle. Red and black. 14. Anatomical line drawing of a heart on sternum. Black ink. 15. 3/4 sleeve consisting of the Philippine star in the inner ditch of the left arm, with a raven on top of a skull amid a background of kudzu leaves. Black and green 16. Philippine eagle, full color, left wrist 17. "Inhale" on left wrist and "Exhale" on right wrist. Black ink 18. "Everything changes, everything's undone" script across upper chest. Black ink 19. Tattoo of a monkey in a sitting

position, upper right shoulder, red ink 20. Morton salt girl, upper, inner left arm. Full color

On the whole, it would seem that the content of "librarian tattoos" does not
skew heavily toward the literary. What is perhaps more important than the
(iconic, indexical, denotative) sign of the tattoo, then, is the body it adorns
and the framing social context of interpersonal interaction and visibility. Lena
Dunham, writer and star of the HBO series *Girls*, has tattoos from the children's book *Eloise*; the singer Rihanna has a "S-h-h-h" finger tattoo. Both of
these women, however, are patently not librarians. If they were, then the professional role might provide an additional lens through which to view their
ink, another layer of implied meaning or significance. Laying aside these hypothetical projections, it should be clear that context, situation, and participant frameworks all contribute to the ways such tattoos can be understood.

Nor would it be fair to assume a one-to-one correlation between a love
of reading and an attraction to library work, though many respondents to
this survey spoke of librarianship as a calling or vocation.[*] A quote can
mean plenty of things. Does it signify a love of books, echo a sentiment
that the wearer holds dear, or serve a purely ornamental purpose? In much
the same way, does a Harry Potter tattoo foreground reading, fandom, a
belief in magic, the power of imagination, or something entirely different?
What tattoos need to make sense, then, is not entirely circumscribed by
the choice of design. They demand both audience and context. Even more
to the point, they have to be anchored in a narrative where the audience,
specifically a person other than the self, is given narrative exposition for
the context. This connects to the idea of rites of passage, where tattoos are
memoirs of inscription for moments of personal significance.

Here, the limitations of the virtual survey become readily apparent: if
the import of a tattoo depends on how the wearer positions it in the narrative of selfhood, then a method that elicits biographical history would be
preferable to a simple survey. It should be noted, however, that multiple
respondents took full advantage of the open-ended questions and essentially combined the answers into their own story. Instead of breaking down

---

[*] Tattoo statistics are based on sampling, and while numbers and demographics are easy to obtain,
there do not seem to be ready statistics about what kinds of designs people choose.

the components of age, placement, design, and significance, they created narratives, which have a very recognizable structure. Narratives also foreground the self as an acting agent, determining the biographical course of an individual's life. Put another way, tattoos can be a way of inscribing difference and taking note of oppositionality. For some respondents, there is a very clear contrast set: the public at large, the parent, the media. In almost all of these cases, the individual is acting upon the surface of the body as an act of reclaiming, of inscription, or of adornment.

Conclusion: Images and Imaginaries

Here, the figure of the tattooed librarian has served as a framing device through which to explore the experiences and self-perceptions of librarians who fit this criterion. Even within the field itself, the tattooed librarian is often a figure of speculation as much as one of directed ire or begrudging respect. Speaking more broadly, of course rampant stereotypy exists with regard to the profession, as has been a near-constant refrain in the library literature. Given the recent uptick of public interest in so-called "hipster" librarians, tattoos neatly demarcate a line of distinction between two stereotypes: old and new; sexless or sexualized; rigid or free.* Whether in photo calendars produced by public libraries to raise funds, or as part of a project where inking en masse symbolizes an allegiance to freedom of information,†

---

* For the definitive treatment of power and gender in the profession, see Marie L. Radford and Gary P. Radford, "Power, Knowledge, and Fear: Feminism, Foucault, and the Stereotype of the Female Librarian," *Library Quarterly* 67, no. 3 (1997): 250–66.

† Kara Jesella, "A Hipper Crowd of Shushers," *New York Times*, July 8, 2007, www.nytimes. com/2007/07/08/fashion/08librarian.html. This is quite the performative moment for the profession, insofar as only when something is "discovered" by the *Times* can it be truly said to exist. The same could also be said for Brooklyn. As of this writing, both the Texas Library Association and the Rhode Island Library Association have produced print calendars featuring librarian ink. Another calendar, "Tattooed Librarians of the Pacific Northwest," was a fundraiser by and for library students at Emporia State. The *8bit* library blog was the impetus behind the "Project Brand Yourself a Librarian," where participants got tattoos of library, literary, or personal significance as a group during 2010 ALA Annual Meeting (Justin Hoenke, "Project Brand Yourself a Librarian," *8bitlibrary.com* [blog], January 13, 2010, http://blog.8bitlibrary.com/2010/01/13/ project-brand-yourself-a-librarian). Of the 10 tattoos on the "Project Brand Yourself a Librarian" Flickr page (www.flickr.com/groups/1376815@N23), two are Dewey numbers, four make use of the public library reading icon, one is of an open book, one is a Douglas Adams reference, one is a visual representation of steampunk gears, and one is an 8bit Nintendo graphic.

the two images of librarians are conceptually and visually opposed.‡

By way of these circulating images and the discourses about them, the body of the librarian becomes contested ground for working out anxieties about the profession, its perception, and its future trajectory. One side clamors for respectability, or at the least concealment, the other for freedom to adorn and display one's body according to individual values and beliefs.[14] We can thus situate the figure of the tattooed librarian within an ongoing conversation about the library profession and understandings of its practitioners. It matters less that these tropic figurations can be mapped onto "real persons" than the ways they communicate meaning about bodies, work, and subjectivity.[15] Talking about the "nontraditional librarian," whose alterity can be signified in a number of ways besides tattoos, invokes the opposing notion of tradition. By establishing a more robust analytic that takes perceptions and reality into account, we can begin to chip away at the sociodiscursive bedrock of these counterpoised stereotypes, and perhaps even begin to trace out their implications in workplace interactions.

Owing to its semiotic power and social history, the tattoo therefore distills anxieties about bodies—often highly gendered ones—enacting agency in a manner that gatekeepers may deem unacceptable. Through both the direct dissemination of images through social media and on-the-ground interactions with patrons, librarians with tattoos can act as representatives for the profession in ways that may not fit with established narratives or figurations. In doing so, they inhabit a mode of personhood that valorizes individual choice over convention and conformity, which may seem openly in opposition to avowed professional values of service, wherein the person is entirely subsumed to their role. This essay represents an initial foray into interrogating tattooed librarians, who hew to the same code of service as their forebears.

---

‡ Though both are likely to be bespectacled.

Notes

1. Terrence S. Turner, "The Social Skin," HAU: Journal of Ethnographic Theory 2, no. 2 (2012): 486–504; reprint from Not Work Alone, ed. Jeremy Cherfas and Roger Lewin, 112–40 (London: Temple Smith, 1980).
2. John A. Rush, Spiritual Tattoo (Berkeley, CA: Frog Books, 2005).
3. Michael Atkinson, *Tattooed: The Sociogenesis of a Body Art* (Toronto, ON: University of Toronto Press, 2003); Harris Interactive, "One in Five US Adults Now Has a Tattoo" (news release), February 23, 2012, 1, www.harrisinteractive.com/vault/Harris%20Poll%2022%20-Tattoos_2.23.12.pdf.
4. Harris Interactive, "One in Five," 1.
5. Jane Caplan, Introduction to *Written on the Body*, ed. Jane Caplan (Princeton, NJ: Princeton University Press, 2000), xi–xxii; Jacques Derrida. *Writing and Difference*, trans. Alan Bass (London: Routledge, 1978); Claude Levi-Strauss, *Structural Anthropology*, vol. 1 (New York: Basic Books [1963] 1974); Enid Schlidkrout, "Inscribing the Body," *Annual Review of Anthropology* 33 (2004): 319–44; Turner, "Social Skin"; Susan Benson, "Inscriptions of the Self: Reflections on Tattooing and Piercing in Contemporary Euro-America," Caplan, *Written on the Body*, 234–54; Marge DeMello, *Bodies of Inscription* (Durham, NC.: Duke University Press, 2000); Mindy Fenske, *Tattoos in American Visual Culture* (New York: Palgrave, 2007); Arnold Rubin, *Marks of Civilization* (Los Angeles: Museum of Cultural History, UCLA: 1988).
6. Larry R. Oberg, "The Emergence of the Paraprofessional in Academic Libraries: Perceptions and Realities," *College and Research Libraries* 53, no. 2 (1992): 99–112.
7. Brian K. Miller, Kay McGlashan Nicols, and Jack Eure, "Body Art in the Workplace: Piercing the Prejudice?" *Personnel Review* 38, no. 6 (2009): 621–40; Jeff W. Totten, Thomas J. Lipscomb, and Michael A. Jones, "Attitudes toward and Stereotypes of Persons with Body Art: Implications for Marketing Management," *Academy of Marketing Studies Journal* 13, no. 2 (2009): 77–96.
8. Rachel Singer Gordon, *The Nextgen Librarian's Survival Guide* (Medford, NJ: Information Today, 2006); Ashanti White, *Not Your Ordinary Librarian* (Witney, UK: Chandos, 2012).
9. Lee Barron, "Semiotics and Tattooing," in *Social Theory in Popular Culture* (Basingstoke, UK: Palgrave Macmillan, 2013), 122.
10. Erving Goffman, *Stigma* (New York: Touchstone, 1963): 146.
11. Atkinson, *Tattooed*, 158; see also Rush, *Spiritual Tattoo*.
12. Goffman, *Frame Analysis*, 573–74.
13. Michael Warner, "The Mass Public and the Mass Subject," in *Habermas and the Public Sphere*, ed. Craig Calhoun, 377–401 (Cambridge, MA: MIT Press, 1991).
14. "Shattering Those Stereotypes," *Annoyed Librarian* (blog), *Library Journal*, November 11, 2012, http://lj.libraryjournal.com/blogs/annoyedlibrarian/2012/11/19/shattering-those-stereotypes.
15. Adi Hastings and Paul Manning, "Introduction: Acts of Alterity," Language and Communication 24, no. 4 (2004): 291–311.

Bibliography

American Library Association. "ALA Library Fact Sheet 2: Number Employed in Libraries." Last updated April 2014. www.ala.org/tools/libfactsheets/alalibraryfactsheet02.

Annoyed Librarian. "Shattering Those Stereotypes." *Annoyed Librarian* (blog), *Library Journal*, November 11, 2012. http://lj.libraryjournal.com/blogs/annoyedlibrarian/2012/11/19/ shattering-those-stereotypes.

Annoyed Librarian. "Tattooed Librarians Are Diverse." *Annoyed Librarian* (blog), *Library Journal*, August 3, 2009. http://lj.libraryjournal.com/blogs/annoyedlibrarian/2009/08/03/ tattooed-librarians-are-diverse.

Atkinson, Michael. *Tattooed: The Sociogenesis of a Body Art*. Toronto, ON: University of Toronto Press, 2003.

Barron, Lee. "Semiotics and Tattooing." In *Social Theory in Popular Culture*, 108–24. Basingstoke, UK: Palgrave Macmillan, 2013.

Benson, Susan. "Inscriptions of the Self: Reflections on Tattooing and Piercing in Contemporary Euro-America." In *Written on the Body. The Tattoo in European and American History*, edited by Jane Caplan, 234–54. Princeton, NJ: Princeton University Press, 2000.

Brush, Pippa. "Metaphors of Inscription: Discipline, Plasticity, and the Rhetoric of Choice." *Feminist Review* 58 (Spring 1998): 22–43.

Caplan, Jane, ed. *Written on the Body: The Tattoo in European and American History*. Princeton, NJ: Princeton University Press, 2000.

Dalrymple, Theodore. "Exposing Shallowness," review of *Bodies of Inscription*, by Marge DeMello. *New Criterion* 18(June 2000): 74.

DeMello, Marge. "'Not Just For Bikers Anymore': Popular Representations of American Tattooing." *Journal of Popular Culture*. no. 3 (1995): 37–52.

DeMello, Marge. *Bodies of Inscription: A Cultural History of the Modern Tattoo Community*. Durham, NC: Duke University Press, 2000.

Department of Professional Employees, AFL-CIO. "Fact Sheet 2011: Library Workers: Facts and Figures." http://ala-apa.org/files/2012/03/Library-Workers-2011.pdf

Derrida, Jacques. *Writing and Difference*, translated by Alan Bass. London: Routledge, 1978.

Fenske, Mindy. *Tattoos in American Visual Culture*. New York: Palgrave, 2007.

Gaonkar, Dilip Parameshwar, and Benjamin Lee, eds. "New Imaginaries." Special issue, *Public Culture* 14, no. 1 (2002).

Goffman, Erving. *Frame Analysis*. Cambridge, MA: Harvard University Press, 1974.

———. *The Presentation of Self in Everyday Life*. New York: Anchor, 1959.

———. *Stigma: Notes on the Management of Spoiled Identity*. New York: Touchstone, 1963.

Gordon, Rachel Singer. *The Nextgen Librarian's Survival Guide*. Medford, NJ: Information Today, 2006.

Harris Interactive. "One in Five US Adults Now Has a Tattoo" (news release). February 23, 2012, 1. www.harrisinteractive.com/vault/Harris%20Poll%2022%20-Tattoos_2.23.12.pdf.

Hastings, Adi, and Paul Manning. "Introduction: Acts of Alterity." *Language and Communication* 24, no. 4 (2004): 291–311.

Jesella, Kara. "A Hipper Crowd of Shushers." *New York Times*, July 8, 2007. http://www.nytimes. com/2007/07/08/fashion/08librarian.html.

Levi-Strauss, Claude. *Structural Anthropology*, vol. 1. New York: Basic Books, [1963] 1974.

Lynch, Mary Jo. "Age of Librarians." American Library Association, August 25, 2013. www.ala. org/research/librarystaffstats/librarystaffstudies/ageoflibrarians.

Manning, Paul. "Barista Rants about Stupid Customers at Starbucks: What Imaginary Conversations Can Teach Us about Real Ones." *Language and Communication* 28 (2008): 101–26.

Miller, Brian K., Kay McGlashan Nicols, and Jack Eure. "Body Art in the Workplace: Piercing the Prejudice?" *Personnel Review*, 38, no. 6 (2009): 621–40.

Oberg, Larry R. "The Emergence of the Paraprofessional in Academic Libraries: Perceptions and Realities." *College and Research Libraries* 53, no. 2 (1992): 99–112.

Radford, Marie L., and Gary P. Radford. "Power, Knowledge, and Fear: Feminism, Foucault, and the Stereotype of the Female Librarian." *Library Quarterly* 67 no. 3 (1997): 250–66.

Rubin, Arnold. *Marks of Civilization: Artistic Transformations of the Human Body.* Los Angeles: Museum of Cultural History, UCLA, 1988.

Rush, John A. *Spiritual Tattoo: A Cultural History of Tattooing, Piercing, Scarification, Branding, and Implants.* Berkeley, CA: Frog Books, 2005.

Schlidkrout, Enid. "Inscribing the Body." *Annual Review of Anthropology* 33 (2004): 319–44.

Seale, Maura. "The Neoliberal Library." In *Information Literacy and Social Justice: Radical Professional Praxis*, edited by Lua Gregory and Shana Higgins, 39-61. Duluth, MN: Library Juice, 2013.

Totten, Jeff W., Thomas J. Lipscomb, and Michael A. Jones. "Attitudes toward and Stereotypes of Persons with Body Art: Implications for Marketing Management." *Academy of Marketing Studies Journal* 13, no. 2 (2009): 77–96.

Turner, Terence S. "The Social Skin." *HAU: Journal of Ethnographic Theory* 2, no. 2 (2012): 486–504. Reprint from *Not Work Alone: A Cross-Cultural View of Activities Superfluous to Survival*, edited by Jeremy Cherfas and Roger Lewin, 112–40, London: Temple Smith, 1980.

Warner, Michael. "The Mass Public and the Mass Subject." In *Habermas and the Public Sphere*, edited by Craig Calhoun, 377–401. Cambridge, MA: MIT Press, 1991.

White, Ashanti. *Not Your Ordinary Librarian: Debunking the Popular Perceptions of Librarians.* Witney, UK: Chandos, 2012.

CHAPTER 10

At the Corner of Personality and Competencies

Exploring Professional Personas for Librarians

Lauren Pressley, Jenny Dale, and Lynda Kellam

Cultural representations of the profession are familiar to librarians. Stereotypes are common, and when librarians appear in the media—whether in song, television, or film—there are certain assumptions about what librarians should look like (e.g., cardigans, buns, and glasses) as well as how they should act (e.g., timidity, rigid adherence to rules). One common theme is the personalities of library workers, and this chapter will examine how assumptions and stereotypes about personality do not necessarily hold true in the field—and even across specialties within it. This discussion will also provide an explanation and exploration of a library worker's "professional persona," which is defined as the intersection of an individual's personality, competencies, and professional interests. An individual's persona is a complex system that might include some traits, perspectives, and tendencies that align with librarian stereotypes and some that are at odds with those stereotypes. This chapter will situate the concept of persona in the existing literature on core competencies and career selection and then examine the implications of personas in the profession with a specific eye toward organizational design.

Our interest in this area has grown from the collaborative work that we have done on presentations and writing projects. We find that we collaborate effectively because each of us brings a unique persona to the team. For instance, when preparing for a recent presentation on personas and core competencies, we found that we naturally split the work based on our personas. Pressley, who focuses on systems and design thinking, immediately jumped in on the design of the presentation and on how our idea of personas could apply to organizational design. Kellam, our relationship builder, took on the task of talking with colleagues and soliciting short video interviews from other librarians for our presentation. Dale, who has a preference for teaching and performing, took on the role of breaking down content and concepts for effective presentation to our audience. The authors have found that our personas come to bear on the work that we do in our own institutions as well, both in the roles that we play and in the ways that we contribute to teams.

Literature Review

This framing of personas is partially based on the idea of applying the concept of core competencies to individual professionals. This concept, which originated in the business world, can be traced back to a 1990 article in the *Harvard Business Review* entitled, "The Core Competence of the Corporation." The authors, C. K. Prahalad and Gary Hamel, describe core competencies as those competencies of an organization that can be applied in various markets, that "make a significant contribution to the perceived customer benefits of the end product," and that "should be difficult for competitors to imitate."[1] One of their examples that still resonates today is the corporation 3M, whose lasting success is based on a core competence in producing sticky tape.[2] In her book *168 Hours*, author Laura Vanderkam argues that people have core competencies, just as companies do. Vanderkam applies the Prahalad and Hamel definition to individuals: "An individual's core competencies are best thought of as abilities that can be leveraged across multiple spheres. They should be important and meaningful. And they should be things we do best and that others cannot do nearly as well."[3]

Based on Vanderkam's definition, core competencies are the activities a person can leverage the most effectively and should spend most of their time doing. For example, Venus Williams is best served in her career by focusing on tennis, while employing someone else to design her website. Vanderkam focuses primarily on core competencies as they relate to home and time management, but these principles can also be applied to the workplace in terms of the types of jobs individuals are good at and enjoy doing as opposed to the types of jobs those same individuals consider dull or tedious. Each individual's core competencies intersect with personality and professional interests to form a professional persona.

Librarianship as a profession has shown an interest in identifying professional competencies. In fact, the American Library Association (ALA) has published a statement on core competencies entitled *ALA's Core Competences of Librarianship*.[4] Examples of these competencies include knowing and being able to employ "the ethics, values, and foundational principles of the library and information profession" and "the principles involved in the organization and representation of recorded knowledge and information."[5] Unlike Vanderkam's idea of personal core competencies, which focuses on honing a small number of competencies that an individual can do best, this list is a broad framework of what students graduating from ALA-accredited library schools "should know and, where appropriate, be able to employ."[6] Other professional organizations within librarianship, including divisions of ALA, have published similar statements that include competencies specific to a particular type or function of librarianship.[*] Generally, these statements on competencies focus on the broad knowledge and skills required for a particular segment of the profession (e.g., law librarians, children's services librarians, etc.). While these statements speak to the broad-based knowledge and wide range of skills that librarians are expected to have after completing a graduate education, the use of the term *core competencies* in this chapter refers to the specific skills that emerge as critical for individual librarians in their positions.

While competencies are critical to the formation of the professional person, personality is another dimension that has a significant impact. Career literature tends to focus on stereotypes of various professions and to match those stereotypes up with a person's personality. For example, in the book *What's Your Type of Career? Find Your Perfect Career by Using your Personality Type*, Dunning matches the personality types in the Myers-Briggs Type Indicator (MBTI) with specific careers.[7] Rather than present-

---

[*] For a comprehensive list, see American Library Association, "Knowledge and Competencies Statements Developed by Relevant Professional Organizations," www.ala.org/educationcareers/careers/corecomp/corecompspecial/knowledgecompetencies.

ing librarianship in terms of the full spectrum of possible roles within an organization (e.g., instruction librarians, systems librarians, etc.), librarians are represented by a single category. Dunning also includes categories for library technicians and library assistants, but does not explain the distinctions between these three careers. Interestingly, Dunning matches several personality types with librarianship but does not explain why an INFJ (Introverted iNtuitive Feeling Judging) versus an ENTJ (Extroverted iNtuitive Thinking Judging) might be attracted to librarianship in particular.

While this approach may be helpful to someone just starting to explore potential careers, it gives a very one-dimensional representation of librarianship, which is a truly multidimensional profession. There are many different types of librarians, and different skill sets are required depending on the department or type of library in which the librarian is employed.* While this is true for all professions, librarianship in particular tends to show up as one homogenous category in the career literature. This may be a result of a lack of awareness of librarianship as a profession or the evolving roles of libraries and may also be influenced by long-held stereotypes about librarians and the work that librarians do.

Within the library literature, there has been a long tradition of interest in how professionals' personalities influence their career choices, and that scholarship has shown a more nuanced approach than the general vocational and career guidance literature. In 1992, the Association of College and Research Libraries (ACRL) sponsored a national study of librarians and other information professionals meant to update vocational profiles of the profession. A sample of 3,500 librarians were asked to complete a demographic questionnaire, the Strong Interest Inventory, and the MBTI.[8] The respondents fell into three groups: American Library Association (ALA) officers and committee members, ALA members, and Special Libraries Association (SLA) members.[9] Participants represented a wide range of different specializations within librarianship as well as a range of different institutional settings, though academic and public libraries were the most heavily represented at 41 percent and 30 percent respectively.[10] This study generated a great deal of nuanced data, including the finding

---

* Again, for examples see American Library Association, "Knowledge and Competencies."

that the top two personality types among surveyed librarians were ISTJ (Introverted Sensing Thinking Judging) and INTJ (Introverted iNtuitive Thinking Judging).[11]

The Strong Interest Inventory is a vocational interest and career guidance instrument based on the idea that "personality traits have a bearing on occupational behavior, affecting both one's choice of and success in a particular occupation."[12] This instrument has been revised and updated frequently since its original development. John Holland's theory that vocational interests are actually an aspect of an individual's personality was integrated into the Strong Interest Inventory in the 1950s and has been considered integral to the inventory since then.[13] There are six "Holland types" or "General Occupational Themes" described by the Strong Interest Inventory: Realistic types (with "technical and outdoor interests"), Investigative types (focused on "scientific or laboratory work"), Artistic types (with "dramatic, self-expressive interests"), Social types (people who "like to help others and have people-oriented interests), Enterprising types (salespersons, leaders, and managers), and Conventional types (who are drawn to activities like scheduling and bookkeeping).[14]

While Holland originally placed librarians in the Conventional category in the 1950s, studies since the 1970s (and including the ACRL study) have shown that librarians actually tend to have preferences aligning them with the Artistic category. In their ACRL-sponsored study, David and Scherdin explain that the Strong Interest Inventory guide indicates "that some people who score high in the Artistic category may be involved in the arts as spectators or observers rather than direct participants. Their potential competencies include creativity, imagination and verbal-linguistic skills."[15]

As mentioned earlier, in the MBTI phase of the study, Scherdin found that out of the 1,600 responses analyzed, the top two personality types were ISTJ (Introverted Sensing Thinking Judging) at 17 percent and INTJ (Introverted iNtuitive Thinking Judging) at 12 percent.[16] This reality is at odds with popular representations of librarians in films as explored in Jeanine Williamson's study of MBTI types of librarian characters in popular films, indicating that popular personality stereotypes of librarians are as inaccurate or at least as incomplete as other common stereotypes of our profession.[17] Williamson found that ISTJ and INTJ were actually among the underrepresented personality types in her sample of 28 films.[18] The real librarians in Scherdin's study showed a significant preference for introversion, with 63 percent of respondents favoring introversion, compared to 35 percent of the general population.[19] It is critical to note, however, that, among the 1,600 responses analyzed, all 16 possible MBTI types were represented, supporting the idea that the field has a diversity of personality types within it.[20] This diversity is also at odds with the representations described by Williamson, as she found that six of the 16 types (ISTP, ISFP, INTP, ESFP, ENFJ, and ENTJ) were not represented in the films she analyzed at all.[21] She concludes that these films "fail to represent the rich variety of personality characteristics found in real librarians."[22] While no one has conducted another personality study of practicing librarians on the same scale as Scherdin's since the 1990s, several have discussed the importance of having a variety of personalities in librarianship.[23]

Personality Types and Personas in Libraries

This diversity of personality types and thus personas is critical because libraries as organizations depend on professionals who can successfully complete a wide variety of tasks. To give an idea of the variety in the academic library, instruction librarians should be good at working with people (and hopefully like it) and have the ability to present in front of groups. The ability to perform in front of an audience is a great skill to make instruction sessions more engaging. Working in technical services, a librarian must still be service-minded, but having the ability to present well to large audiences may be less of a priority. A higher priority would be attention to detail and project management skills.

While it may not be possible to find a job within librarianship that is a perfect fit with a given persona, being cognizant of one's own personality, traits, and skills will help in understanding better why some tasks are easy to complete and others are put off until the last moment. If professionals can understand this, they can better structure their time (and rewards) to get the job done as needed. On the organizational level, supervisors and employees who are keyed into personalities and competencies may be able to reassign aspects of work to those who most enjoy them and are best skilled in them so as to free up the efforts of employees for whom the time to do those tasks would be better spent in other ways. In a perfect world, our organizations would be open and flexible about personas in a way that would help maximize the potential and effectiveness of individuals and of the larger organization. There is much to be said for encouraging employees to expand their skill sets and areas of work. While reassigning tasks might appear to be a foray into narrowed jobs, it can better be seen as giving other workers more opportunities for growth by picking up new areas to explore.

Personas and Organizational Design

Individuals' core competencies and professional personas, or the competencies, personality, and interests that a person brings to their job, impact organizations in a number of ways. For example, Vanderkam's assertion that core competencies are the abilities an individual can leverage the most effectively and should spend most of their time doing has significant implications for effective use of time. If *time* is an individual's most valuable resource, a manager has to ask: is any given employee using their time in a way that maximizes their potential contribution to the organization?[24] In all likelihood, given the wide distribution of duties most library professionals perform and the broad-based knowledge that library professionals are expected to have, many people probably are not focusing on their core competencies. If a manager is concerned about employee satisfaction, that manager should also be thinking about helping people reach their potential and professional goals and assessing whether employees are happy in the work they do. Understanding personas and organizational design allows administrators to think about how to help library employees participate in the organization in a way that makes the most sense for both the institution and the individual.

Can an organization be created around the concept of personas? Can the library be reimagined based on this idea? Several institutions are beginning to do this, specifically academic libraries looking at ways to increase specialization in liaison duties, allowing those who have strong preferences or skill sets to focus on specific aspects of liaisonship such as collections, reference, and instruction.

Personas and Liaison Models

One way to think about how to design an organization around personas is to think about how one aspect of the organization—such as liaison support—is currently structured. As librarians take on new responsibilities, such as scholarly communication duties, liaison models have begun to evolve in response.[25] The section below will discuss a spectrum of three possible liaison models: an informal approach that could be implemented at a library just beginning to explore this concept, formalized teams that give structure to the idea, and individualized liaisonships that push the concept of liaison to very specific designations.

Informal

A common approach for a smaller library, or a library that is just beginning to consider this type of structure, is an informal one. For instance, if two colleagues find that they have very different interests and skill sets, they might informally split up duties accordingly. If one of the two librarians has an interest in collection development and a core competency in analyzing and building a collection that serves the institution, that librarian might take on the bulk of collection duties and do less teaching. At the same time, the other colleague might have an interest in pedagogy and a core competency in teaching information literacy skills. That person might assume primary responsibility for instruction and reduce collections responsibilities. Or, in a team where one person loves the reference desk and has developed a core competency in one-on-one reference assistance while the rest of the team members find that they prefer not to work it, that one person might take on the majority of reference hours and push instruction and collection duties to other librarians freed up by the lack of desk shifts. Or, even more simply, if a teaching request comes in during a time that an instruction-leaning librarian is working the desk, they might see if someone would be willing to take the desk shift instead of the class so that they might use the time to teach instead. Of course, in this scenario, a department would need to be very careful that work is balanced equitably. Most libraries deal with this now and work to create workplace equity with uneven work demands from different departments or colleges.

Formalized Teams

A more formalized approach is the liaison model that the University of North Carolina at Greensboro (UNCG) University Libraries is currently implementing.* In this model, there are three subject teams (Humanities, Social Science, and Science teams) and several functional teams (Instruction, Collections, Reference Desk, and Scholarly Communications at the time of writing). Each subject team has at least one representative on each functional team, affording the subject teams the opportunity to adequately support all of their academic liaison areas while allowing specific liaisons to specialize in a particular function reflecting that person's area of interest. This team-based liaison model was based on research conducted by a liaison task force.[26] Many other libraries have also transitioned to a team-based liaison model, some with more emphasis on functional teams, and some with more emphasis on subject teams.[27]

These formalized teams provide a path to specialization that also includes some flexibility for continued involvement in the areas that people enjoy but may not want to specialize in. Many liaison librarians want to give up some part of their job but do not want to walk away forever for any number of reasons, not the least of which is that there is job security in maintaining a broad skill set. In some cases, the broad spectrum of duties might provide a rare chance to interact with users for an otherwise internally facing position. Or, in the reverse case, this broad spectrum of duties might provide a liaison librarian with a chance to be with or away from users at times. In this team-based model, each team has the flexibility and autonomy to divide the labor of liaisonship as the team members see fit. This model is in the very early stages of implementation at UNCG University Libraries at the time of writing, but plans are in place to reflect on this model at the end of the first year and to design an assessment plan to evaluate its effectiveness and sustainability.

---

* Chapter authors Jenny Dale and Lynda Kellam are liaisons at UNCG University Libraries.

Individualized Liaisonships

A third model involves the creation of highly specialized liaisonships. This is one model that Virginia Tech University Libraries is exploring due to a new administration and a changing vision for what the library ought to be.* This library system is driven by a start-up culture that embraces pilot projects, agile development, and a build-measure-learn philosophy, and the libraries will use this perspective to evaluate the success of the program.[28] In this model, liaisons will choose an area of professional specialty: instruction and reference, collections, liaising with colleagues, etc. Most librarians would choose one, but some might choose to have two or to have a primary and secondary area as well. The framework the institution is considering is to think of these as analogous to academic majors and minors.

In this model, roles would determine departmental affiliations. For instance, most librarians with a primary focus in instruction and reference would be located in the reference and instruction department. Likewise, collections would be located in technical services. Academic department liaison roles, separate from reference and instruction, would be the primary point people and consultants, facilitating partnerships between teaching faculty and librarians.

The power of this model is that it also allows the library to bring other areas of expertise on board as they emerge. An example from recent years is scholarly communications. As the need for this expertise has grown in academic libraries, so has the number of librarians interested in this type of work. This model makes it very easy to bring on liaisons in new areas of interest, as identified by the libraries or the larger university community. Virginia Tech University Libraries have already hired liaisons with expertise in data and visual literacy, for example. The visual literacy liaison can work faculty members interested in introducing visual concepts like poster design in their assignments, and the data services librarian can liaise around issues of data literacy for undergraduates and graduate students.

---

* Chapter author Lauren Pressley is a manager at the Virginia Tech University Libraries.

Adaptability, Fit, and Attitude of Professionals

Perhaps the most important thing any manager does in their work is to find future colleagues. Jeffrey J. Fox, author of *How to Become a Great Boss*, speaks at length about the dangers of hiring the wrong person for a job. The costs include stress, lost resources, disruption to the organization, decreased energy from goals and organizational strategy, and low morale.[29] New hires might work in the organization for many years, and managers certainly want to be sure they have the skills they need to be successful in their jobs. But perhaps more important, administration needs to know that a new employee is the type of person that existing employees can work with, that they will be a good fit for the local community of users, and that they will be able to adapt to the current rapidly changing information environment.

In recruitment and hiring, soft skills are arguably more important than the hard skills we look for on transcripts and curricula vitae.[30] A frequent refrain from library professionals is that they learned as much on the job as they did in graduate school. Librarianship as a profession relies heavily on on-the-job training that is either community- or organization-specific. A library cannot expect everyone it hires to come in the door knowing how to do everything that is important for their specific context. If they did, they would likely find the job unstimulating and quickly grow bored. Learning the hard skills required to complete certain tasks is usually part and parcel of any library job. Soft skills, on the other hand, can be difficult to teach. Some people have a generally positive or negative view of the world that impacts their approach to work. Some people have an interest in playing around to figure out new things on their own, while others prefer to be taught. These examples simplify the complex nature of a personality and create a false sense of dualistic choices. However, being able to think about the soft skills and approaches that a given organization needs will allow a manager to be able to look for employees with appropriate attitudes.

There are several general traits that many libraries would be likely to seek out. For example, library literature and conference presentations are filled with claims that a general inclination toward learning, and aptitude for learning new technologies, effective communication, systems thinking, and comfort with ambiguity or change are necessary in today's information professionals. For instance, Reeves and Hahn conducted a content analysis of over 1,000 entry-level job advertisements in 2009 and found that, in addition to specific training, experience, and skills, many of these advertisements specifically mentioned personal traits.[31] More than half of the advertisements analyzed mentioned communication skills, and 20 percent mentioned service orientation, collaboration, and "team capabilities."[32] These are essential traits that will help people be successful in their work, but they are not necessarily traits that we can teach or instill externally.

Once there is evidence that candidates possess the skills required for the job, many managers claim the attitude and fit they bring to the organization becomes the next most important variable to consider.[33] A library might find itself with a candidate who has the background that is needed, would be an excellent fit, and also has additional areas of expertise. In a case like this the library might want to hire the candidate, but also consider how to shift work within the organization to allow the job to evolve to fit the employee and to allow other jobs in the organization to evolve to maximize the skills and strengths of the employees in them.

In informal interviews with library workers, the chapter authors are often asked if assigning job duties based on personas will lead to everyone wanting to take on the "good" jobs, leaving entire areas of service unassigned. The authors have found, though, that in conversations about what people would like to emphasize in their work, librarians tend to express preferences covering the broad spectrum of existing services. For instance, one colleague asserted that she would gladly take over library instruction responsibilities for others if it meant no longer having regularly scheduled reference desk shifts or collection management assignments. In conversations with her colleagues, she found that there were several with opposing preferences. If this group of colleagues shifted duties around, everyone would be able to focus on their core competencies and become true experts in those areas rather than attempting to be competent in a broad spectrum of tasks. On a larger scale, the literature supports the idea that librarians generally have a wide range of professional interests. In the demographic component of the ACRL study conducted in the early 1990s, respondents were asked which activities they preferred to spend time on.[34] While Collection Development/Acquisitions and Reference/Reader Services were the two highest areas of interest, both at 18 percent, respondents showed individual preferences for a wide variety of other activities that represent the broad spectrum of tasks required in an organization.[35]

Conclusion

Libraries are not the homogenous organizations that the general career literature might suggest; they are shaped by the different—and, ideally, complementary—personas of their employees. Knowing this, it should be a priority of library management to think about the hiring processes and consider the implications of any assumptions about how a library worker ought to process information, engage with others, or work. Hiring managers should consider personas within their own organization in order to plan for greater diversity in the candidate pool. For example, does a phone interview serve as an impassable threshold to people who would not typically communicate via phone in their day-to-day job? Does relying too heavily on the face-to-face interview enable high-energy extroverts to overshadow more reserved candidates? Does a behaviorally based interview bias the committee against new professionals? Considering the unintended consequences of an interview process can enable an organization to avoid hiring a homogeneous workforce for their diverse community.

Once a library worker is hired, it is useful to consider how she can integrate into the team. For example, with the aid of tools like the MBTI, the Strong Interest Inventory, or even a popular press option like *Strengths-Finder 2.0*,[36] team members can learn more about each other and how they can maximize their effectiveness by leveraging their individual personas and strengths. Related to this, as a professional grows in their position and skill set, it is likely that their persona may shift as well. Continued individual reflection and team building can give the organization the opportunity to evolve as its members do. This type of organizational growth can allow professionals to continue to gain new skills and add expertise to their work while keeping the employees' interest and enabling growth in their work.

The authors' interest in this idea of the professional persona has grown as they have considered the implications that these personas could have on their own careers, institutions, and the profession as a whole. The theory presented here, rooted in the idea that libraries are organizations built around the diverse professional personas of library professionals, calls into question cultural representations of librarians that tend to homogenize us based not just on our appearance and attire, but also on our personalities. Discarding this notion of librarians as reflections of any broad stereotype is essential for moving the profession forward and building in the flexibility required to truly embrace the many personas necessary for a vibrant and thriving 21st-century library.

Notes

1. C. K. Prahalad and Gary Hamel, "The Core Competence of the Corporation," *Harvard Business Review* 68, no. 3 (May 1990): 83–84.
2. Ibid., 82.
3. Laura Vanderkam, *168 Hours* (New York: Portfolio, 2010), Kindle edition, chap. 2, loc. 557.
4. See American Library Association, *ALA's Core Competences of Librarianship,* approved January 27, 2009, www.ala.org/educationcareers/sites/ala.org.educationcareers/files/content/careers/corecomp/corecompetences/finalcorecompstat09.pdf.
5. Ibid., 1–2.
6. Ibid., 1.
7. Donna Dunning, *What's your Type of Career?* (Boston: Nicholas Brealey, 2010).
8. Mary Jane Scherdin, "From Children's Books to CD-ROMs: Life for Librarians Today," in *Discovering Librarians,* ed. Mary Jane Scherdin, 65–101 (Chicago: Association of College and Research Libraries, 1994).
9. Ibid., 67.
10. Ibid., 70.
11. Mary Jane Scherdin, "Vive la Difference: Exploring Librarian Personality Types," in Scherdin, *Discovering Librarians,* 132.
12. Indra David and Mary Jane Scherdin, "Librarians in Transition: Profiles on the Strong Interest Inventory," in Scherdin, *Discovering Librarians,* 102.
13. Ibid., 102–103.
14. Ibid., 104.
15. Ibid., 109.
16. Scherdin, "Vive la Difference," 132.
17. Jeanine Williamson, "Jungian/Myers-Briggs Personality Types of Librarians in Films," *Reference Librarian* 78 (2002): 47–59, doi:10.1300/J120v37n78_04.
18. Ibid., 51.
19. Scherdin, "Vive la Difference," 132.
20. Ibid., 134.

21. Williamson, "Jungian/Myers-Briggs Personality Types," 51.
22. Ibid., 55.
23. See Jennifer A. Bartlett, "New and Noteworthy," *Library Leadership and Management* 26, no. 1 (March 2012): 1–5; Robin Milford and Tania Wisotzke, "Introverts and Customer Service in the Library: An Unexpected Fit," *OLA Quarterly* 17, no. 3 (Fall 2011): 22–26.
24. Richard Koch, *The 80/20 Principle* (New York: Doubleday, 1998).
25. Kara J. Malenfant, "Leading Change in the System of Scholarly Communication: A Case Study of Engaging Liaison Librarians for Outreach to Faculty," *College and Research Libraries* 71, no. 1 (January 2010): 63–76; Prahalad and Hamel, "Core Competence of the Corporation," 83–84; Craig Gibson and Jamie Wright Coniglio, "The New Liaison Librarian" in *The Expert Library*, ed. Scott Walter and Karen Williams (Chicago: Association of College and Research Libraries, 2010), 93–126.
26. Steve Cramer et al., "Great Expectations: New Organizational Models for Overworked Liaisons Based on the UNCG Libraries Liaison Collections Responsibilities Task Force," in *Accentuate the Positive: Charleston Conference Proceedings, 2012*, ed. Beth R. Bernhardt, Leah H. Hinds, and Katina P. Strauch, 278–91 (West Lafayette, IN: Purdue University Press, 2013), doi:10.5703/1288284315112.
27. Ibid.
28. Brian Mathews, "Think Like a Startup: A White Paper to Inspire Library Entrepreneurism," last modified April 3, 2012, http://vtechworks.lib.vt.edu/handle/10919/18649.
29. Jeffrey J. Fox, *How to Become a Great Boss* (New York: Hyperion, 2002), 21–22.
30. Michael Stephens, "Essential Soft Skills," *Library Journal* 138, no. 3 (February 15, 2013): 39.
31. Robert K. Reeves and Trudi Bellardo Hahn, "Job Advertisements for Recent Graduates: Advising, Curriculum, and Job-Seeking Implications," *Journal of Education for Library and Information Science* 51, no. 2 (Spring 2010): 103–119.
32. Ibid., 112.
33. Marcus Buckingham and Curt Coffman. *First, Break All the Rules* (New York: Simon and Schuster, 1999), 90.
34. Scherdin, "From Children's Books to CD-ROMs."
35. Ibid., 78.
36. Tom Rath, *StrengthsFinder 2.0* (New York: Gallup Press, 2007).

Bibliography

American Library Association. *ALA's Core Competences of Librarianship.* Approved January 27, 2009. www.ala.org/educationcareers/sites/ala.org.educationcareers/files/content/careers/corecomp/corecompetences/finalcorecompstat09.pdf.

———. "Knowledge and Competencies Statements Developed by Relevant Professional Organizations." Accessed October 18, 2013. http://www.ala.org/educationcareers/careers/corecomp/corecompspecial/knowledgecompetencies

Bartlett, Jennifer A. "New and Noteworthy." *Library Leadership and Management* 26, no. 1 (March 2012): 1–5.

Buckingham, Marcus, and Curt Coffman. *First, Break All the Rules: What the World's Greatest Managers Do Differently.* New York: Simon and Schuster, 1999.

Cramer, Steve, Beth Bernhardt, Mike Crumpton, Amy Harris, and Nancy Ryckman. "Great Expectations: New Organizational Models for Overworked Liaisons Based on the UNCG Libraries Liaison Collections Responsibilities Task Force." In *Accentuate the Positive:*

Charleston Conference Proceedings, 2012, edited by Beth R. Bernhardt, Leah H. Hinds, and Katina P. Strauch, 278–291. West Lafayette, IN: Purdue University Press, 2013. doi:10.5703/1288284315112.

David, Indra, and Mary Jane Scherdin. "Librarians in Transition: Profiles on the Strong Interest Inventory." In Scherdin, *Discovering Librarians*, 102–24.

Dunning, Donna. *What's Your Type of Career? Find Your Perfect Career by Using Your Personality Type.* Boston: Nicholas Brealey, 2010.

Fox, Jeffrey. *How to Become a Great Boss: The Rules for Getting and Keeping the Best Employees.* New York: Hyperion, 2002.

Gibson, Craig, and Jamie Wright Coniglio. "The New Liaison Librarian." In *The Expert Library: Staffing, Sustaining, and Advancing the Academic Library in the 21st Century*, edited by Scott Walter and Karen Williams, 93–126. Chicago: Association of College and Research Libraries, 2010.

Koch, Richard. *The 80/20 Principle: The Secret to Success by Achieving More with Less.* New York: Doubleday, 1998.

Malenfant, Kara J. "Leading Change in the System of Scholarly Communication: A Case Study of Engaging Liaison Librarians for Outreach to Faculty." *College and Research Libraries* 71, no. 1 (January 2010): 63–76.

Mathews, Brian. "Think Like a Startup: A White Paper to Inspire Library Entrepreneurism." Last modified April 3, 2012. http://vtechworks.lib.vt.edu/handle/10919/18649.

Milford, Robin, and Tania Wisotzke. "Introverts and Customer Service in the Library: An Unexpected Fit." *OLA Quarterly* 17, no. 3 (Fall 2011): 22–26.

Prahalad, C. K., and Gary Hamel. "The Core Competence of the Corporation." *Harvard Business Review* 68, no. 3 (May 1990): 79–91.

Reeves, Robert K., and Trudi Bellardo Hahn. "Job Advertisements for Recent Graduates: Advising, Curriculum, and Job-Seeking Implications." *Journal of Education for Library and Information Science* 51, no. 2 (Spring 2010): 103–19.

Scherdin, Mary Jane, ed. *Discovering Librarians: Profiles of a Profession.* Chicago: Association of College and Research Libraries, 1994.

———. "From Children's Books to CD-ROMs: Life for Librarians Today." In Scherdin, *Discovering Librarians*, 65–101.

———. "Vive la Difference: Exploring Librarian Personality Types." In Scherdin, *Discovering Librarians*, 125–56.

Stephens, Michael. "Essential Soft Skills." *Library Journal* 138, no. 3 (February 15, 2013): 39.

Vanderkam, Laura. *168 Hours: You Have More Time Than You Think.* New York: Portfolio, 2010. Kindle edition.

Williamson, Jeanine. "Jungian/Myers-Briggs Personality Types of Librarians in Films." *Reference Librarian* 78 (2002): 47–59. doi:10.1300/J120v37n78_04.

CHAPTER 11

Student Perceptions of Academic Librarians

The Influence of Pop Culture and Past Experience

Melissa Langridge, Christine Riggi, and Allison Schultz

> A warning: If you rip, tear, shred, bend, fold, deface, disfigure, smear, smudge, throw, drop, or in any other manner damage, mistreat, or show lack of respect towards this book, the consequences will be as awful as it is within my power to make them.
>
> —Madam Irma Pince, Hogwarts Librarian[1]

In "The Perception of Image and Status in the Library Profession," Deirdre Dupré notes, "It's not the stereotype that's the problem, it's the *obsession* with the stereotype."[2] She argues that this obsession with public perception of librarianship actually stems from an overall sense of insecurity and unworthiness within the profession itself. Although librarians may have unintentionally assisted in the creation and preservation of some negative stereotypes, visual mass media—namely film and television—have contributed to the adverse perceptions cultivated by the public in regard to librarians and their role in society.[*]

---

[*] While we do see the irony in writing about librarian stereotypes—and that we, by participating in this book, are presumably perpetuating the concept of stereotype-obsessed librarians even further—we conducted this study in order to better understand preconceived ideas of gender roles, ageism, and occupational bias and how to avoid them in library services.

In the article "Librarians, Professionalism and Image," Abigail Luth-mann writes a succinct overview of librarian representations in mass media throughout the 20th century. She explains that the "infamous negative stereotypes" of librarians are often quite old. The common media-generated representation of a librarian is an older, single, white woman, generally adorned with one or more of the following: cardigan, pearls, tweed skirt, hair in a bun, and dark-rimmed glasses.[3] These pop culture images found on television, are woven into the fabric of the student subconscious for years prior to entering college.

Niagara University Library was interested in assessing whether or not there is a difference between freshman and senior undergraduate student perceptions of academic librarians and evaluating why this does or does not occur. We sought to discover whether there is a strong connection between childhood television viewing experiences and expectations of librarians. Furthermore, we wanted to know if direct and indirect experiences contribute to the stereotypes created by the mass media in regard to undergraduate students' impressions of perceived librarian usefulness.

Understanding this information will help library staff assess how we can become more approachable and develop various strategies when assisting the 21st-century student population. Quantitative and qualitative methods were employed to assess student perceptions of librarians; these perceptions were sought from of willing undergraduates attending our small, private northeastern university. Students were given a survey to gauge whether or not television played a role in the formation of their perceptions of librarians. If no media influence was found, the authors' secondary assessment factor was perceived service ability based solely on the librarian's outward expression through clothing and related aspects of appearance. Additionally, the authors surveyed a national sample of librarians to compare reports of the clothing they wore versus what students expected them to wear based on portrayals of librarians in media. Responses represent typical daily work attire selected by librarians who were surveyed.

Surveys for both the students and the librarians were developed based on research conducted by Peluchette, Karl, and Rust in 2006.[4] Their study describes individual differences in the beliefs and attitudes regarding workplace attire among MBA students. Emphasis is placed on the attitudes of the wearer and the extent to which they might use their clothing to influence the perceptions of others or to achieve certain workplace objectives. We based our survey on this approach in an attempt to assess how undergraduate students perceive themselves and if their survey response is a direct reflection of what they expect from others. We hypothesized that academic librarians use clothing to influence others. We looked for evidence of how and why they may do so and of whether their clothing choices perpetuate the media-generated stereotypes.

Perceived Approachability of Librarians Based on Media Influence

Cultivation theory is the idea that "television viewing affects beliefs and influences the judgments of viewers based on frequency."[5] This theory, developed by George Gerbner and Larry Gross in 1976, was derived from several research projects conducted to determine if there was a correlation between the amount of violent television viewed and people's perceptions of violence in the real world.[6] Not only did their article conclude that those who watched more TV perceived the world to be a more violent place, it also led others in the mass communication field to explore the thought processes that led to these cultivated beliefs.

Current research builds on Gerbner and Gross's original theory. According to L. J. Shrum, television viewing affects the construction of real-world judgments through its effect on the accessibility of information from memory.[7] Heavy viewers are able to easily recall these familiar media constructs as a basis for their judgments based on the frequency, recency, and vividness of stereotype.[8] These findings suggest that television viewing supports typical archetypes rather than changing attitudes, which is consistent with Gerbner's view of long-term television effects.[9]

Additionally, media has more of an impact if the content is perceived to be realistic.[10] RoskosEwoldsen, Davis, and RoskosEwoldsen note that Gerbner and his colleagues observed that "men are characters in TV shows at about a 2 to 1 ratio to women, and women's roles are more stereotypical than men's."[11] As a result, people who are heavy viewers of television, for whom the experience of "reality" is more filtered through impressions from television, tend to have more sexist views of women. Research conducted by Prentice, Gerrig, and Bailis states that information contained in fictional messages can influence beliefs about social groups.[12]

Mainstreaming and resonance are two variables that have been incorporated into general cultivation theory in response to the methodological and theoretical critiques of Gerbner and Gross's original work on the subject and its effects.[13] Building on the social cognitive theory developed by Albert Bandura, mainstreaming suggests that our actions are guided by what we observe in others.[14] This indirect learning, coupled with exposure to media-generated behaviors, allows us to interpret events and model our actions and responses to similar situations by what we have observed. We are influenced by our perceptions to different stimuli, for example attractiveness or functional need.[15] Television portrayals of particular actions, events, or groups tend to be more vivid than real-world experiences. However, if direct exposure to these real-world experiences is not possible, we gain our understanding of these events through media depictions. A "script" or "episode model" can be used in order to interpret the event and discern how to react to it.[16] Essentially, we utilize media depictions to make sense of and react to actions, events, and groups we have not previously encountered.

Resonance proposes that television viewing reaffirms a person's belief that was originally cultivated based on their own life experiences.[17] For example, people who have interactions with crime, violence, and drama tend to acquire long-lasting impressions, and as a result, a larger cultivation effect is created based on those encounters.[18] This begs the question, do daily social interactions contribute to the creation of a cultivated effect in the same way as exposure to a more significant event would? How much do nondescript outings such as going to the dentist, going grocery shopping, or even visiting the local library influence the way we assess information and formulate stereotypical cultivations?

Roskos-Ewoldsen, Davis, and Roskos-Ewoldsen agree that cultural models influence how the media are understood.[19] Although no research has investigated this phenomenon yet, they take the cultivation theory one step further and suggest that a stronger effect of heavy TV viewing may be found if researchers measure television exposure during childhood and early adolescence. This is a critical period in a child's life. Repeated exposure to a stimulus, such as heavy television viewing, has stronger effects on perceptions of social reality.[20]

Librarian Approachability Based on Wardrobe

Does the repeated image of a mean older lady with a bun and thick-rimmed glasses influence a student's decision to approach or avoid a librarian? Research shows that library users consider two types of information about librarians when they consider initiating a reference encounter. In a 1998 *Library Trends* article, Marie Radford explains, "First, they receive an impression of the librarian attending the reference desk informed by their appearance and nonverbal behavior. Secondly, previous experience with and/or opinions of librarians."[21] Solutions proposed to increase reference interactions often include improving a librarian's interpersonal skills at the desk. However, there is relatively little research on the effect of a librarian's appearance.

Patricia Glass Schuman makes an argument that many librarians, including us, agree with—that image concerns should "not be about physical stereotypes, but about librarians' usefulness and necessity."[22] Patrons need a clear idea of the range of services the library provides. However, the image we convey is more influential than what we say or how we say it.[23] A recent study conducted by Bonnet and McAlexander suggests that librarians can easily increase their approachability by adapting their affect and clothing.[24] By incorporating certain characteristics into their wardrobe and behavior, such as wearing comforting colors or a friendly smile, librarians can help ease students' anxieties and increase patron interactions.

In addition to appearance and behavior, another stereotypical factor that may come into play, whether or not students realize it, is ageism. Usually, age discrimination refers to those in the workforce who are over the age of 50, but Melanie Chu notes, "Young, new librarians face age discrimination, including disrespectful treatment in the workplace and unrealistic expectations of performance."[25] Unfortunately, there has been little research conducted into student perceptions of young or novice librarians' abilities. Librarianship is one of the professions where the average number of workers aged 45 and older is higher than in the rest of the general workforce.[26]

Crosby, Evans, and Cowles apply the notion of psychological "mirroring" and "matching" in the service context.[27] Their research study found that if a salesperson and customer were similar in appearance, lifestyle, and socioeconomic status, there was a positive effect on trust and satisfaction. Customers also tend to match their expectations of what a person with technical knowledge should look like based on the age or gender of a frontline employee. In many cases, this led to customers approaching staff based on both age- and gender-related stereotypes. Age was associated with experience, while one's sex was related to gender-normative roles and occupations. Furthermore, a study conducted by Johnson-Hillery, Kang, and Tuan found that older consumers prefer to be served by older retail staff because they perceived them to be more helpful than younger employees and more likely to suggest products that related to their personal needs.[28] White-collar professional services that are high in status, such as dentistry, are difficult for customers to evaluate.[29] As with reference librarians, customers must rely solely on the service provider's knowledge in the service encounter. These preferences influence patron interactions and the perceived usefulness of librarians.

Survey Administration

In order to assess student perceptions, we created an online image-rating survey to display visible characteristics of librarians varied by gender, age, ethnicity, and attire (see figure 1). First, we tracked the participants' demographic characteristics to assess for matching or mirroring in terms of librarian approachability. Next, students were asked to evaluate their current use of the library and perceived customer satisfaction with library services. This acted as a baseline assessment to compare actual versus perceived notions of the library and librarian usefulness. Lastly, the students were given hypothetical research scenarios and were prompted to select which librarian would be most useful in assisting them with a specific task and to provide reasoning for their selection.

FIGURE 1

The student survey included their rating of librarian approachability based on images of actual librarians and examples of their wardrobes.*

For the images used, we recruited librarians who fit the demographics associated with a stereotype. In addition, to control for bias, we sought out librarians not associated with our own institution. Their images represent typical daily work attire choices confirmed by the sample of librar-

* Special thank you to Natalie Bennett as well as the pictured librarians: David Bertuca, Carolyn Klotzbach, Christopher Hollister, Glendora Johnson-Cooper, A. Ben Wagner, Helen Farralo, Ken Fujiuchi, Lauren Woody, and Krishna Grady.

ians who were surveyed. All librarians were photographed with their gaze directed toward the camera, with a smiling facial expression to seem more approachable and to attempt to control for perceived differences in expression.[30]

Additionally, two librarians were chosen to represent a uniformed look that is a standard in service-oriented businesses. This included blue button-down shirts and a name tag that identified their professional status clearly. We chose the shirt color on the basis of color theory that suggests that blue inspires calm and tranquility. Bonnet and McAlexander's study echoes this theory that blue increases the approachability of the wearer.[31] Because we thought that library anxiety is a major inhibitor to student library use, we opted to have our "librarians-in-uniform" wear the most comforting color to appear more accessible.

Study Variables

Our dependent variable was the perceived usefulness of librarians based on student perceptions. The independent variables noted in our study were the amount of television viewing and time spent at local libraries during childhood, young adulthood, and college years. The amount of television watched was measured through self-reported hours of viewing based on long-term autobiographical memory.*

Seven demographic variables were measured to compare television viewing and perceptions of social reality based on past experience: race, education level, gender, GPA, perceived family income level, major, and age.[32] This demographic content accounted for individual differences independent of any media variables. Assessment of these measures was intended to provide understanding of how different conditions influence the judgment-construction process.[33]

Educational television is expected to influence individuals' beliefs and attitudes in distinctive ways.[34] Based on the research conducted by Dahlstrom and Scheufele, we wanted to measure the types of television content

---

* Cultivation effects are typically observed for judgments of societal norms, but not for personal experiences (L. J. Shrum, "The Implications of Survey Method for Measuring Cultivation Effects," *Human Communication Research* 33, no. 1 (2007): 66.)

students were familiar with.[35] This way, we could pinpoint student content viewing. Fifteen popular cable channels were included as a way to measure the potential interaction between exposure amount and how particular media content influenced their judgments.

Student Results

In September 2013, a 30-question survey was sent to approximately 2,900 undergraduate students via the university-wide e-mail system. In order to increase participation, a nominal monetary incentive was awarded by random lottery to one student who completed the entire survey. Four hundred twenty-six students attempted the 30-question survey. Three hundred sixty students completed the majority of the survey, while only 199 students completed the survey in its entirety. We believe that there was a high attrition rate due to the length of the survey. However, all responses were considered regardless of whether the respondent completed the entire survey. While every academic level was represented, the largest group of respondents were freshmen (34 percent); female (81 percent); from the largest departments on campus, namely business or education (42 percent combined); between the traditional college student ages of 17 and 21 (86 percent); and self-identified as non-Hispanic white or Euro-American (90 percent). This sample is representative of the general undergraduate student population.[†]

Our results indicate that there is not a direct link between exposure amount and particular media content and student judgments of librarian usefulness. It is important to keep in mind that student responses may be skewed based on the accuracy of long-term autobiographical memory. This information was collected as a means to place their prior experiences in perspective.

The cultivation effect may be skewed due to a student's ability (or inability) to process information during survey administration. Shrum

---

† Overall, Niagara University last reported to the National Center for Education Statistics that 60 percent females and 40 percent males were enrolled in 2012. The majority of students identify themselves as Caucasian (66 percent). In addition, 5 percent identify themselves as African American, 3 percent as Hispanic, and less than 2 percent as American Indian/Alaskan Native or Asian/Pacific Islander. Twenty-four percent of the students did not identify their ethnicity. ("IPEDS Data Center," National Center for Education Statistics, last modified 2012, http://nces.ed.gov/ipeds/datacenter/SnapshotX.aspx?unitId=acb4aeb4b2ae).

found that a majority of college students given surveys are usually in a hurry to complete them and are therefore more likely to use heuristics, or mental shortcuts. These judgments are able to be recalled due to their vividness, frequency, or recency in the memory and tend to show a larger cultivation effect because they retrieve only a small amount of the cognitive information available. Heuristics are easy to apply and make few demands on cognitive resources, so they are more likely to be used in instances in which either the ability to process information is impaired (e.g., time pressure, distraction) or the motivation to process information is low (e.g., low involvement).[36] This lack of processing may cause source discounting errors because students are either unmotivated or unable to determine the source of the information they retrieve.[37]

The largest groups of our students reported having watched between two and three hours of television a day throughout the years, regardless of their educational status (elementary school, 52 percent; high school, 47 percent; college, 40 percent). A small group (less than 7 percent at each developmental level) reported watching television six hours or more a day. The most popular television channels viewed during their early childhood years were the Disney Channel (66 percent), Nickelodeon (60 percent), and ABC/ABC Family (34 percent). However, the majority of the students surveyed could not name specific examples of librarians in the media. In general, students identified librarian media portrayals to be female and older. Fifty-five percent of students recalled that librarians rarely appeared in media, but mostly remembered it to be negative. Comments provided below this question offered a dichotomy either of an "old," "mean," or "shushing woman," or of a "young, sexy woman." One student stated in her comment that while most examples were of these types, she had "yet to meet [a librarian] that fit these stereotypes."

In an effort to compare social reality based on past experience, we asked students to recall childhood experiences. The majority of students stated that they grew up in the middle-income households (83 percent) and their parents both worked full-time (59 percent). Students estimated that they went to the library weekly during elementary school (64 percent). During that time, they remember asking the librarian for assistance monthly (43 percent). Library use decreased to monthly as they progressed through high school (35 percent), while their use of the librarian slightly decreased as their age increased (38 percent).

When asked to reflect on their own opinions, the largest group of respondents stated that a librarian's wardrobe has no effect on their approachability (45 percent). However, their responses about their own approachability fared very differently (figure 2). For example, when asked if they felt that their own wardrobe affects their approachability, comments included, "You need to present the way you want people to see you" and "Education is a very professional and personable profession. You have to have an air of respect for yourself, and it's definitely represented through your attire." With this in mind, a professional wardrobe and presentation are imperative for potential interactions with staff and patrons.

Students: Attire, Effort, and Influences					
	Strongly Agree	Agree	Disagree	Strongly Disagree	Total
I put a lot of effort into my clothing attire	15.01%	54.42%	27.61%	2.95%	
	56	203	103	11	373
I expect others to put effort into their attire as well.	4.56%	46.11%	43.97%	5.36%	
	17	172	164	20	373
The way I dress affects my personal interactions.	15.05%	54.57%	26.34%	4.03%	
	56	203	98	15	372
Clothing influences a librarians approachability.	5.36%	32.98%	45.58%	16.09%	
	20	123	170	60	373

FIGURE 2

Students' self-perceptions and beliefs were assessed to reflect psychosocial matching and mirroring in librarian approachability.

At the time of survey administration, 45 percent of students reported frequenting the campus library on a weekly basis. Students stated that they have received assistance from a librarian weekly (4 percent), monthly (6 percent), a couple of times a semester (37 percent), or never (35 percent). Of those asked, 16 percent of students did not respond. These results may be skewed due to the fact that a large number of the student respondents were freshmen and the survey was administered during the first two weeks of their first college semester. A few students (5 percent) mentioned that they could not locate a staff member when they needed help or that they did not know who to approach for assistance.

The results of our survey coincide with Luthmann's contention that the "image" of a profession is created by people's personal experience of it.[38] No matter the academic level, our students have a positive outlook toward librarians in general (figure 3). Overall, students reported being either satisfied or very satisfied with the way they are treated at the campus library (92 percent) and the quality of service they are provided (88 percent), even if they had yet to receive direct service.

Student Perception of Librarian Ability					
	Strongly Agree	Agree	Disagree	Strongly Disagree	Total
Librarians aid my advancement in my academic discipline.	17.88%	67.58%	13.64%	0.91%	
	59	223	45	3	330
Librarians enable me to be more efficient in my academic pursuits.	19.39%	66.06%	13.64%	0.91%	
	64	218	45	3	330
Librarians help me distinguish between trustworthy and untrustworthy information.	22.05%	66.16%	10.27%	1.51%	
	73	219	34	5	331
Librarians provide me with the information skills I need in my work or study.	18.60%	70.12%	10.06%	1.22%	
	61	230	33	4	328

FIGURE 3

A majority of students surveyed felt that librarians were beneficial to their academic research.

While our results do not contain enough data to prove or disprove our hypothesis that student satisfaction with the library increases throughout one's academic career, students who left comments with this question suggest a confirmation of service quality. A few juniors stated, "I love the librarians," "I got help today :)," and "If I need help the librarians are always nice and help." These comments indicate that older students were more inclined to explicitly endorse librarians based on positive experiences accumulated since freshman year.

When given a choice, more male and female users chose to approach female librarians, supporting Kazlauskas's findings in 1976 that users prefer to approach a female when given a choice.[39] Comments included these:

> When I am seeking reference I put my trust in someone who I feel is intellectual, and I don't know why I pick female, I just feel most librarians are female. That's how I have seen them so that's how they should be.

> * * *

> Because this is what I have grown up with and am used to. I want someone who is like me and knows what she is talking about.

Conversely, it was surprising to find that a few females made comments that suggested that they do not think their gender knows as much as males do in certain areas of academia. One female respondent stated

> I would chose person number seven. He looks very young and fashionable, thus he seems up to date with all sorts of technology. Him being a guy also adds into my decision because I stereotypically think more males know more about technology than females.

Another stated, "Three, men are usually better at/like more statistical data." In fact, one female simply stated her selection was not at all based on the wardrobe so much as "because he is a male."

Mirroring and matching in the service context of an academic library was confirmed in our study. One male student stated he would select librarian "three or seven. Both are closest to my age and male so they'd probably think more like I do, making it easier to communicate." Another male stated

> I would ask number three for statistical help. All my stats professors have been male, so I associate males with understanding math. Again, he is young enough to be approachable and since he is not wearing a tie, I feel that he has time to help, whereas a man with a suit and tie would seem too busy to help.

Many of the responses related their librarian selections solely to past experience, for example, "Three, honestly it's because he looks like my high school physics teacher who spent quite a bit of time helping me analyze data and work with graphs and tables." It is clear that it is not only occupational stereotyping at issue. The results of our student survey show gender biases as well. The issue with statements such as these is a continuing unwillingness of patrons to pose STEM-related questions to female librarians.* As this is a female-dominated profession, the resulting risk is that the librarian is underutilized.

Our student sample selected the youngest librarian as the most approachable (34 percent) and the overall best example of an ideal librarian (32 percent). The majority of reasons provided may be summarized in this statement:

> As a female, approaching another female is a lot easier for me. Also approaching someone who is older than a student but not too old where they might struggle with the current trends. She looks like a normal person who is distinguished by her unique top, so I don't have to worry about approaching the wrong person.

Another female stated

> Person number two seems extremely friendly and wanting to help her students. She is also young and pretty. Also, her

---

* STEM: Science, Technology, Engineering, and Math.

clothes won't distract anyone because they aren't revealing or too showy, but she is very approachable.

The fewest students said that they would approach librarian eight (9 percent) and nine (8 percent). Surprisingly, the main reasons were these librarians' "young" age and outfit worn. Comments were similar to this one:

> They are younger and don't seem to be in the professional setting based on their casual apparel. Though dressed acceptably, there's really nothing that sets them apart from anybody else who might be using the library (images seven, eight and nine). I am more likely to approach someone who looks the role of a staff member—semi-formally dressed with a name-tag or "librarian" tag.

Based on these comments, it appears that a professional appearance is more approachable than personal style.

Librarian five was rated as the most professional-looking (84 percent) while appearing to have the most knowledge required to provide quality research assistance (31 percent). In contradiction to these statements, other students determined that librarian five also appears the most business-like or impersonal (45 percent) as well as unapproachable (32 percent). These student responses indicated that it was because he was wearing a tie. While this inhibited his approachability for a large number of students, others claimed that the tie associated him with the ranks of a professor as "most of our male faculty wear ties daily." Second to him in every statement was librarian one. These selections of preferences demonstrate that a professional look is generally preferred among the sample. However, it is worth mentioning that appearing too professional, for example, wearing a tie, is a detriment to increased patron interactions. Therefore, moderately professional dress seems to be functional, in terms of professionalism, and friendlier, in terms of approachability.

When it came to assisting with online technologies, librarian seven was considered the best librarian for the job (36 percent). This seemed to be the only time that ethnicity stood out as an issue. There were numerous student comments similar to the following, "Number seven. He seems the youngest out of all of them and therefore having the most experience. The fact that he is Asian also influenced my decision." Other reasons seemed to be influenced by his personal style, for example, "I would choose person seven because of his mail carrier bag. It just seems like he has his laptop on him at all times and would be most likely to find and be able to interpret statistical data." Note that this selection was chosen based on a belief that he had some type of statistical as well as technological knowledge. This belief corresponds with the previous comments applied to males and their supposedly greater STEM-related knowledge.

Some students preferred their ideal librarian to be "older" and "wiser," selecting librarians one, five, and six. One student proclaimed, "Six, because she portrays a typical librarian in my mind because she is older and looks like a librarian from the movies." However, there was no connection between those who watched more television as children (i.e., six hours or more a day) and those who preferred the traditional media-generated stereotype of an older woman. In fact, most of our respondents indicated that in their past experience, real-life librarians have been older (51 percent), intellectual (44 percent), and female (81 percent).

Thus, our hypothesis that there is a higher cultivation effect in those who watched more television as children has been deemed null. Students based their judgments on perceived librarian usefulness solely on their prior experiences in a reference encounter. This was noted based on their high frequency rates of attendance in libraries growing up (64 percent attended the library during elementary school once a week) as well as their positive ratings of their current library without necessarily having used it yet.

Academic Librarian Results

It is important to compare media-derived stereotypes and student perceptions with actual characteristics of the professional librarian image. Are we, in fact, caught perpetuating these media stereotypes ourselves? During the summer of 2013, we surveyed a sample of academic librarians (715 respondents) using an online self-assessment that was distributed through various e-mail lists. Librarians replied to 19 questions concerning self-perceptions of their actual work environment and office attire.

The majority of the respondents identified themselves as non-Hispanic white or Euro-American (92 percent) and female (87 percent). There is a range of ages in those who completed the survey. Of the academic librarians surveyed, 17 percent stated that they are in their 20s while the largest group of respondents are in their 30s (38 percent). Members of the second-largest group are at least 50 years of age (29 percent; see figure 4).

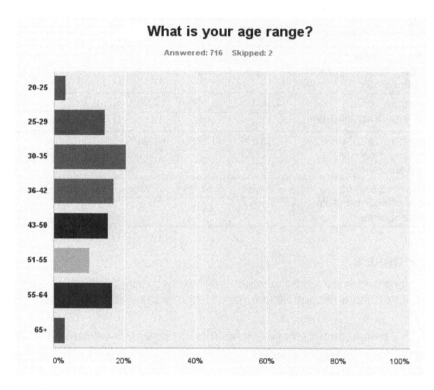

FIGURE 4

Librarian demographic survey response—age range

Eighty-one percent agreed that their wardrobe selection is influenced by their job duties. Respondents indicated that their choice of dress might influence colleagues' perception of their professionalism and abilities (80 percent). However, they did not seem to see it influencing promotions or pay raises (41 percent; see figure 5). One librarian asserted, "I feel that interpersonal politics has more to do with departmental advancement and respect than dress does," though one might argue that dress can certainly influence or at least be part of interpersonal politics.

Librarians: Attire, Effort, and Influences					
	Strongly Agree	**Agree**	**Disagree**	**Strongly Disagree**	**Total**
Librarian attire influences impressions.	33.61%	57.98%	7.42%	0.98%	
	240	414	53	7	714
Librarian attire influences promotions or raises.	12.32%	37.68%	40.37%	9.63%	
	87	266	285	68	706
Librarian attire influences colleagues.	22.03%	58.33%	17.23%	2.40%	
	156	413	122	17	708
I spend a lot of time and effort on my workplace attire.	10.13%	41.35%	41.21%	7.31%	
	72	294	293	52	711
The way I feel at work affects positive interactions.	42.42%	53.37%	3.93%	0.28%	
	302	380	28	2	712

FIGURE 5

Librarians were asked whether they felt their workplace attire represented them accurately in regard to numerous variables.

Depending on the workday schedule, 75 percent of respondents stated that they tend to wear business casual outfits to work, mainly because various projects, such as moving boxes or shifting the collection, call for less formal attire. Most librarians claimed their outfits are both professional and modest while not limiting their personal style that adds to one's approachability. Many discuss their attempt to thwart the frumpy librarian stereotype by adding "cool" and "funky" accessories as a way to build rapport with students. In fact, one librarian quipped

> I mostly make an effort as I hate the stereotype of librarians as
> fussy older women only interested in cardigans and the impor-

tance of complete silence being maintained at all times. Also I work with a lot of students who are around 10 years younger than me—quite a gap to them at 18, but not to me! I'd like to be thought of as approachable and current, not over-the-hill.

The same ideal holds true for more experienced information workers. One librarian reflected

> I think the world has changed and the libraries I worked in 30 years ago are a different environment from those we work in now. The conservative look is not required, and is more for those whose personality it fits, not because you have to wear it. Hair color, tattoos, bigger jewelry, statement colors in clothes, are much more accepted. I think it is great!

Another expressed

> I believe that wearing stylish and appealing clothing has a positive effect on my interactions with students, faculty, staff and the larger community. As I'm an older librarian (over 65), my apparel also helps me to avoid being automatically cast as a senior who's possibly less cool and knowledgeable than some of the younger staff.

The youngest generation of librarians surveyed unanimously admitted to an attempt to stand out from the student population and tend to dress formally (17 percent); simply put, "I try to dress up more so students realize that I am actually a librarian and not a student worker." In another example, one respondent explained

> I work on a college campus and look young for my age, so I do want to distinguish myself from looking like a student. I also want to send the message that I am professional and confident. Further, I think dressing nicely sends a message that you care about being there and helps put you in the "work" mindset.

Another pointed out, "I began wearing a coat and tie to work when I started my first library job because I felt I looked young and wanted to make it obvious to patrons that I was a library employee." Those who identified themselves as library directors reported that they also dress formally as it is considered the norm among other campus directors. One director summed up the situation well:

> It is not the library specifically, but the university enforces a dress code. The university tries to demonstrate professionalism. I want to look like a leader but an approachable person who can be helpful.

Some librarians reported that their ideal work outfit is very different from what they normally wear day to day (24 percent). Most of the responses stated that they wanted to be more relaxed in their attire or that they simply cannot afford the expensive contents of their ideal wardrobes. Twenty-seven percent of academic librarians stated that there is a dress code in effect at their institution; less than one percent of those stated that it included a uniform.

Future Research Opportunities

While the librarian survey offered geographically diverse responses, the nature of the student survey warranted the use of a voluntary sample that was geographically narrow and limited in sample size. Due to the demographics of Niagara University, these results are not generalizable. Replication of the student survey with a larger sample and a more diverse population is warranted.

In regard to the images, it is yet unclear how librarians one and two were interpreted by the student population. The images were intended to represent a uniformed look. However, it is unclear whether or not the images were viewed in that sense or simply as professional-looking. Likewise, expanding the pictured librarians to rotate the clothing styles across more librarians and depicting individuals in multiple styles of dress could allow for more refined observations of how our user population encounters librarians.

Additionally, future studies may include moving beyond a survey to actual application of the hypothetical research scenarios with practicing research librarians and surveys taken after reference interactions. These real-life observations can be used to measure how action reflects self-reporting of students in terms of avoiding and initiating reference interactions. The implementation should be sure to control for gender, age, ethnicity, and attire.

Conclusion

The media presents us with what seems to be a constant stream of images and representations, often stereotyped, of aspects of daily life. Through our formative years, we absorb the images we see on television, in the movies, and in other media. These images help shape the way in which we react to and interpret our world. Ideally, every perception, idea, and interpretation we have would be based on prior experience. As this is not always possible, these images then become the basis for our opinions and perceptions of similar situations, people, professions, and other traits associated with the images. However, past experience cannot be discounted when considering the foundation for a person's perceptions, biases, and opinions concerning a certain topic. If an individual interacts with a person demonstrating stereotypical behavior, including wardrobe and appearance, of their profession, gender, age, or other identifiable characteristics, that stereotype will influence all other interactions that individual has with any other member of that group.

Acknowledging that self-reporting gets at only one aspect of students' encounters with librarians, we can come away from this study with some useful observations. Through the surveys administered, it is clear that a student's past personal experience with a librarian is more powerful than media representations. Based on these results, the authors found that cultivation theory does not necessarily apply to the students surveyed in their decision to approach a reference librarian. It appears that prior experience has a stronger effect than media representation when it comes to student perception of librarian service quality. It is clear that the students surveyed, regardless of academic year, perceive our librarians in a positive manner.

However, stereotypes have not been entirely removed from their perceptions. These views are only somewhat influenced by mass media–derived stereotypes of librarianship. Instead, there is a greater emphasis on gender, age, and ethnicity.

Our study suggests that the majority of the college students surveyed prefer librarians to be similar to, or mirror, themselves.[*] Students feel that these librarians will be able relate to common student issues. This mirroring enables students to feel more comfortable and less anxious when asking questions. However, it is not realistic to have only younger staff on hand. The librarian workforce requires diversification. Recently, there has been a record increase of minority student enrollment.[40] If students want librarians who are reflections of themselves, one logical conclusion is that increased diversity among librarians will improve our service to an increasingly diverse student body.

After numerous attempts made by the ALA, the profession remains largely unchanged in terms of gender, disability, age, and ethnicity, to name a few.[41] Perhaps a reevaluation of MacAdam and Nichols's Peer Information Counseling programs could be instituted.[42] The original program consisted of minority upperclassmen who were hired and trained by a librarian supervisor to act as information specialists for their peers. This program was found to be a successful way to lessen student library anxiety through mirroring in the reference encounter. Reimplementation of this program would provide diversification of the library workforce until the profession begins to look like the rest of US population.[†]

Some librarians may be guilty of a self-obsession with existing stereotypes. Even with an occasional accoutrement, librarians' adoption of the stereotypical signifiers does more to encourage the stereotype than it does to assuage it. As evidenced through our study, a patron's perception of a librarian is fundamentally formed through their direct experience. It stands to reason that, when confronted with the stereotypical librarian im-

---

[*] Some students also preferred assistance from mature librarians because those librarians reminded them of former instructors or others they held in high regard. However, this was not the majority.

[†] For more discussion of diversifying the academic library workforce, see chapters 7 and 12 in this volume.

age, a patron's preexisting ideas of the stereotype will be emphasized and become ingrained in their perception of the profession thereafter. In short, through our own reinforcement of these media-generated images, either intentionally or otherwise, we are cultivating these stereotypes ourselves.

Notes

1. J. K. Rowling, "Hogwarts Library Checkout Card," in *Quidditch through the Ages* (New York: Arthur A. Levine Books, 2001), 2.
2. Deirdre Dupré, "The Perception of Image and Status in the Library Profession," *New Breed Librarian* 1, no. 4 (August 2001): 4.
3. Abigail Luthmann, "Librarians, Professionalism and Image: Stereotype and Reality," *Library Review* 56, no. 9 (2007): 775.
4. Joy V. Peluchette, Katherine Karl, and Kathleen Rust, "Dressing to Impress: Beliefs and Attitudes Regarding Workplace Attire," *Journal of Business and Psychology* 21, no. 1 (2006): 45–63.
5. L. J. Shrum, "Media Consumption and Perceptions of Social Reality: Effects and Underlying Processes," in *Media Effects*, 3rd ed., ed. Jennings Bryant and Mary Beth Oliver (New York: Taylor and Francis, 2009), 52.
6. George Gerbner and Larry Gross, "Living with Television: The Violence Profile," *Journal of Communication* 26, no. 2 (1976): 172–94.
7. L. J. Shrum, "Processing Strategy Moderates the Cultivation Effect," *Human Communication Research* 27, no. 1 (2001): 96.
8. L. J. Shrum, "The Cognitive Processes Underlying Cultivation Effects Are a Function of Whether the Judgments Are On-line or Memory-Based," *Communications: The European Journal of Communication Research* 29, no. 3 (2004): 332–33; Shrum, "Processing Strategy," 112; Rick W. Busselle and L. J. Shrum, "Media Exposure and Exemplar Accessibility," *Media Psychology* 5, no. 3 (2003): 256.
9. Michael Morgan, James Shanahan, and Nancy Signorielli, "Growing Up with Television: Cultivation Processes," in Bryant and Oliver, *Media Effects*, 34–49.
10. Marsha L. Richins, "Media, Materialism, and Human Happiness," *Advances in Consumer Research* 14, no. 1 (1987): 355.
11. Beverly RoskosEwoldsen, John Davis, and David R. RoskosEwoldsen, "Implications of the Mental Models Approach for Cultivation Theory," *Communications: The European Journal of Communication Research* 29, no. 3 (2004): 347.
12. Deborah A. Prentice, Richard J. Gerrig, and Daniel S. Bailis, "What Readers Bring to the Processing of Fictional Texts," *Psychonomic Bulletin and Review* 4, no. 3 (1997): 419.
13. George Gerbner, Larry Gross, Michael Morgan, and Nancy Signorielli, "The 'Mainstreaming' of America: Violence Profile No. 11," *Journal of Communication* 30, no. 3 (September 1980): 10–29. doi:10.1111/j.1460-2466.1980.tb01987.x.
14. Albert Bandura, "Social Cognitive Theory of Mass Communications," in *Media Effects*, 3rd ed., ed. Jennings Bryant and Mary Beth Oliver (Mahwah, NJ: Lawrence Erlbaum, 2009), 94–124.
15. Robin L. Nabi and Marina Krcmar, "Conceptualizing Media Enjoyment as Attitude: Implications for Mass Media Effects Research," *Communication Theory* 14, no. 4 (November 2004): 302.

16. Robert S. Wyer Jr., "Principles of Mental Representation," in *Social Psychology*, 2nd ed., ed. Arie W. Kluglanski and E. Tory Higgins (New York, Guilford, 2007), 289.

17. L. J. Shrum and Valerie Darmanin Bischak, "Mainstreaming, Resonance, and Impersonal Impact," *Human Communication Research* 27, no. 2 (2001): 191.

18. L. J. Shrum, Robert S. Wyer Jr., and Thomas C. O'Guinn, "The Effects of Television Consumption on Social Perceptions: The Use of Priming Procedures to Investigate Psychological Processes," *Journal of Consumer Research* 24, no. 4 (1998): 455.

19. RoskosEwoldsen, Davis, and RoskosEwoldsen, "Implications of the Mental Models Approach," 353.

20. Ibid.; Karyn Riddle, "Cultivation Theory Revisited: The Impact of Childhood Television Viewing Levels on Social Reality Beliefs and Construct Accessibility in Adulthood" (paper presented at annual meeting of International Communication Association, Chicago, IL, May 21, 2009), 4.

21. Marie L. Radford, "Approach or Avoidance? The Role of Nonverbal Communication in the Academic Library User's Decision to Initiate a Reference Encounter," *Library Trends* 46, no. 4 (Spring 1998): 699.

22. Patricia Glass Schuman, "The Image of Librarians: Substance or Shadow?" *Journal of Academic Librarianship* 16, no. 2 (1990): 87; Luthmann, "Librarians, Professionalism, and Image," 776.

23. For instance, see Eleri Sampson, "First Impressions: The Power of Personal Style," *Library Management* 16, no. 4 (1995): 28.

24. Jennifer L. Bonnet and Benjamin McAlexander. "First Impressions and the Reference Encounter: The Influence of Affect and Clothing on Librarian Approachability," *Journal of Academic Librarianship* 39, no. 4 (2013): 336.

25. Melanie Chu, "Ageism in Academic Librarianship," *EJASL: Electronic Journal of Academic and Special Librarianship* 10, no. 2 (Summer 2009): sec.1, http://southernlibrarianship.icaap.org/content/v10n02/chu_m01.html.

26. John Edge and Ravonne Green, "The Graying of Academic Librarians: Crisis or Revolution?" *Journal of Access Services* 8, no. 3 (June 21, 2011): 99.

27. Lawrence A. Crosby, Kenneth R. Evans, and Deborah Cowles, "Relationship Quality in Services Selling: An Interpersonal Influence Perspective," *Journal of Marketing* 54, no. 3 (July 1990): 68-81, cited in Carley Foster and Sheilagh Resnick, "Service Worker Appearance and the Retail Service Encounter: The Influence of Gender and Age," *Service Industries Journal* 33, no. 2 (2013): 241–43.

28. Julie JohnsonHillery, Jikyeong Kang, and WenJan Tuan, "The Difference between Elderly Consumers' Satisfaction Levels and Retail Sales Personnel's Perceptions," *International Journal of Retail and Distribution Management* 25, no. 4 (1997): 126–37.

29. Karolina Wägar and LarsJohan Lindqvist, "The Role of the Customer Contact Person's Age in Service Encounters," *Journal of Services Marketing* 24, no. 7 (2010): 511, doi:10.1108/08876041011081069.

30. Bonnet and McAlexander, "First Impressions and the Reference Encounter," 336; Radford, "Approach or Avoidance?" 699–717; Lynden K. Miles, "Who Is Approachable?" *Journal of Experimental Social Psychology* 45 (2009): 262–66.

31. Bonnet and McAlexander, "First Impressions and the Reference Encounter," 337.

32. Michael Hughes, "The Fruits of Cultivation Analysis: A Reexamination of Some Effects of Television Watching," *Public Opinion Quarterly* 44, no. 3 (1980): 291; Michael Morgan and James Shanahan, "The State of Cultivation," *Journal of Broadcasting and Electronic Media* 54, no. 2 (2010): 339, doi:10.1080/08838151003735018.

33. Shrum, "Processing Strategy," 97.
34. Michael D. Slater and Donna Rouner, "Entertainment—Education and Elaboration Likelihood: Understanding the Processing of Narrative Persuasion," *Communication Theory* 12, no. 2 (May 2002): 174.
35. Michael F. Dahlstrom and Dietram A. Scheufele, "Diversity of Television Exposure and Its Association with the Cultivation of Concern for Environmental Risks," *Environmental Communication* 4, no. 1 (2010): 59.
36. Shrum, "Processing Strategy," 99; Shrum, "Implications of Survey Method," 66; Shrum, "Media Consumption," 60.
37. Danny Axsom, Suzanne Yates, and Shelly Chaiken, "Audience Response as a Heuristic Cue in Persuasion," *Journal of Personality and Social Psychology* 53, no. 1 (July 1987): 38.
38. Luthmann, "Librarians, Professionalism and Image," 778.
39. Edward Kazlauskas, "An Exploratory Study: A Kinesis Analysis of Academic Library Service Points," *Journal of Academic Librarianship* 2, no. 3 (July 1976), 130-34, cited in Radford, "Approach or Avoidance," 710.
40. Richard Fry, *Minorities and the RecessionEra College Enrollment Boom* (Washington, DC: Pew Research Center, 2010), 4–5, www.pewsocialtrends.org/2010/06/16/minorities-and-the-recession-era-college-enrollment-boom.
41. E. J. Josey and Ismail Abdullahi, "Why Diversity in American Libraries," *Library Management* 23, no. 1 (2002): 10–16; Camila A. Alire and Frederick J. Stielow, "Minorities and the Symbolic Potential of the Academic Library: Reinventing Tradition," *College and Research Libraries*56, no. 6 (November 1995): 509–17.
42. Barbara MacAdam and Darlene P. Nichols, "Peer Information Counseling: An Academic Library Program for Minority Students," *Journal of Academic Librarianship* 15, no. 4 (1989): 204–209.

Bibliography

Alire, Camila A., and Frederick J. Stielow. "Minorities and the Symbolic Potential of the Academic Library: Reinventing Tradition." *College and Research Libraries* 56, no. 6 (November 1995): 509–17.

Axsom, Danny, Suzanne Yates, and Shelly Chaiken. "Audience Response as a Heuristic Cue in Persuasion." *Journal of Personality and Social Psychology* 53, no. 1 (July 1987): 30–40.

Bandura, Albert. "Social Cognitive Theory of Mass Communications." In *Media Effects: Advances in Theory and Research*, 3rd ed., edited by Jennings Bryant and Mary Beth Oliver, 94-124. Mahwah, NJ: Lawrence Erlbaum, 2009.

Bonnet, Jennifer L., and Benjamin McAlexander. "First Impressions and the Reference Encounter: The Influence of Affect and Clothing on Librarian Approachability." *Journal of Academic Librarianship* 39, no. 4 (2013): 335–46.

Busselle, Rick W., and L. J. Shrum. "Media Exposure and Exemplar Accessibility." *Media Psychology* 5, no. 3 (2003): 255–82.

Chu, Melanie. "Ageism in Academic Librarianship." *E-JASL: Electronic Journal of Academic and Special Librarianship* 10, no. 2 (Summer 2009): 1–4. http://southernlibrarianship.icaap.org/content/v10n02/chu_m01.html.

Dahlstrom, Michael F., and Dietram A. Scheufele. "Diversity of Television Exposure and Its Association with the Cultivation of Concern for Environmental Risks." *Environmental Communication* 4, no. 1 (2010): 54–65.

Dupré, Deirdre. "The Perception of Image and Status in the Library Profession." *New Breed Librarian* 1, no. 4 (August 2001): 1–8.

Edge, John, and Ravonne Green. "The Graying of Academic Librarians: Crisis or Revolution?" *Journal of Access Services* 8, no. 3 (June 21, 2011): 97–106.

Foster, Carley, and Sheilagh Resnick. "Service Worker Appearance and the Retail Service Encounter: The Influence of Gender and Age." *Service Industries Journal* 33, no. 2 (2013): 236-47.

Fry, Richard. *Minorities and the Recession-Era College Enrollment Boom.* (Washington, DC: Pew Research Center., 2010). www.pewsocialtrends.org/2010/06/16/minorities-and-the-recession-era-college-enrollment-boom.

Gerbner, George, and Larry Gross. "Living with Television: The Violence Profile." *Journal of Communication* 26, no. 2 (1976): 172–94.

Gerbner, George, Larry Gross, Michael Morgan, and Nancy Signorielli. "The 'Mainstreaming' of America: Violence Profile No. 11." *Journal of Communication* 30, no. 3 (September 1980): 10–29. doi:10.1111/j.1460-2466.1980.tb01987.x.

Hughes, Michael. "The Fruits of Cultivation Analysis: A Reexamination of Some Effects of Television Watching." *Public Opinion Quarterly* 44, no. 3 (1980): 287–302.

Institute of Education Sciences. "IPEDS Data Center." National Center for Education Statistics. Last modified 2012. http://nces.ed.gov/ipeds/datacenter/SnapshotX.aspx?unitId=acb4aeb4b2ae.

Johnson-Hillery, Julie, Jikyeong Kang, and Wen-Jan Tuan. "The Difference between Elderly Consumers' Satisfaction Levels and Retail Sales Personnel's Perceptions." *International Journal of Retail and Distribution Management* 25, no. 4 (1997): 126–37.

Josey, E. J., and Ismail Abdullahi. "Why Diversity in American Libraries." *Library Management* 23, no. 1 (2002): 10–16.

Luthmann, Abigail. "Librarians, Professionalism and Image: Stereotype and Reality." *Library Review* 56, no. 9 (2007): 773–80.

MacAdam, Barbara, and Darlene P. Nichols. "Peer Information Counseling: An Academic Library Program for Minority Students." *Journal of Academic Librarianship* 15, no. 4 (1989): 204–209.

Miles, Lynden K. "Who Is Approachable?" *Journal of Experimental Social Psychology* 45 (2009): 262–66.

Morgan, Michael, and James Shanahan. "The State of Cultivation." *Journal of Broadcasting and Electronic Media* 54, no. 2 (2010): 337–55. doi:10.1080/08838151003735018.

Morgan, Michael, James Shanahan, and Nancy Signorielli. "Growing Up with Television: Cultivation Processes." In *Media Effects: Advances in Theory and Research*, 3rd ed., edited by Jennings Bryant and Mary Beth Oliver, 34–49. New York: Taylor and Francis, 2009.

Nabi, Robin L., and Marina Krcmar. "Conceptualizing Media Enjoyment as Attitude: Implications for Mass Media Effects Research." *Communication Theory* 14, no. 4 (November 2004): 288–310.

Peluchette, Joy V., Katherine Karl, and Kathleen Rust. "Dressing to Impress: Beliefs and Attitudes Regarding Workplace Attire." *Journal of Business and Psychology* 21, no. 1 (2006): 45–63.

Prentice, Deborah A., Richard J. Gerrig, and Daniel S. Bailis. "What Readers Bring to the Processing of Fictional Texts." *Psychonomic Bulletin and Review* 4, no. 3 (1997): 416–20.

Radford, Marie L. "Approach or Avoidance? The Role of Nonverbal Communication in the Academic Library User's Decision to Initiate a Reference Encounter." *Library Trends* 46, no. 4 (Spring 1998): 699–717.

Richins, Marsha L. "Media, Materialism, and Human Happiness." *Advances in Consumer Research* 14, no. 1 (1987): 352–56.

Riddle, Karyn. "Cultivation Theory Revisited: The Impact of Childhood Television Viewing Levels on Social Reality Beliefs and Construct Accessibility in Adulthood." Paper presented at annual meeting of International Communication Association, Chicago, IL, May 21, 2009.

Roskos-Ewoldsen, Beverly, John Davis, and David R. Roskos-Ewoldsen. "Implications of the Mental Models Approach for Cultivation Theory." *Communications: The European Journal of Communication Research.* 29, no. 3 (2004): 345–63.

Rowling, J. K. "Hogwarts Library Checkout Card." In *Quidditch through the Ages.* New York: Arthur A. Levine Books, 2001.

Sampson, Eleri. "First Impressions: The Power of Personal Style." *Library Management* 16, no. 4 (1995): 25–28.

Schuman, Patricia Glass. "The Image of Librarians: Substance or Shadow?" *Journal of Academic Librarianship* 16, no. 2 (1990): 86–89.

Shrum, L. J. "The Cognitive Processes Underlying Cultivation Effects Are a Function of Whether the Judgments are On-line or Memory-Based." *Communications: The European Journal of Communication Research* 29, no. 3 (2004): 327–44.

———. "The Implications of Survey Method for Measuring Cultivation Effects." *Human Communication Research* 33, no. 1 (2007): 64–80.

———. "Media Consumption and Perceptions of Social Reality: Effects and Underlying Processes." In *Media Effects: Advances in Theory and Research,* 3rd ed., edited by Jennings Bryant and Mary Beth Oliver, 50–72. New York: Taylor and Francis, 2009.

———. "Processing Strategy Moderates the Cultivation Effect." *Human Communication Research* 27, no. 1 (2001): 94–120.

Shrum, L. J., and Valerie Darmanin Bischak. "Mainstreaming, Resonance, and Impersonal Impact." *Human Communication Research* 27, no. 2 (2001): 187–215.

Shrum, L. J., Robert S. Wyer Jr., and Thomas C. O'Guinn. "The Effects of Television Consumption on Social Perceptions: The Use of Priming Procedures to Investigate Psychological Processes." *Journal of Consumer Research* 24, no. 4 (1998): 447–58.

Slater, Michael D., and Donna Rouner. "Entertainment—Education and Elaboration Likelihood: Understanding the Processing of Narrative Persuasion." *Communication Theory* 12, no. 2 (May 2002): 173–91.

Wägar, Karolina, and Lars-Johan Lindqvist. "The Role of the Customer Contact Person's Age in Service Encounters." *Journal of Services Marketing* 24, no. 7 (2010): 509–517. doi:10.1108/08876041011081069.

Wyer, Robert S., Jr., "Principles of Mental Representation." In *Social Psychology: Handbook of Basic Principles,* 2nd ed., edited by Arie W. Kluglanski and E. Tory Higgins, 285-307. New York: Guilford, 2007.

CHAPTER 12

The Revolution Will Not Be Stereotyped

Changing Perceptions through Diversity

Annie Pho and Turner Masland

Introduction

Librarianship has long had a complex relationship with professional image and identity.[1] Stereotypes about libraries and the people who work in them are often rooted in images of poor customer service, outdated materials, and lack of diversity.[2] Stereotypes can be indicators of cultural norms, portraying what people perceive to be a truth. For academic libraries, these stereotypes can influence and misinform the opinions of students who are not familiar with what the library can provide. We should ask ourselves what we can do to change how our patrons see us and how they understand the work that we do as librarians. Whether in "public service" or not, as much as librarians work with providing access to information, they also work with the public.

Providing our students with rich and dynamic experiences in our libraries will only help contribute to deconstructing stereotypes. Many academic libraries are striving to do so, adding innovative services, new uses of space, and new material types. However, a key factor, which may be overlooked in these efforts, is that in higher education, there is a widening gap between the rising number of diverse student populations and the hiring of minority librarians.[3] Diversity on college and university campuses allows for opportunities for students to learn from each other. Seeing diversity in faculty and staff is important on an academic campus because it communicates that the institution is inclusive. The employees who work in an institution have a capacity to impact it, not just by sitting behind a desk as a face, but by changing structures and culture and atmosphere behind the scenes. Changing user perceptions about librarians is a long process and isn't solved with any quick answers. But having a diverse library workforce helps create an environment that is potentially more comfortable for a diverse community of patrons. The workforce shapes the leadership of the library, helps build a culture of inclusion, and educates our students on library research.

In this chapter, we examine the connection between increasing diversity in the library workplace and dispelling stereotypes. We explore how diversity in the academic library workforce can have positive effects in dispelling stereotypes through visibility, outreach, and education. We also want to rethink what we mean when we discuss diversity and what it entails. This is important to the process of examining library diversity initiatives and how they can fall short of complete inclusion. We also explore how activist librarians have defied the librarian stereotype and what we can learn from them. In order to create desired changes, we also need to see what the field is currently doing in terms of recruiting for diversity and what we can do to create a culture of inclusion at our institutions.

Academic libraries are in the position to reimagine their place on campus to be more than just a warehouse for books, and many are well along in this process. Librarians with different and diverse backgrounds, who are able to effectively communicate with a wide variety of individuals, will dispel antiquated library stereotypes. Students' perceptions will change once dynamic, diverse, and future-thinking librarians start working directly with them. The answer to dispelling stereotypes and increasing diversity in library staff is not simple, but by better understanding our past endeavors, we can create better steps for the future.

Complexities and Definitions of Diversity

Discussions about diversity can be challenging due to the inconsistent understanding of what that means. In the existing literature on diversity in libraries, there are a variety of ways that researchers choose to define diversity, but most only look at visible group identities, excluding the invisible.

Therefore, many assume diversity to mean race and ethnicity, but as the researchers Jaeger, Bertot, and Franklin point out, diversity encompasses a wide spectrum: "Diversity is certainly about more than issues of ethnicity, encompassing gender and sexual orientation, for example. However, no meaningful attempts have been made to determine the representation in librarianship and LIS of many diverse populations—including persons with disabilities; the socioeconomically and geographically disadvantaged; and gay, lesbian, bisexual, transgender, and questioning (GLBTQ) individuals, among others."[4]

Going beyond racial and ethnic diversity, we want to look at other groups who have been marginalized throughout history. Instead of focusing on visible differences, we understand diversity to be more than what we can see. We want to focus on diversity as points of difference, and when we discuss "minorities," we are focusing on factors that create a difference in treatment between a majority group and a minority group, in which the minority group can be viewed less favorably than the majority. This understanding of diversity also refers to differences that are not visible, such as sexual orientation or socioeconomic background. Other examples can include being a veteran, having a disability, being a first-generation American, belonging to a minority religion—the list is extensive. The focus we want the reader to consider is not just on these individual factors, but on the power dynamic between the majority and minority. How can we shift the power dynamics to balance out the inequalities between different groups? To confine diversity to a few labels denies the richness of the human condition and ignores the fact that people can have varied backgrounds. We must also consider the idea of intersectionality—how having multiple group identities shape one's experiences in life.[5] Intersectionality has been a key theory in feminism as a way to explore the influence of multiple identities and provides a framework for understanding that diversity is complex. Intersectionality is an area that needs further research in our field, and many library diversity initiatives do not take these kinds of experiences into account. They instead focus on quantifiable quotas, which is easier to do when one recruits based on race and ethnicity. It is much harder to recruit for invisible diversity.

What makes increasing diversity in librarianship even more complicated is the role of gender in the profession. Librarianship has been (and still is) primarily made up of women, and there are many equity issues related to this situation.[6] Male librarians are more likely to move into leadership positions and be paid more than women.[7] Considering the fact that female librarians compose the majority, it is an indicator that sexism in the workplace is present in librarianship. Christine Williams, sociologist and professor at University of Texas at Austin, states, "Men take their gender privilege with them when they enter predominantly female occupations: this translates into an advantage in spite of their numerical rarity."[8] Understanding gender inequality in librarianship is pertinent to understanding the climate for diversity in our field.

We are not arguing that our industry needs a certain number of men, or of racial or ethnic minorities, for librarian stereotypes to be lifted. Efforts to change stereotypes have to be multifold. If we want to change them through diversity, we have to understand what diversity is and how intersectionality shapes one's experience in the field. Take, for example, the authors of this chapter—one is an Asian American woman who has experienced prejudice based on her gender and race while working at the reference desk. Once, when she referred a student to the IT help desk for a printing question, she received the sexist comment "I shouldn't ask you about tech stuff, that's too complicated. I should ask the guys." Comments like this are an example of microaggression that she has faced while working in public services. The other author is an openly gay white man. As he was searching for his first professional job after library school, he was often told to remove his work with GLBT organizations from his resume. The justification was that anything "too gay" would alienate potential employers. This left him conflicted. Excluding it reinforces the privilege many gay, lesbian, and bisexual individuals have: being able to hide their differences whereas members from other groups cannot. As a white gay man, he can easily "pass" in both gay and straight worlds, but he also understands the fear and anxiety that comes from being an "other." Our experiences with intersectionality inform our understanding of how being different from the majority can affect our presence in the library world.

Diversity and Visibility in Higher Education

The discussion of diversity in institutions of higher education often focuses on the student population while missing the importance of faculty populations. John Brooks Slaughter, president emeritus of Occidental College and CEO of the National Action Council for Minorities in Engineering, agrees that recruiting and building a diverse student body is essential, but he argues that in order for true progress to be made, the students' education must be provided by a diverse faculty and supported by a diverse staff.[9] Robert Canida and Adriel Hilton continue the argument for more diverse faculty body in a recently released editorial in *Diverse Issues in Higher Education*, making the case that without the presence of diverse faculty on campus, students from diverse backgrounds begin to feel alienated and are less likely to persist.[10]

Diverse faculty not only represent an opportunity for visibility, but also give students the opportunity to learn from someone who is different from them. These same arguments can be made for library faculty and staff as well. Professional organizations have also realized the importance of institutional diversity. In 2012, the Association of College and Research Libraries (ACRL) developed Diversity Standards: Cultural Competencies for Academic Libraries, which demonstrated the importance of diversity to academic libraries. It states in the guidelines: "ACRL understands that if libraries are to continue being indispensable organizations in their campus communities, they must reflect the communities they serve and provide quality services to their increasingly diverse constituencies."[11] If libraries want to remain relevant and important to their communities, they need to make sure their employees understand the needs of that community.

To promote the recruitment of diversity in the field, we need to assess what is currently happening. Since 2007, ALA's Office for Diversity has been tracking diversity statistics through its Diversity Counts Study, which includes both public and academic librarians. This study found that the number of minority librarians has gone up over the past few years, but that the majority of degreed librarians are still white and female.[12] Hui Feng Chang, associate professor and librarian at Oklahoma State University, reported, "Overall minority students have increased from 19.6 percent in 1980 to almost 40 percent in 2010."[13] Yet, academic libraries in the Association of Research Libraries (ARL) have seen a 4.2 percent increase in the hiring of minority librarians.[14] Four percent is a low rate of increase in comparison to the rise in diversity of student populations. Slaughter highlighted the fact that creating a more diverse student body in higher education is becoming a reality, but that these achievements are not reflected by the hiring of diverse faculty. The number of diverse faculty members in higher education has plateaued over the past two decades.[15] The diversity trends in academic librarianship mirror what is happening in higher education: there is an increasing gap between the numbers of diverse faculty members and of students.

The need for diverse faculty extends beyond teaching faculty and into libraries. Libraries often serve as the heart of the institution, playing an integral part in student success. Megan Oakleaf described student success as a combination of learning, engagement, and retention. Specifically on retention, she states, "Most retention and graduation rate studies have focused on explanations for student persistence or departure, either due to personal characteristics or institutional practices. . . . Because most librarians are not in positions that enable them to influence students' personal traits, they can focus on creating institutional environments that foster retention and eventual graduation."[16]

Diversity among library staff creates an institutional environment that supports student learning. A study on librarian approachability in academic libraries found that African American participants were more likely to rank African American and Asian American images of librarians as more approachable than images of white librarians. The researchers Bonnet and McAlexander concluded that "racially underrepresented populations in higher education may be better served when the librarian population is also racially diverse."[17] This study supports the idea that racial and ethnic diversity behind a service desk can improve librarian approachability and ease library anxiety for underrepresented students. It's a matter of having a choice of whom to approach, as some of the students in the study felt more comfortable approaching librarians who were from similar racial backgrounds.

The authors argue that this form of visibility extends beyond racial and ethnic diversity, and that what is visible to one group of people can be invisible to another. For example, transgender individuals can potentially go unnoticed by members of the cisgendered community, but can be beacons of inclusion for other members of the trans* community.* The authors can also see how a conversation about visibility might be problematic. Ideally, we should be able to look past diversity and feel comfortable approaching those who are different from us. But we do not live in that reality. Visibility is still a factor when discussing diverse communities. It should also be noted that we are not arguing that black students should be helped by black librarians nor gay students by gay librarians. Rather, librarians should be prepared to effectively serve diverse communities and students should be able to see a variety of faces behind service desks. The librarian's role in a student's life is manifold: librarians are teachers, research counselors, and role models, making the importance of diversity in these supporting roles so significant. There are actions library professionals can take to include more diverse staff members in their organizations. But before we offer examples of how academic libraries can best support diverse communities, we should examine how stereotyping librarians affects our profession.

Librarian Stereotypes

There is a major disconnect between how librarians view themselves and how the public perceives them, creating tension in the way students interact with libraries and librarians. Librarians in popular media are often portrayed as females who are "introverted, unmarried, prim, shy and young."[18] Google image searches for *librarian* results in numerous pictures of females wearing buns and glasses with a finger raised to their lips. For individuals who have not stepped into a library in a long time, this imagery is what informs them about what a library is. These stereotypes are still quite present in media and applied to our profession. This cultural misunderstanding can be problematic for public service librarians who are working to build relationships with students and want to provide research

---

* *Cisgender* refers to a group of individuals whose self-identity conforms with the gender they were assigned at birth. *Trans** refers to all identities under the gender spectrum.

help. It puts a predisposed negative connotation in a patron's head before they walk into the library, creating a hurdle for librarians before they interact with that patron. Gary P. Radford and Marie L. Radford have argued, "Fear is the fundamental organizing principle, or code, through which representations of libraries and librarians are manifest in modern popular cultural forms such as novels, movies, and television shows. Fear is the means by which the presence of the library setting, and the librarian characters within them, are to be understood."[19]

Students may approach the library with certain expectations because this imagery of library fear and anxiety is communicated to them through media. For example, students may have anxiety about approaching the reference desk for help or expect the library to have only books to aid them in research. Studies have shown library anxiety to be a real phenomenon among college students, and a lack of understanding of library resources can result in visiting the library less frequently.[20]

One way to change a stereotype is to reverse the stereotype itself and to "challenge the image of the librarian, by showing that the opposite is true. In the LIS context this would involve media images of librarians as the reverse of their stereotypical images that is, as young, cool, and hip."[21] However, this creates more stereotypes, which is not helpful or positive. In 2007, the *New York Times* featured an article on the new image of librarians, detailing how librarians now use technology, are younger, and are socially conscious.[22] The presentation of librarians in this way suggests that the *New York Times* and some portion of the collective unconscious have begun to see librarians in a new light. Stuart Hall, acclaimed cultural theorist, argues that there are benefits to using positive imagery in reversing stereotypes: "Underlying this approach is an acknowledgement and celebration of diversity and difference in the world."[23] This alternative image of "hip" librarians is the revelation that there are different kinds of people who work in this industry.

Yet Hall also notes that positive imagery alone is not enough to displace all negative connotations. While some might find this new "hip" librarian image to be a relief, there is still something problematic about this portrayal—the lack of diversity. The same *New York Times* article featured pictures of librarians, but none of them were librarians of color. The lack of diversity can shut out those who do not fit into a mainstream, widely accepted profile. Flipping our professional image to be seen as cool or hip, as opposed to stuffy, is just a cosmetic change. Showing the public that our work has depth and that academic librarians are diverse will help dissolve harmful stereotypes altogether. The larger problem is that the public does not know what librarians do, which produces misconceptions about our professional image.

It is not easy to pinpoint the unease that stereotypes of librarians can evoke. It may seem trivial to discuss librarian stereotypes at all. Those who make up the majority of the profession (i.e., white, cisgender, and female) may feel that stereotypes of librarians are lighthearted or humorous and not view these stereotypes as harmful. Stereotypes affect the way that minority groups are treated by coworkers and patrons. For example, a student might approach the reference desk and not believe the person at the desk to be a librarian because he or she does not fit the stereotype. Stereotypes distill a few simple, widely recognized traits and erroneously simplify them to create a false representation.[24] They create the idea that there is a "normal" and that anything that deviates from that norm does not belong to that group. This creates tension between the majority group and the "other," which produces inequality as a result of not understanding the "other."[25]

The harmful impact of stereotypes derives from the fact that external groups pigeonhole the individual, removing the ability to create his or her own identity. While professional identity stereotypes do not seem as heavy as racial or gender stereotypes, they can be related. Librarians have an understanding of their professional duties but do not communicate outwardly what their job entails. Visual representation in popular culture and everyday life is a factor in the way stereotypes are formed and upheld. There is a need to get outside the echo chamber and show the public what librarians actually do for a living. By changing the public's perception, we can cause these stereotypes to begin to dissipate. Librarians can work with the public to show that our profession is comprised of many dynamic individuals who are doing important work. If students see individuals from a wide range of backgrounds in faculty roles, it is going to be much easier for them to have role models and envision themselves in similar positions.[26]

Going against the Grain: Activist Librarians

Several groups of librarians have worked hard throughout the years to combat discrimination in librarianship and raise awareness of issues pertaining to underrepresented librarians. In the late 1960s through the 1970s, several groups began to form within ALA to address issues of diversity and social justice in the profession. Many of these groups now comprise the ethnic caucuses of ALA and the Social Responsibilities Round Table (SRRT). The civil rights movement, the women's liberation movement, the gay rights movement, and many other activist movements during this period influenced how librarians shaped the future of their profession. Organizing these divisions was a way to increase visibility in libraries, create community with each other, and recruit other diverse candidates to the profession. Although librarianship has not always been a diverse profession in terms of race and ethnicity, there have been many diverse groups that have grown out of ALA and the library community. In fact, there have always been librarians in the margins who have organized themselves to bring the disparities experienced by minorities to the attention of the profession at large.

One interesting case was the formation of the Task Force on Gay Liberation, which was the foundation for the group now known as the Gay, Lesbian, Bisexual, and Transgender (GLBT) Round Table. Round Tables are groups with a specialized focus that do not fall within a larger division of the American Library Association, but unlike a task force, they have a permanent stature. The Task Force on Gay Liberation was the first professional organization in the country to openly address issues of sexual orientation.[27] This group compiled the first GLBT bibliographies and gay book awards, brought awareness of GLBT issues to the public eye, fought discrimination in employment, and helped to create ways for other librarians to support GLBT initiatives in their own libraries through the collection of materials. This happened in the 1970s when the discussion of GLBT rights was not as prevalent in the mainstream as it is today. Activist groups like this truly felt it was their responsibility as librarians to engage the profession and the public in these civil rights issues. Librarians have a professional duty to provide access to information, but they do not have to be neutral in their work. We can be social activists and librarians who incorporate our interests into our work.

Many of the founding leaders of these caucuses and round tables are role models for librarians today. Janet M. Suzuki was the cofounder of the Asian American Librarian Caucus, the first pan–Asian American librarian group. She took the responsibility of speaking out against social injustices very seriously. She saw the need to create a group for Asian American librarians that could meet and discuss issues related to their experiences in the profession. Additionally, her dedication to social justice went beyond librarianship. She was also an activist who spoke out against racism. In 1974, Suzuki worked with other Asian American activists "to convince the Pekin (Illinois) High School basketball team to change its name from the 'Chinks' to something less offensive."[28] Suzuki used her leadership skills to improve librarianship and spoke out against the injustices experienced by the Asian American community.

The work these divisions have done within ALA, and for their communities, overwhelmingly shows that these librarians were critically engaged and outspoken. These were not meek, docile, shushing librarians. Barbara Gittings, one of the first founding organizers of ALA's Task Force for Gay Liberation, described her work with the Task Force as "a heady time! We were activists. We were innovative, bold, imaginative, full of fun and energy, full of love for promoting our cause."[29] Her self-description reflected the important groundbreaking work that she and others had accomplished in this time period. These librarians were asking for others to speak up and change the injustices of society. They have set the path for other underrepresented groups to have a place and community in the library profession.

There are many contemporary examples of librarians fighting for social justice. In 2011, during the Occupy Wall Street movement, an image of a woman holding a sign that said "You know things are messed up when librarians start marching" circulated online.[30] This single image suggested that there is juxtaposition between being an activist and being a librarian, and that it is humorous that a librarian could be both. Yet it showed that librarians do take action and are involved in political movements. We do not have to march to promote social justice in our library communities. Librarians can incorporate critical pedagogy into their library instruction, work with underrepresented groups to help disseminate information to their communities, promote open access, or just be advocates for issues we deeply care about.

Despite the courageous actions that these activist librarians have taken, their passion and conviction for social change have somehow been lost in translation. Currently, library schools do not often focus on teaching their students library history; so new professionals start their careers without having background knowledge about how librarians have incorporated social justice into their everyday work. Knowing the profession's history helps guide its future. A clear understanding of the actions that librarians have taken and initiatives they are working on will diminish sweeping generalizations about librarians' work and roles. Looking at the work of these activist librarians, we see that they do not fit into the stereotype of the quiet librarian. They are not meek; they are outspoken and use their passion for social justice to organize their communities beyond the library realm. The way that these librarians have defined themselves and their work is far from cultural stereotypes, making it more important for current librarians to be aware of this part of library history. As a result, new professionals may lack the context for why so many diversity initiatives exist in our field. By understanding the relationship between social justice and libraries, we can fight for equality in our profession and for our students. For activist librarians like Gittings and Suzuki, creating social change went beyond librarianship; they were concerned about fighting for equal rights in society as well.

Working in libraries is not always easy for librarians from minority groups. Despite the trailblazing efforts of activist librarians in the 1960s and 1970s, issues of discrimination were still present, which created barriers in the hiring of diverse candidates in libraries. Minority librarians have experienced limited opportunities for growth once they were hired.[31] Additionally, open acts of bigotry in the workplace and in job interviews have prevented those who might have been great candidates from moving further up in the field. John Barnett, in his discussion of interviewing at academic libraries as an openly gay man in the 1980s, wrote: "My experiences in interviewing at colleges and universities were overwhelmingly negative, cynical, and demoralizing events."[32] For Barnett, there was never any open indication that his sexual orientation was what barred him from getting certain jobs, but being different from the majority was enough to eliminate his candidacy during interviews. Colleagues advised him to blend in and not give any impression that he was different; however, a crucial part of one's self-identity like sexual orientation or cultural background is not something someone should have to hide or be ashamed of. Putting in effort to hide an individual's sexuality can be harmful and potentially lead to mental health issues and internalized homophobia. Recent studies claim that it is in our nature to be drawn to those who are like-minded or similar to us, which creates homogeneous work environments.[33] This is why it is important to be cognizant when trying to hire people who bring unique perspectives to our institutions.

Learning about the experiences of underrepresented librarians reveals the consequences of stereotypes: how they form the ideas of cultural norms and how that can create difficulties in the workplace. If someone does not fit the mold of the norm, then that person is subject to being treated differently. Although this situation has improved over the past few decades, there are still many ways to help ensure inclusivity and openness in the workplace for underrepresented librarians. We should examine what may contribute to the conditions that keep these numbers small and find ways to retain and encourage these librarians to succeed once they are in the field.

Supporting Diversity

Despite years of effort of trying to recruit more underrepresented groups into libraries, libraries have still not come close to achieving equitable employment for all. There is much room for improvement in diversifying the workforce. We will not be changing any user perceptions if the stereotypes of librarians still hold a grain of truth. It is not enough to collect data and notice discrepancies in hiring; we need to take action to seriously change our own demographics for the benefit of our industry. The level of change needed is not an easy process to undertake because there are many challenges in trying to increase diversity. Many of the programs we are going to discuss in this section explicitly state that they are geared for racial and ethnic minority groups, but we should consider those with invisible diversity. Diversity encompasses a wide range of characteristics, and there is no accurate way to determine how many librarians identify with any of these subcategories.

While hiring a diverse staff is a clear answer, there are many other approaches to supporting diversity in academic libraries. We have to consider creating a culture for diversity, mentoring and retaining underrepresented librarians, training employees to be sensitive to other cultures in the workplace, and building a bridge between the library and the campus. This section will highlight different actions libraries can consider to recruit more diverse employees and support more diverse student groups.

Before Library School

When discussing the efforts to increase diverse communities, most practitioners talk about the need to start efforts early. A modern example is the Harlem Children's Zone, initiated by Geoffrey Canada, a social activist and leader in the American education reform movement.[34] While most education practitioners start with the problem and attempt to create a solution, Canada started with his ideal outcome and worked backwards. He wanted individuals from Harlem to escape from the cycles of poverty, violence, and crime endemic to their communities. Working from that goal, he created an organization that provides education, counseling, and health care for children and their families. The program has been so successful that President Obama incorporated it into his 2007 plan to end education disparity in the United States.[35] Taking a cue from Canada's outcome-based approach, managers of academic libraries should also think about sustainable solutions—such as reaching out to undergraduate students—to create a more diverse group of faculty and staff. By providing members of diverse communities with opportunities to build their experience, hiring committees will have more candidates to select from.

For example, academic libraries can take Canada's approach by introducing librarianship to students before they enter a master's program. The Discovering Librarianship project, offered through ALA, was an Institute of Museum and Library Services (IMLS) Laura Bush 21st-Century Librarian Program to fund a three-year project (2010–2013) to recruit ethnically diverse high school and college students to careers in libraries.[36] Early-career librarians who had graduated from previously successful diversity recruitment programs were enlisted in this program to go to speak to high school and college students and act as ambassadors for the profession. The hope was that early-career librarians from diverse backgrounds could plant a seed in the minds of these underrepresented students and convince them that librarianship is a viable career.

Work experience is a significant factor in making library school graduates competitive in the job market, so providing students from underrepresented groups the opportunity to work in academic libraries would aid them in their job search once they graduate. Academic libraries can provide internships specifically tailored to these individuals. Internships would allow undergraduate students from underrepresented communities (who might never have thought to become a librarian) to gain experience working in a library before entering an MLS/MLIS program, making them competitive candidates when applying for graduate programs and jobs. A few university libraries, like the Washington University Library and the University of Illinois, Urbana-Champaign, provide these opportunities.[37] In the Washington University Libraries Diversity and Inclusion Grant program, undergraduate interns work in various areas of the library with assigned mentors and develop a research project based on aspects related to the University Library.[38] The University of Illinois Undergraduate Library hires interns from diverse backgrounds to work specifically on information technology/informatics projects. This practice is not limited to libraries, and is used in other professions as well, such as in medical education at Johns Hopkins and the National Park Service.[39]

Undergraduate outreach initiatives increase minority students' library usage and improve their attitudes toward the library. The University of Michigan Undergraduate Library created the Peer Information Counseling Program to aid in the retention of minority students, hiring undergraduates from underrepresented groups and training them in basic reference services.[40] These students worked at the reference desk, answered basic reference questions, and helped their peers with writing papers. The library's intent was for the peer counselors to "serve as role models for minority students who might initially feel more comfortable asking for assistance from another minority student than from a librarian."[41] This is a significant aspect of the peer counseling program, and one downside is that the students graduate after a few years. Libraries could also focus on hiring permanent library staff from minority groups, especially if they found the peer counseling program to aid in minority student retention. Having permanent staff would offer a sustainable option, as opposed to relying on student workers.

During Library School

Recruiting diverse candidates to the field needs to start somewhere, and a critical examination of library and information science (LIS) education is a step in the right direction. Diversifying librarianship should begin with the recruitment of underrepresented groups into library school. Anajli Gulati, library science lecturer, argues that "increased levels of diversity among LIS faculty would also help to reinforce to Master's students from underrepresented populations that they too could become LIS faculty, leading to more diversity in LIS doctoral programs."[42] Interestingly, the *ALA Policy Manual* states, "The American Library Association, through the Committee on Accreditation, will encourage graduate programs in library and information studies seeking accreditation or re-accreditation to ensure that their student bodies, faculties, and curricular effect the diverse histories and information needs of all people in the United States," showing that diversity in LIS education is a high priority on a professional organizational level.[43] There are many programs in place to address diversity gaps in library and information science education.

Diversity initiatives like the Spectrum Scholarship Program and the ARL Initiative to Recruit a Diverse Workforce (IRDW) aim to recruit more underrepresented candidates into library school programs.[44] Targeting potential students who are identified as racial and ethnic minorities, these programs provide them with scholarships to attend library schools, leadership training, and career mentoring. The hope is that these programs will diversify LIS education and that program participants will be well prepared to be gainfully employed in the field upon graduation. We must note that these programs are focused solely on racial and ethnic minorities and not on other minority groups. Library school is the time for students to explore their interests in librarianship, gain work experience, and learn from experienced colleagues in the field. Several diversity initiatives provide students with gaining real-life experience, building their resumes, and increasing their employability.

For those who do not identify as underrepresented, there are still many ways to be an ally to those who are. Students can take classes in serving special populations, such as learning about accessibility and creating tailored online tools or developing resources for bilingual communities. Students can also volunteer to provide library services for underserved populations. The iDiversity program at University of Maryland is an example of how library school students can build a culture of inclusion. Its mission is to "create and maintain a dialogue between iSchool students, alumni, and faculty, as well as information professionals outside the university, to ensure that issues of diversity are addressed in practice, research, and technology."[45] This project is just one of many examples of efforts that students can undertake to enrich their education.

After Library School

Most diversity initiatives are focused on helping future librarians find employment in the field, which can be difficult any professional, particularly recent graduates. One way that academic libraries have striven to support diversity among new librarians is through residency programs. Geared toward new graduates, these programs hire individuals who "bring new perspectives, ideas, and training to jump start the academic library's entry into the twenty-first world [*sic*] of global scholarship, learning methods, and high tech means of communication."[46] Typically, these academic appointments are on a fixed term so that the residents can get a couple years of experience and explore academic librarianship. Positions that are focused on recruiting new professionals are rare, so these programs are competitive to get into but should provide the librarians with valuable experience. Ideally, these types of programs could extend job security beyond what is typically offered in a residency program. If we want to recruit more diversity, shouldn't these librarians be placed in permanent positions in libraries instead of temporary programs? On the other hand, residents leave their programs with employment experience that makes it much easier for them to find other positions down the road or find employment at the institution where they did their residency.

Training Programs

Creating training programs and library services aimed at diverse populations are activities beyond hiring practices that libraries can implement. For example, SafeZone or Safe Space training, which aims to educate employees on GLBT issues, is found at many academic institutions.[47] This training enables employees to become allies and promotes openness about supporting GLBT individuals at work. Participants put up signs to indicate that their office or building is a designated SafeZone, a visual cue to GLBT individuals that they are welcome and should feel safe in that space. Employees usually go through an orientation to learn about the GLBT community in order to dispel stereotypes and misinformation that might be associated with those communities. As John Barnett explained in describing his experiences of being a gay librarian, feelings of displacement and being treated differently are problems in the workplace.[48] Providing diversity training promotes cultural competency and helps employees prepare to work with different groups. Increased sensitivity toward other cultures and groups assists in the retention of underrepresented librarians and allows us to learn from others, building social empathy toward colleagues from different backgrounds.

Because minority librarians still make up a small percentage of the profession, it's even more important that libraries provide opportunities for these individuals to grow into leadership roles. Academic libraries can do this for underrepresented students, helping them gain work experience in order to be more marketable in the job hunt, creating inclusive environments for all librarians, and providing training for all staff members to be more aware of the issues of marginalized groups.

Creating a Culture for Inclusion

Libraries should be creating a culture for inclusion and retention of diverse librarians: investing in long-term employment, providing mentors, being explicit in the hiring process that different backgrounds are valued. Academic institutions should have open lines of communication to foster honest relationships with all of their employees. In the best-case scenario, librarians wouldn't feel out of place in their institution. They would feel supported and, as a result, would have the freedom to express their individuality. This positive environment trickles down into all functions of the library. Creating this culture benefits the library employees, faculty, and students.

In terms of supporting students and other library professionals, we need to remember that diversity goes beyond race and ethnicity. Students may be dealing with issues pertaining to disability, sexuality and gender, being a nontraditional student, being a first-generation college student, etc. By being aware that diversity is inclusive and intersectional, our organizations will be better prepared to meet students' needs. Many of the examples in this chapter examined specific facets of diversity, but this does not get to the complex, rich nature of someone's identity. We are not defined by just one factor; we can identify with many, which is why the idea of intersectionality is important to the discussion of diversity initiatives. Intersectionality is defined as "the interactivity of social identity structures such as race, class, and gender in fostering life experiences, especially experiences of privilege and oppression."[49] For example, a student who is a woman of color might have life experiences shaped by her race and gender. Campuses should have centers for individuals with various cultural backgrounds so they have resources and a community to support them.

Cultural centers on campus provide students with programming, a safe space to hang out, academic support, and opportunities to meet others. There may be a number of separate offices for these centers, but there's potential for these places to better serve their students by combining forces. These offices for diversity often operate in competition for limited resources but often have common goals.[50] Instead of allowing them to compete with each other, colleges and universities could move toward combining these offices to support students' intersectional experiences.

Academic librarians can work closely with these diversity groups to develop relevant resources and promote library services to these students. By creating connections with these other offices and with their students, librarians can get out beyond the library and become more visible. As mentioned previously, if students see librarians who are from similar backgrounds, they may be more likely to see the library as a welcoming space, especially if the librarian makes an effort to create a relationship with that group of students.

Conclusion

In order to change public perception of who we are, we need to take a critical look at the structures that contribute to these perceptions and work together to find solutions. Stereotypes work against librarians and influence the way that some students approach the academic library. Shifting the discourse of our professional identity must produce new "knowledge that shapes perceptions and practice. It is part of the way in which power operates. Therefore, it has consequences for both those who employ it and those who are subjected to it."[51] Redefining this conversation goes beyond showing patrons how we look: it includes how we act, how we teach, and how we reach out to those we help. As professionals, we need to tell our own stories and talk about social justice issues. We can work together to communicate to the public the dynamic aspects of our work. We should build strong relationships with our students to give them a better sense of how we can help them. By providing our communities with an understanding of our work, we can build public knowledge of what we do as librarians.

The way we approach diversity in our field is in need of a paradigm shift. Instead of focusing on inputs like recruitment, we should be look at outputs: determining how many underrepresented library school students get jobs, how many stay in the field, and what barriers are in place that continue to keep the numbers low for underrepresented librarians. By identifying the desired outcomes, we can manifest systems that help overcome current inequalities.

In an article on rethinking diversity in libraries, Yeo and Jacobs stated, "While recruitment is important, it is much more crucial to engage in and create space for dialog to challenge our consciousness and dominant ideas within the community—however uncomfortable this may be."[52] This dialog is our opportunity to confront stereotypes head on, redefining our public representation and moving the spotlight from who we are to the innovative ways we serve our community in the 21st century. If discourse produces knowledge, then we need to have conversations about how we see ourselves and how we would like to be seen by others, and continue to find solutions to make our vision a reality.

We are now at a point where discussions about the intersectionality of gender, sexuality, race, and ethnicity in librarianship are happening among a wider audience. Those who have historically been shut out of the conversation now have the chance to speak up and be heard. These difficult conversations about diversity are the first steps toward a plan of action. It is our duty as academic librarians to encourage our students and our peers to think critically and to support them no matter their background. Through open dialog and listening, we can all strive to be better allies for those whose voices are not often heard, for our students and our colleagues.

Notes

1. James V. Carmichael Jr., "Introduction: Makeover without a Mirror—A Face for Lesbigay History," in *Daring to Find Our Names*, ed. James V. Carmichael Jr. (Westport, CT: Greenwood, 1998), 3.
2. Katherine C. Adams, "Loveless Frump as Hip and Sexy Party Girl: A Reevaluation of the Old-Maid Stereotype," *Library Quarterly* 70, no. 3 (2000): 288.
3. Hui-Fen Chang, "Ethnic and Racial Diversity in Academic and Research Libraries: Past, Present, and Future" (presentation, Association of Research and College Libraries biannual conference, Indianapolis, IN. April 10–13, 2013), 183.
4. Paul T. Jaeger, John Carlo Bertot, and Renee E. Franklin, "Diversity, Inclusion, and Un-

derrepresented Populations in LIS Research," *Library Quarterly* 80, no. 2 (2010): 175. doi:10.1086/651053.

5. Kimberle Crenshaw, "Mapping the Margins: Intersectionality, Identity Politics, and Violence against Women of Color," *Stanford Law Review* 42, no. 6 (1991): 1244.

6. George Bobinski, *Libraries and Librarianship* (Lanham, MD: Scarecrow, 2007), 60.

7. Jean Weihs, "Women in Libraries: The Long Struggle for Equality," *Technicalities* 28, no. 3 (2008): 12.

8. Christine Williams, "The Glass Escalator: Hidden Advantages for Men in the 'Female' Professions," *Social Problems* 39, no. 3 (1992): 263.

9. John Brooks Slaughter, "Diversity and Equity in Higher Education: A New Paradigm for Institutional Excellence" (presentation, Diversity Leadership Council Conference, Johns Hopkins University, Baltimore, MD, November 1, 2004), http://web.jhu.edu/dlc/dlc_old/pdfs/conference-pdfs/john-slaughter-presentation.pdf.

10. Robert L. Canida II and Adriel A. Hilton. "Diversity within the Academy: Where Is the Balance?" *Diverse Issues in Higher Education* 30, no. 10 (2013): 28.

11. *Diversity Standards: Cultural Competency for Academic Libraries (2012)*, Association of College and Research Libraries, www.ala.org/acrl/standards/diversity.

12. ALA Office for Diversity, "Diversity Counts," American Library Association, May 5, 2014, www.ala.org/offices/diversity/diversitycounts/divcounts.

13. Chang, "Ethnic and Racial Diversity," 185

14. Ibid.

15. Slaughter, "Diversity and Equity."

16. Megan Oakleaf, *The Value of Academic Libraries* (Chicago: Association of College and Research Libraries, 2010), 106

17. Jennifer L. Bonnet and Benjamin McAlexander, "Structural Diversity in Academic Libraries: A Study of Librarian Approachability," *Journal of Academic Librarianship* 38, no. 5 (2012): 282, doi:10.1016/j.acalib.2012.06.002.

18. Stephen Walker and V. Lonnie Lawson, "The Librarian Stereotype and the Movies," *MC Journal: The Journal of Academic Media Librarianship* 1, no. 1 (1993): 24.

19. Gary P. Radford and Marie L. Radford, "Libraries, Librarians, and the Discourse of Fear," *Library Quarterly* 71, no. 3 (2001): 300.

20. Qun G. Jiao and Anthony J. Onwuegbuzie, "Antecedents of Library Anxiety," *Library Quarterly* 67, no. 4 (1997): 384.

21. Marie L. Radford and Gary P. Radford, "Librarians and Party Girls: Cultural Studies and the Meaning of the Librarian," *Library Quarterly* 73, no. 1, (2003): 67.

22. Kara Jesella, "A Hipper Crowd of Shushers," *New York Times*, July 8, 2007, www.nytimes.com/2007/07/08/fashion/08librarian.html.

23. Stuart Hall, "The Spectacle of the Other," in *Representation*, ed. Stuart Hall (London: Sage Publications, 1997), 237.

24. Ibid., 258.

25. Ibid., 259.

26. Daryl Smith, *Diversity's Promise for Higher Education* (Baltimore: Johns Hopkins University Press, 2009), 143.

27. Cal Gough, "The Gay, Lesbian, and Bisexual Task Force of the American Library Association: A Chronology or Activities, 1970–1995," in Carmichael, *Daring to Find Our Names*, 122.

28. Kenneth A. Yamashita, "Asian/Pacific American Librarians Association: A History of APALA and Its Founders," *Library Trends* 49, no. 1 (2000): 91.

29. Barbara Gittings, "Gays in Library Land: The Gay and Lesbian Task Force of the American Library Association: The First Sixteen Years," in Carmichael, *Daring to Find Our Names*, 82.

30. "You Know Things Are Messed Up When Librarians Start Marching," *Ouno Design* (blog), October 5, 2011, http://blog.ounodesign.com/2011/10/05/occupy-wall-street.

31. Evan St. Lifer and Corinne Nelson, "Unequal Opportunities: Race Does Matter," *Library Journal* 122, no. 18 (1997) 44.

32. John Barnett, "Out Publicly," in Carmichael, *Daring to Find our Names*, 210.

33. Lauren A. Rivera, "Hiring as Cultural Matching: The Case of Elite Professional Service Firms," *American Sociological Review* 77, no. 6 (2012): 1017.

34. Paul Tough, *Whatever It Takes* (Boston: Houghton Mifflin Harcourt, 2009).

35. Barack Obama, "The Government Can Help End the Cycle of Urban Poverty," in *Urban America*, ed. Roman Espejo, 20–31 (Detroit, MI: Greenhaven, 2011).

36. "Discovering Librarianship: The Future Is Overdue," American Library Association, accessed May 5, 2014, www.ala.org/offices/diversity/imls.

37. "Washington University Libraries' Diversity and Inclusion Grant Interns," Washington University Libraries, last updated July 16, 2013, http://libguides.wustl.edu/diginterns; BD, "Summer Diversity Internship at the UGL!" *Undergraduate Library Blog*, University of Illinois, April 8, 2012, http://publish.illinois.edu/undergradlibrary/2012/04/08/summer-diversity-internship-at-the-ugl.

38. Lauren Todd, "Diversity and Inclusion Grant Funds Summer Internships," *Off the Shelf* (Washington University Libraries) 9, no. 1 (2013): 10, http://library.wustl.edu/offtheshelf/pdf/2013spring.pdf.

39. "Summer Internship Program," Johns Hopkins Medicine, accessed May 5, 2014, www.hopkinsmedicine.org/graduateprograms/sip.cfm; "Cultural Resources Diversity Internship Program," National Park Service, last updated June 15, 2013, www.nps.gov/crdi/internships/intrnCRDIP.htm.

40. Barbara MacAdam and Darlene P. Nichols, "Peer Information Counseling at the University of Michigan Undergraduate Library," *Journal of Academic Librarianship* 14, no. 2 (1988): 80.

41. Barbara MacAdam and Darlene P. Nichols, "Peer Information Counseling: An Academic Library Program for Minority Students," *Journal of Academic Librarianship* 15, no. 4 (1989): 205.

42. Anjali Gulati, "Diversity in Librarianship: The United States Perspective," *IFLA Journal* 36, no. 4 (2010): 291. doi:10.1177/0340035210388244.

43. "B.3 Diversity (Old Number 60)," *ALA Policy Manual*, American Library Association, accessed May 5, 2014, www.ala.org/aboutala/governance/policymanual/updatedpolicymanual/section2/diversity#B.3.6.

44. "Spectrum Scholarship Program," *American Library Association*, accessed May 5, 2014, www.ala.org/offices/diversity/spectrum; "Initiative to Recruit a Diverse Workforce (IRDW)" Association of Research Libraries, accessed May 5, 2014, www.arl.org/leadership-recruitment/diversity-recruitment/initiative-to-recruit-a-diverse-workforce-irdw.

45. iDiversity "About" page, University of Maryland, accessed May 5, 2014, http://idiversity.umd.edu/about.

46. Barbara Dewey and Jillian Keally, "Recruiting for Diversity: Strategies for Twenty-First Century Research Librarianship," *Library Hi Tech* 26, no. 4 (2008): 622–29.

47. "SafeZone Training Programs," Gay Alliance, accessed May 5, 2014, www.gayalliance.org/safezonet.html.

48. Barnett, "Out Publicly," 219.

49. Ahir Gopaldas, "Intersectionality 101," *Journal of Public Policy and Marketing* 32, no. 1

(2013): 90.
50. Ibid., 93.
51. Stuart Hall, "The West and the Rest: Discourse and Power," in *The Indigenous Experience*, ed. Roger Maaka and Chris Andersen (Toronto, ON: Canadian Scholars' Press, 2006), 173.
52. ShinJoung Yeo and James R. Jacobs, "Diversity Matters? Rethinking Diversity in Libraries," *Counterpoise* 9, no. 2 (2006): 7.

Bibliography

Adams, Katherine C. "Loveless Frump as Hip and Sexy Party Girl: A Reevaluation of the Old-Maid Stereotype." *Library Quarterly* 70, no. 3 (2000): 287–301.

ALA Office for Diversity. "Diversity Counts." American Library Association, May 5, 2014. www.ala.org/offices/diversity/diversitycounts/divcounts.

American Library Association. "B.3 Diversity (Old Number 60)." *ALA Policy Manual*, American Library Association, accessed May 5, 2014. www.ala.org/aboutala/governance/policymanual/updatedpolicymanual/section2/diversity#B.3.6.

American Library Association. "Discovering Librarianship: The Future Is Overdue." American Library Association, accessed May 5, 2014. www.ala.org/offices/diversity/imls.

Association of College and Research Libraries. *Diversity Standards: Cultural Competency for Academic Libraries (2012)*. Association of College and Research Libraries, www.ala.org/acrl/standards/diversity.

Association of Research Libraries. "Initiative to Recruit a Diverse Workforce (IRDW)." Association of Research Libraries, accessed May 5, 2014. www.arl.org/leadership-recruitment/diversity-recruitment/initiative-to-recruit-a-diverse-workforce-irdw.

BD. "Summer Diversity Internship at the UGL!" *Undergraduate Library Blog*, University of Illinois, April 8, 2012. http://publish.illinois.edu/undergradlibrary/2012/04/08/summer-diversity-internship-at-the-ugl.

Bobinski, George. *Libraries and Librarianship: Sixty Years of Challenge and Change,1945–2005*. Lanham, MD: Scarecrow, 2007.

Bonnet, Jennifer L., and Benjamin McAlexander. "Structural Diversity in Academic Libraries: A Study of Librarian Approachability." *Journal of Academic Librarianship* 38, no. 5 (2012): 277–86. doi:10.1016/j.acalib.2012.06.002.

Canida, Robert L., II, and Adriel A. Hilton. "Diversity within the Academy: Where Is the Balance?" *Diverse Issues in Higher Education* 30, no. 10 (2013): 28.

Carmichael, James V., Jr., ed. *Daring to Find Our Names: The Search for Lesbigay Library History*. Westport, CT: Greenwood, 1998.

Chang, Hui-Fen. "Ethnic and Racial Diversity in Academic and Research Libraries: Past, Present, and Future." Presentation, Association of Research and College Libraries biannual conference, Indianapolis, IN, April 10–13, 2013.

Crenshaw, Kimberle. "Mapping the Margins: Intersectionality, Identity Politics, and Violence against Women of Color." *Stanford Law Review* 42, no. 6 (1991): 1241–99.

Dewey, Barbara and Jillian Keally. "Recruiting for Diversity: Strategies for Twenty-First Century Research Librarianship." *Library Hi Tech* 26, no. 4 (2008): 622–29.

Gay Alliance. "SafeZone Training Programs. Gay Alliance, accessed May 5, 2014. www.gayalliance.org/safezonet.html.

Gopaldas, Ahir. "Intersectionality 101." *Journal of Public Policy and Marketing* 32, no. 1 (2013): 90–94.

Gulati, Anjali. "Diversity in Librarianship: The United States Perspective." *IFLA Journal* 36, no. 4 (2010): 288–93. doi:10.1177/0340035210388244.

Hall, Stuart. "The West and the Rest: Discourse and Power." In *The Indigenous Experience: Global Perspectives*, edited by Roger Maaka and Chris Andersen. 165–73. Toronto, ON: Canadian Scholars' Press, 2006.

———, ed. *Representation: Cultural Representations and Signifying Practices*. London: Sage Publications,1997.

Jaeger, Paul T., John Carlo Bertot, and Renee E. Franklin. "Diversity, Inclusion, and Underrepresented Populations in LIS Research." *Library Quarterly* 80, no. 2 (2010): 175–81. doi:10.1086/651053.

Jesella, Kara. "A Hipper Crowd of Shushers." *New York Times*, July 8, 2007. www.nytimes.com/2007/07/08/fashion/08librarian.html.

Jiao, Qun G., and Anthony J. Onwuegbuzie. "Antecedents of Library Anxiety." *Library Quarterly* 67, no. 4 (1997): 372–89.

Johns Hopkins Medicine. "Summer Internship Program." Johns Hopkins Medicine, accessed May 5, 2014. www.hopkinsmedicine.org/graduateprograms/sip.cfm.

MacAdam, Barbara, and Darlene P. Nichols. "Peer Information Counseling: An Academic Library Program for Minority Students." *Journal of Academic Librarianship* 15, no. 4 (1989): 204–9.

———. "Peer Information Counseling at the University of Michigan Undergraduate Library." *Journal of Academic Librarianship* 14, no. 2 (1988): 80–81.

National Park Service. "Cultural Resources Diversity Internship Program." National Park Service, last updated June 15, 2013. www.nps.gov/crdi/internships/intrnCRDIP.htm.

Oakleaf, Megan. *The Value of Academic Libraries: A Comprehensive Research Review and Report.* Chicago: Association of College and Research Libraries, 2010.

Obama, Barack. "The Government Can Help End the Cycle of Urban Poverty." In *Urban America,* edited by Roman Espejo, 20–31. Detroit, MI: Greenhaven, 2011.

Ouno Design. "You Know Things Are Messed Up When Librarians Start Marching." *Ouno Design* (blog), October 5, 2011. http://blog.ounodesign.com/2011/10/05/occupy-wall-street.

Radford, Gary P., and Marie L. Radford. "Libraries, Librarians, and the Discourse of Fear." *Library Quarterly* 71, no. 3 (2001): 299–329.

Radford, Marie L., and Gary P. Radford. "Librarians and Party Girls: Cultural Studies and the Meaning of the Librarian." *Library Quarterly* 73, no. 1 (2003): 54–69.

Rivera, Lauren A. "Hiring as Cultural Matching: The Case of Elite Professional Service Firms." *American Sociological Review* 77, no. 6 (2012): 999–1022.

Slaughter, John Brooks. "Diversity and Equity in Higher Education: A New Paradigm for Institutional Excellence." Presentation, Diversity Leadership Council Conference, Johns Hopkins University, Baltimore, MD, November 1, 2004. http://web.jhu.edu/dlc/dlc_old/pdfs/conference-pdfs/john-slaughter-presentation.pdf.

Smith, Daryl. *Diversity's Promise for Higher Education*. Baltimore: Johns Hopkins University Press, 2009.

St. Lifer, Evan, and Corinne Nelson. "Unequal Opportunities: Race Does Matter." *Library Journal* 122, no. 18 (1997): 42–46.

Todd, Lauren. "Diversity and Inclusion Grant Funds Summer Internships." *Off the Shelf* (Washington University Libraries) 9, no. 1 (2013): 10. http://library.wustl.edu/offtheshelf/pdf/2013spring.pdf.

Tough, Paul. *Whatever It Takes: Geoffrey Canada's Quest to Change Harlem and America*. Boston: Houghton Mifflin Harcourt, 2009.

University of Maryland. iDiversity "About" page, University of Maryland, accessed May 5, 2014.

http://idiversity.umd.edu/about.

Walker, Stephen, and V. Lonnie Lawson. "The Librarian Stereotype and the Movies." *MC Journal: The Journal of Academic Media Librarianship* 1, no. 1 (1993): 17–28.

Washington University Libraries. "Washington University Libraries' Diversity and Inclusion Grant Interns." Washington University Libraries, last updated July 16, 2013. http://lib-guides.wustl.edu/diginterns.

Weihs, Jean. "Women in Libraries: The Long Struggle for Equality." *Technicalities* 28 no. 3 (2008): 9–12.

Williams, Christine L. "The Glass Escalator: Hidden Advantages for Men in the 'Female' Professions." *Social Problems* 39, no. 3 (1992): 253–67.

Yamashita, Kenneth A. "Asian/Pacific American Librarians Association: A History of APALA and Its Founders." *Library Trends* 49, no. 1 (2000): 88–108.

Yeo, ShinJoung, and James R. Jacobs. "Diversity Matters? Rethinking Diversity in Libraries." *Counterpoise* 9, no. 2 (2006): 5–8.

Toward a New Inclusion in Library Work

K. R. Roberto

We can and will worry about externally projected stereotypes of library workers all we'd like, but the ones we project upon each other are ultimately most concerning. Critiques that come from outside of the profession are difficult, but can be contextualized as ignorance about the field, a public relations problem and not a professional one. Actions toward our colleagues that betray our own internal biases, however, are more immediate and arguably more lasting. It's like the difference between playground bullies calling you names and your parents doing so; the latter hits you where you live—or work, as the case may be.

Library workers tend to pride ourselves on being tolerant of diversity; in the best cases, we are accepting and inclusive. As such, we are much more likely to commit microaggressions that transgress our attempts at the respect of diversities, rather than overt acts of hostility. The term *microaggressions* comes from psychiatric literature and was initially coined to refer to subtle acts and statements that insidiously contribute to racism against people of color;[1] the concept has been extended to encompass passive hostility with regard to gender and sexual orientation and can expand to include virtually any marginalized group.[2] Imagine a backhanded compliment based on a biased assumption about a specific population, and there you have it.

These behaviors belie some underlying assumptions that need to be unpacked. Libraries are a microcosm of a society as a whole, and library workers often unwittingly mirror the overgeneralizations that we all make based on other people's backgrounds—more accurately, on our perceptions of other people's backgrounds. Much of our internal stereotyping assumes that library workers of various identities have common lived experiences—and that library workers have common lived experiences at all. Didn't we all grow up as solitary bookworms who loved puzzles and science fiction? (Personally, I happen to be terrible at puzzles. I hope this doesn't mean that I have to leave the profession.) One salient example is the idea that white librarians mostly grew up middle class, but librarians of color mostly grew up poor. There are fleeting strands of an invisible, painfully racialized narrative where white people go into library work because they love books, while people of color go into library work because they want to give back to their communities (presumably by making them love books). Many library workers have accepted the reality that our patrons live within many different races, ethnicities, class backgrounds, genders, sexual orientations, abilities, and so many other ways of being; we have considerably more difficulty accepting that these differences are found on both sides of the desk.

There is very little in the LIS literature about these microaggressions, which is arguably a microaggression in and of itself.* Examples from the field are plentiful, however. Here are a few common examples, some uglier than others:

- Any statement involving the phrase "just a paraprofessional."
- "I'm different. I'm a cataloger with social skills!"
- "Do you go by an 'American name' that we can have our patrons use?"
- "People in Tech Services have no idea what our patrons need."
- Assuming that one of your female coworkers will take the notes at the staff meeting.
- "You work in children's services? Do you ever get a *real* reference question?"
- Automatically assuming that every library worker of color will serve on the diversity committee or be interested only in diversity and inclusion.

---

* An April 2014 search of EBSCO's Library and Information Science Source found two articles and a book review.

- "I know that you hate it when the patrons ask if you're a he or a she, but sometimes it can be hard to tell"
- Assuming that people who are not native English speakers want to work only in cataloging or systems.
- "LIS programs are so worthless. Nobody ever learns anything useful!"[†]
- "It's okay if you want to do a Pride exhibit, but make sure everything in it is family-friendly."
- Assuming that every newly degreed librarian of color was a Spectrum Scholar.
- "I know that you can't get your wheelchair through the stacks, but you know we can't afford a renovation right now. Why don't you just have a staffer get things for you to work on?"

I Didn't Do It on Purpose, So That Makes It Okay

Many of these statements come out of good intentions, but that does not lessen the need for accountability. For example, if I were pushing a book truck around the library and accidentally run it over your foot, my lack of intent to do so does not minimize its impact; your toe is still broken, whether I meant it or not. Intent does not excuse offensive behavior, either ethically or legally.[‡] Disenfranchising library workers is less visible—at least at first—but it still involves breaking. Even if we work as classifiers by trade, we might want to consider keeping our personal ontologies to ourselves. Classifying items is difficult and controversial enough,[§] let alone applying the same techniques to our colleagues.

While working on the above list, I posted a query on Facebook asking for examples of microaggressions in the profession.[¶] Many of the people who initially replied were white, and many of them mentioned the librar-

---

† This type of microaggression is particularly impressive because it manages to disparage professors, students, practitioners, and the entire library profession in 10 words.

‡ See http://www2.ucsc.edu/title9-sh/intent.htm for an explanation of how intent is not relevant when discussing legal matters such as sexual harassment.

§ See the work of Sanford Berman, Emily Drabinski, and Hope Olson, among others.

¶ Not the most rigorous research method, I fully admit.

ian/library staff divide as the foremost example. I greatly respect these colleagues and am always grateful for any sort of input, but this reaction epitomizes a certain variety of white privilege where class issues are the only type of oppression that is ever articulated. It also reflects our work-place culture,* where we remain uncomfortable in engaging in self-reflection; we can explain economic inequity among library workers as a result of educational level without having to ever address the societal processes that created the inequality in the first place. It's always easier to invoke our perceived commonalities than to make social change.

I Was a Hipster Librarian Before Hipster Librarians Were Cool

Speaking of sci-fi and other shared librarian references, it seems that the nascent librarian stereotype is to love it completely and wholeheartedly. These days, it appears that the most prevalent librarian archetypes embrace fandoms and a certain type of detail-oriented geekiness, the latter being a perpetual favorite in libraryland. There is a parallel trend involving DIY makerspaces and 3-D printing, but that may ultimately play out to be a community-oriented variation of the same trope. While these images are undoubtedly an improvement over the widely disliked hipster librarian stereotype, as they substitute sincerity for that former perceived smugness, is there a real difference? After all, they continue to enforce the same type of values as the earlier versions did, those of the frighteningly intelligent sexless spinsters and ironic shushers. The images that we currently prize are those that celebrate our arcane knowledge as opposed to our useful skills, ultimately arguing for an expert-based model instead of a service-based one. As Ayanna Gaines observes in chapter 4, these preferences devalue the feminization of labor, replacing it with an allegedly gender-neutral (i.e., masculine) know-it-all image. Maybe that explains the fondness for science fiction, with its penchant for emotionless robots.[†]

---

* Which is shaped by life under neoliberalism and late capitalism.

† Yes, I am stereotyping science fiction. No, that is not a microaggression. Please feel free to substitute for *emotionless robots* the more accurate term of your choice; for Haraway readers, *cyborg* may work well.

I Can't Tell If I'm Being Ironic Anymore

Another eternally popular trend in library work is rampant technophilia. We appear to be continually working to create the algorithms that will ultimately render our work redundant. At the same time, our digital love affair manages to accommodate self-conscious irony, and possibly outright nostalgia, for all things nondigital. The fetishization of outdated library technology is perplexing. It is a truly interesting experience to hear someone praise automatic indexing and express their love of *Desk Set* in the same breath. I have a secret suspicion that anyone who adores card catalogs has never had to file in one. They probably have never spent hours proofreading cards with a bottle of Wite-Out in Antique White nearby, ready to correct typographical errors.

This all dovetails nicely with the current fad of regarding all print items as objects and all digital items as data. It sometimes appears that the future librarian stereotype will be to venerate the past as a dead artifact, disparage all current technology, and yearn for a new future where librarians are either CIOs or programmers or work in special collections. Libraries have been beloved by most people (barring extreme libertarians), if increasingly underused, for generations now, indicating that our LIS ancestors were doing *something* right.

Putting the Pieces Back Together

Library work is often found to lack a sense of cohesion, also known as a "shared vision" in corporate speak. This is unfortunate, since many of us seem to have the same goals with wildly divergent opinions on the methods to get there. It seems safe to argue that the work cannot be cohesive until the workers are, so how can we start this process? As various contributors to this book have stated, increased visibility and inclusion of library workers from diverse backgrounds and lived experiences is a key starting point. A hugely important act is to acknowledge that our internal prejudices and antipathies can unknowingly affect our words and behaviors; being mindful of potential impact and expressing willingness to remain accountable is incredibly valuable and speaks volumes (print or digital!) about creating an inclusive space. A desire for inclusion needs to be established before coalition building can begin, and coalition building needs to begin before we can move toward any type of change based on shared needs and goals.

As Gretchen Keer and Andrew Carlos state in chapter 3 of this volume, "[T]he most effective way to combat the negative effects of librarian stereotypes is to work diligently toward social justice for marginalized groups." Once we are able to articulate that librarians are from marginalized groups, maybe we can get some work done. Library workers already love knowledge organization, so let's organize our own!

Notes

1. Charles Pierce, "Psychiatric Problems of the Black Minority," in *American Handbook of Psychiatry*, ed. Silvano Arieti, 512–23 (New York: Basic Books, 1974).
2. Derald Wing Sue and Christina M. Capodilupo, "Racial, Gender, and Sexual Orientation Microaggressions: Implications for Counseling and Psychotherapy," in *Counseling the Culturally Diverse*, 5th ed., 105–30, ed. Derald Wing Sue and David Sue (Hoboken, NJ: John Wiley and Sons, 2008).

Bibliography

Pierce, Charles. "Psychiatric Problems of the Black Minority." In *American Handbook of Psychiatry*, edited by Silvano Arieti, 512–23. New York: Basic Books, 1974.

Sue, Derald Wing, and Christina M. Capodilupo. "Psychiatric Racial, Gender, and Sexual Orientation Microaggressions: Implications for Counseling and Psychotherapy." In *Counseling the Culturally Diverse: Theory and Practice*, 5th ed., edited by Derald Wing Sue and David Sue, 105-30. Hoboken, NJ: John Wiley and Sons, 2008.

Author Bios

Terry Baxter: Terry Baxter is an archivist with the Multnomah County Records Program in Portland, Oregon. He has worked as an archivist for nearly 30 years, first at the Oregon State Archives, then at PacifiCorp, and since 1998 at Multnomah County. He has served in a variety of roles with both Northwest Archivists and the Society of American Archives, currently serving as a council member for SAA. He loves archives and archivists very much and works hard to see them both change the world for the better.

Amanda Brennan: Amanda Brennan graduated with her MLIS from Rutgers University in 2011. For the next two years, she combined her library studies with her love of Internet culture during her tenure as cat expert the website Know Your Meme. She currently works on the Content and Community team at Tumblr in New York City. She blogs at http://memelibrarian.com.

Andrew Carlos: Andrew is one of the STEM and Web Services Librarians at California State University, East Bay. He is the liaison for the Computer Science, Earth and Environmental Sciences, Engineering, and Psychology departments, as well as an instructor for LIBY 1210: Introduction to Information Literacy. His interests including emerging technology, popular culture, user experience, and mobile technology.

James V. Carmichael: James V. (Jim) Carmichael Jr. is Professor of Library and Information Studies at the University of North Carolina at Greensboro. He received his undergraduate and master's degrees from Emory University and his doctorate from the University of North Carolina at Chapel Hill. He has written extensively on southern library history, gender issues, and gay library history.

Jenny Dale: Jenny Dale is the Coordinator of First-Year Programs at the University of North Carolina at Greensboro. When she's not busy coordinating or teaching information literacy sessions for 100-level courses, she serves as liaison to the departments of English, Communication Studies, and Kinesiology and focuses on campus outreach efforts. While she enjoys writing about librarian personalities and core competencies, most of her research has focused on issues related to pedagogy in libraries.

Dorothy Gambrell: Dorothy Gambrell makes pictures and words together in different combinations. The swift, meaningless arms of the Internet find her at http://catandgirl.com and www.verysmallarray.com.

Ayanna Gaines: Ayanna Gaines is an Associate Librarian at Ventura College in Ventura, California. She has a bachelor's degree in English from Brown University and a master's degree in library and information science from Dominican University. She owns several cardigans and two cats, but swears that is purely coincidental.

Isabel Gonzalez-Smith: Isabel Gonzalez-Smith is an Academic Resident Librarian in reference and instruction at her alma mater, the University of Illinois of Chicago. Isabel has experience working in a public library, rare books store, special collections/archives, and academic libraries. She graduated with an MLIS from the University of Illinois at Urbana-Champaign in 2011 and is a 2012 Minnesota Institute for Early Career Librarians alumna.

Julie M. Jones: Julie M. Jones is a law librarian in Atlanta and one of the founding members of the Atlanta Emerging Librarians group.

Gretchen Keer: Gretchen Keer thinks and writes about issues related to the intersections between social justice and information science, including critical information literacy, access to online learning, and community knowledge production. Gretchen is Online Learning and Outreach Librarian at CSU East Bay in Hayward, California.

Lynda Kellam: Lynda Kellam is the Data Services and Government Information Librarian at the University of North Carolina at Greensboro's University Libraries and Adjunct Lecturer in the political science department. In addition to providing research assistance and instruction on data and government sources, she is the liaison to the political science department, environmental studies program, and pre-law program. She received her MA in political science from the University of Wisconsin, Madison and her MLIS from the University of North Carolina at Greensboro.

Melissa Langridge: Melissa Langridge is the User Education Coordinator at Niagara University Library. She holds her master's in library science from the University at Buffalo and is currently obtaining her master's in literacy instruction at Niagara University. Her research focuses on online instruction, active and participatory learning, and instructional game design.

J. Turner Masland: J. Turner Masland graduated from Emporia State University with an MLS in 2012. Having worked for a number of academic libraries in the Portland area, currently he is the Resource Sharing Supervisor for Portland State University, were he oversees interlibrary loan andinterconsortial borrowing and has implemented a document delivery service. His research interests include access services, management, and effective use of emerging technologies. In his free time he enjoys exploring the Pacific Northwest.

Nicole Pagowsky: Nicole Pagowsky is an Instruction Librarian at the University of Arizona. She has a BA in communication science and rhetorical studies from the University of Wisconsin–Madison and her MLIS and soon-to-be MS in educational technology and instructional design from the University of Arizona. Her research centers on game-based learning, critical library pedagogy, and student motivation.

Erin Pappas: Erin Pappas is Librarian for Social Sciences and European Languages at Georgetown University in Washington, DC. She holds degrees in Russian literature, library science, and anthropology from Reed

College, the University of Kentucky, and the University of Chicago. She currently has only one tattoo, but a pile of Pinterest boards for inspiration.

Annie Pho: Annie Pho is an Academic Resident Librarian at the University of Illinois at Chicago, where she works in reference and instruction. She was also a 2014 ALA Emerging Leader. She has a bachelor's in art history from San Francisco State University and graduated from Indiana University–Indianapolis with her master's in library science. Her research interests include diversity and professional representation, information literacy, and critical pedagogy.

Lauren Pressley: Lauren Pressley is the Associate Director for Learning and Outreach at Virginia Tech University Libraries. She is the author of *So You Want to Be a Librarian* and *Wikis for Libraries* and holds elected positions on the ALA Council and the LITA Board of Directors. She has been recognized as a *Library Journal* Mover and Shaker and an ALA Emerging Leader and with a Distinguished Alumni Early Career Award from the UNC-G School of Education. She frequently writes and presents on education, instruction, technology, and the future of libraries.

Miriam Rigby: Miriam Rigby is the Anthropology, Sociology, and Ethnic Studies Subject Specialist Librarian and liaison to the Honors College at the University of Oregon. Her undergraduate study and first MA were in cultural anthropology, which continues to guide her research as a librarian. She is especially active in the Anthropology and Sociology Section (ANSS) of ACRL, serving as a chair on a variety of committees and enjoying the camaraderie of the members.

Christine Riggi: Christine Riggi is a Reference Librarian at Niagara University Library. She holds her masters in library science from the University at Buffalo.

K. R. Roberto: K. R. Roberto is a doctoral student in the Graduate School of Library and Information Science at the University of Illinois at Urbana-Champaign. His research areas include institutionalized bigotry in classification systems and queer and transgender advocacy in library work. Before returning to school, he worked as an academic librarian and co-edited several books, including *Radical Cataloging: Essays at the Front* (McFarland, 2008).

Allison Schultz: Allison Schultz is an undergraduate student at Niagara University. She studies English, history, and writing studies, and is known to make *Doctor Who* references, whether they are relevant or not.

David Squires: David Squires is completing a PhD in English at the University at Buffalo. His dissertation, "Archives Unbound: Modern Literature and the Rise of Library Science," investigates modernist writers who appropriated and adapted representational modes pioneered in the emergent discipline of library science. He recently co-edited the volume *Porn Archives* (Duke University Press, 2014), which includes his essay "Pornography in the Library."

Sarah Steiner: Sarah Steiner is the Head of Research and Instruction Services at Western Carolina University. Sarah earned her master of library science degree from the University of South Florida and a master of arts degree in English literature from Georgia State University. She is an Associate Professor who regularly writes and speaks on instruction skills, social media in libraries, and emerging technologies. She is comfortable being struck while on roller skates and flying on a trapeze, but is afraid to try Chatroulette.

Juleah Swanson: Juleah Swanson is an Assistant Professor and Acquisitions Librarian for Electronic Resources at the Ohio State University Libraries, where she began her librarian career as a Mary P. Key Diversity Resident. In the summer of 2012, Juleah attended the Minnesota Institute for Early Career Librarians from Traditionally Underrepresented Groups, which is where she met her two co-authors. She received her master's in library and information science from the University of Washington.

Azusa Tanaka: Azusa Tanaka is a Japanese Studies Librarian at University of Washington and handles outreach, reference, instruction, and collection development. Born and raised in Kyoto, Japan, she came to the United States to pursue her MA in Korean studies at University of Washington in 2003, where she encountered subject librarians and their helpful guidance. Since then, she gained library experience at Columbia University's East Asian Library as an archivist assistant, earned her MSLIS from Syracuse University, and worked as a Japanese Studies Librarian at Washington University in St. Louis. Her interests include diversity in libraries, information retrieval, instruction, and outreach.